Diversity Quotas, Diverse Perspectives

Diversity Quotas, Diverse Perspectives

The Case of Gender

Edited by

STEFAN GRÖSCHL and
JUNKO TAKAGI

ESSEC Business School, Paris, France

CHAIR OF
LEADERSHIP
& DIVERSITY

LONDON AND NEW YORK

First published 2012 by Gower Publishing

2 Park Square, Milton Park, Abingdon, Oxon OX14 4RN
711 Third Avenue, New York, NY 10017, USA

Routledge is an imprint of the Taylor & Francis Group, an informa business

First issued in paperback 2016

Gower Applied Business Research
Our programme provides leaders, practitioners, scholars and researchers with thought provoking, cutting edge books that combine conceptual insights, interdisciplinary rigour and practical relevance in key areas of business and management.

British Library Cataloguing in Publication Data
Diversity quotas, diverse perspectives : the case of gender.
    1. Affirmative action programs. 2. Sex discrimination in employment.
    I. Groschl, Stefan. II. Takagi, Junko.
    331.1'33–dc23

Library of Congress Cataloging-in-Publication Data
Gröschl, Stefan.
Diversity quotas, diverse perspectives : the case of gender / by Stefan Gröschl and Junko Takagi.
    p. cm.
    Includes bibliographical references and index.
    ISBN 978-1-4094-3619-5 (hardback : alk. paper)
    1. Women's rights. 2. Equality. 3. Reverse discrimination. I.Takagi, Junko. II. Title.

    HQ1236.G69 2011
    323.3'4–dc23

    2012004311

ISBN 978-1-4094-3619-5 (hbk)
ISBN 978-1-138-26164-8 (pbk)

Contents

List of Figures

List of Tables

About the Contributors

Laurent Bibard is Professor and former Dean of MBA programmes at the ESSEC Business School, France/Singapore. Laurent holds a PhD in Economics and a PhD in Political Philosophy. His research is based on this twofold education – questioning management from a philosophical perspective, and exploring philosophical thoughts through management experiences and practices. His most recent research focuses on organizational vigilance interpreted as the organizational conditions favouring collective as well as individual mindfulness on one hand, and gender relations on the other hand. Laurent practices what he teaches. He consults, coaches and accompanies business leaders in organizational change processes. Laurent has frequently been a guest speaker in internationally renowned business schools such as Mannheim Business School (Germany), UQAM (Canada) and Keio Business School (Japan). His most recent publications include *Conducting Business in Viet-Nam: A Brief for International Managers* (2012) and *Towards a Phenomenology of Management: From Modelling to Day-to-Day Moral Sensemaking Cognition (2011)*. Two of Laurent's books are currently being translated, *Sexualité et Mondialisation* (2010) (*Sexuality and Globalization*) into English, and *La Sagesse et le Feminine* (2005) (*Wisdom and Feminity*) into Japanese. For a detailed list of publications please see http://www.essec.fr/professeurs/laurent-bibard.

Elena Doldor is a Senior Research Fellow at Cranfield's International Centre for Women Leaders, where she earned her PhD. Her research interests lie in two core areas: organizational politics and gender diversity at leadership levels. Elena's research examines the notion of political maturation, by exploring how male and female managers develop willingness and ability to engage in organizational politics. She is also involved in research projects examining diversity on public and private sector boards of directors in the UK and internationally, including Cranfield's annual Female FTSE Report. Elena presents her research frequently at international conferences in the UK and abroad. After being presented a Fulbright Award, she spent the academic year 2007–2008 as a visiting researcher in Northwestern University, USA. Elena is a reviewer for academic journals such as the *Journal of Business Ethics and Gender* and *Work and Organization*, and is a member of the American Academy of Management and the British Academy of Management.

Suzette Dyer is a senior lecturer with the Waikato Management School at the University of Waikato, New Zealand. She teaches career development studies, organizational behaviour and feminist organization studies. Her research interests include understanding the impact of the global context on career and community, human resources management and understanding gendered organizations. Suzette can be contacted on sdyer@waikato.ac.nz.

Patricia Gabaldón is currently Associate Professor of Economics at IE Business School, Spain. She holds a PhD in Economics and has developed her research career around the role of women in the economy, gender equality policies, female patterns of consumption and gender differences in the uses of time. She has more than 12 years of diversified experience in research and project development of gender and other social sciences projects from the economic point of view. Patricia is a researcher and academic responsible for the Centre for Diversity in Management at the IE Business School., Patricia is a graduate in Economics of the University of Alcala (Spain), from where she received her PhD in Economics in 2005. She also holds a MSc in Leisure Management from the University of Deusto, Spain. Patricia has participated in UN Woman in Spain and the Global Compact Initiative by the UN as member of the women's empowerment discussion group. She is member of the Academic Committee of The Gender Equality Project, certifying companies' progress on gender equality in equal pay for equivalent work, recruitment and promotion, training and mentoring, work–life balance and company culture. She has also participated in the Global Roundtable on Board Diversity organized by the Corporate Women Directors International and the International Finance Corporation by the World Bank.

Stefan Gröschl is Associate Professor of Human Resources Management and Co-Chair of Leadership and Diversity in the Faculty of Management at ESSEC Business School, France. His primary research interests focus on cross-cultural diversity issues and aspects, and HR policies and practices supporting the integration of disadvantaged and/or minority employee groups into the workforce. Stefan has published widely in international journals, books and book chapters. He serves on a range of editorial boards within the diversity and equality area and within industry specific sectors.

Morten Huse is Professor of Organization and Management at BI Norwegian Business School and President of European Academy of Management. He is also a member of Catalyst Europe Advisory Board. He has been affiliated to various universities in Europe, including Lund University, Bocconi University, St. Gallen University and Tor Vergata University. His main research focus is on behaviour perspectives on boards and governance. This is a topic in which he is widely published, and he is the founder of the annual Norefjell Board Governance workshop. Core contributions include *Boards, Governance and Value Creation: The Human Side of Corporate Governance* (2007) and *The Value Creating Board: Corporate Governance and Organizational Behaviour* (2009). He has studied the impact of women on corporate boards for more than two decades, and during recent years he has followed the discussions about the Norwegian Gender Balance Law. Results of studies about women on boards have been published in several books, *Corporate Governance: An International Review, European Management Review, Journal of Business Ethics*, and so on. His research about boards of directors and women on boards, as well as his presidentship of the European Academy of Management has taken him worldwide as a speaker and as a consultant to policy-makers and activists.

Fiona Hurd is a doctoral researcher in Human Resource Management at the University of Waikato, New Zealand. Her thesis is examining, through an identity lens, the impact of the global division of labour on work, workers and communities. Her wider research and teaching interests include critical management studies and pedagogy, gender and organization, and critical perspectives on career management and development. Fiona can be contacted on fah1@waikato.ac.nz.

Mijntje Lückerath-Rovers is Professor in Corporate Governance at Nyenrode Business University and also Associate Professor in Financial Markets and Supervision at Erasmus University Rotterdam. Her research focuses on the role of the board of directors, corporate governance and board diversity. She is the author of the annual Dutch Female Board Index, co-author of the annual Dutch Non-executive Directors survey and of a Code of Conduct for Non-executive directors. She is editor of the *Yearbook Corporate Governance* (Kluwer), of a Dutch journal on Good Governance (*Tijdschrift Goed Bestuur*) and of a Dutch journal on Supervision (*Tijdschrift voorToezicht*). She is also a member of the Supervisory Boards of Achmea and of the investment and greenfund(s) of the sustainable ASN Bank. Mijntje graduated in 1994 with a Masters degree in Financial Business Economics from the Erasmus University Rotterdam. Afterwards she worked until 2001 at Rabobank International in various financial positions. Since 2001 she worked at the Erasmus University. Her PhD thesis concerned the decisions' usefulness of the (operating) lease accounting standard.

Shora Moteabbed is a doctoral candidate in Organizational Behaviour at ESSEC Business School. Her research focuses on relational identity, gender, diversity and high-quality interpersonal connections. She also collaborates with the Chair of Leadership and Diversity at ESSEC.

Shoma Mukherji was Head of Human Resources with a leading multinational and currently works as a consultant in HR, sales administration, and cross cultural communication training. She is associated with an organization imparting adventure-based training to corporates and holds a voluntary position with an non-governmental organization imparting education to underprivileged children. She is currently pursuing the Executive Fellowship (PhD) programme in Management at the Management Development Institute, Gurgaon, India. She has completed a Masters in International Management from the American Graduate School of International Management, USA. Her research interests are leadership communication, cultural intelligence, gender issues and corporate social responsibility. Her publications include book chapters and research papers in national/international journals/conference proceedings. Shoma can be contacted on shomamukherji@airtelmail.in.

Stella M. Nkomo is a Professor in the Department of Human Resource Management at the University of Pretoria in South Africa. Her internationally recognized work on race and gender and managing diversity appears in numerous journals and edited volumes. She is co-author with Dr Ella L. J. Edmondson Bell of the critically acclaimed Harvard Business School Press book, *Our Separate Ways: Black and White Women and the Struggle for Professional Identity* (2001). She is the recipient of the 2009 Sage Scholarly Contributions Award for her pioneering contributions to gender and diversity research in organizations. She is currently an Associate Editor for *Organization: The Critical Journal of Organization, Theory and Society* and the *British Journal of Management*. Dr Nkomo served on the editorial board of the *Academy of Management Review* (2002–2007); and currently serves on the editorial board of *Leadership, Journal of Management Education, Equality, Diversity* *and Inclusion: An International Journal, South African Journal of Labour Relations, Journal of Managerial Psychology, South African Journal of Human Resource Management, Management Communication Quarterly,* and *The Hispanic Journal of Business Research.* She is a past member of the Board of Governors and former chair of the Women in Management Division of the Academy of Management. In 2010, she received the Distinguished Woman Scholar in the Social Sciences Award from the Department of Science and Technology (South Africa). Most recently, she was elected President of the Africa Academy of Management.

Marjan Radjavi trained as an anthropologist and is the Lead of the Gender Portfolio at the Centre for International Sustainable Development Law, Montreal, Canada. She has worked as a teacher and a gender advocate for over 15 years. During this time she has consulted with Chatham House, the Canadian Government and the World Meteorological Organization, as well as being involved in the UNESCO Chairs programme. She has contributed to the UN World Summit on Sustainable Development, Habitat, and the World Water Forum processes. Most recently, she was Principle Researcher and Director of a five-year Gender, International Law and Justice Project, examining the impacts of human rights advocacy on local human rights outcomes.

Maureen A. Scully is CGO Affiliate at the Center for Gender in Organizations and Assistant Professor in Management at University of Massachusetts, Boston. She is author of numerous articles published in management journals and is co-author of *Managing for the Future: Organizational Behavior and Processes* (with D. Ancona, T. Kochan, J. Van Maanen and E. Westney, second edition 1998). She is currently working on a book, *Luck, Pluck, or Merit? How Americans Make Sense of Inequality.*

Radha R. Sharma is a Senior Professor in Organisational Behaviour and HRD at the Management Development Institute (MDI), India and HR Ambassador for India at the Academy of Management. She has completed research supported by the World Health Organization (WHO), UNESCO, Academy of Management, McClelland Centre for Research and Innovation, Polish Academy of Sciences, Humanistic Management Network, IDRC, Canada and the Government of India. She is recipient of Outstanding Cutting Edge Research Paper Award, 2006, AHRD, (USA); Best Faculty Award: Excellence in Research, 2006 and 2007 at MDI; Outstanding Management Researcher Award, AIMS International (2008). She has been a Visiting Professor to International University, Germany and has taught courses on Intercultural Skills in ESCP–Europe MBA programmes. A recipient of four gold medals for academic excellence, Rhada has Advanced Professional Certification in MBTI from the Association of Personality Type, EI certification from EI Learning Systems (USA), and has completed certificate courses in Corporate Social Responsibility from the British Council and New Academy of Business, UK and the World Bank Institute. She has received certification in participant-centred learning at Harvard Business School, USA. Her research interests are: executive burnout; emotional, social and cultural intelligence; managerial competencies, leadership, spirituality, diversity, humanism and CSR. She has published more than 86 papers with Routledge, Palgrave Macmillan, Information Age Publishing and Edward Elgar. Her books include: *Change Management* (2007); *Change Management & Organisational Transformation* (in Press); *360 Degree Feedback, Competency Mapping & Assessment Centres* (2002); *Organisational Behaviour* with Steven McShane and Mary Ann Von Glinow (three editions – 2006, 2008, 2011). She has edited a special issue of *Vision on Emotional Intelligence* (2008) and another special issue of *Vision: The Journal of Business Perspective on Managerial Competencies* with Professor Richard E. Boyatzis (2011). Rhada can be contacted on radha@mdi.ac.in.

Junko Takagi is Associate Teaching Professor of Management and Chair of Leadership and Diversity at ESSEC Business School. Her primary research interests include identity issues in multicultural settings, global leadership and gender issues in the workplace. Junko has contributed to international journals and books on these topics, and consults to multinational firms.

Preface

In response to the challenges and opportunities created by the diversification of the workforce throughout Europe, the ESSEC Leadership and Diversity Chair was created in 2007 and renewed in 2011 in partnership with Deloitte and L'Oréal. The overall aim of the ESSEC Leadership and Diversity Chair is the creation of knowledge, relevant to both managerial and academic audiences, based on research on diversity and its relationship to leadership issues, taking into account the perspectives of different stakeholders.

The recent European debate on diversity quotas led to the second ESSEC Leadership and Diversity Chair Academic Conference in Paris in 2011. Participants gathered from around the world to present their work, with many contributions focusing on the issue of gender quotas. As with the first ESSEC Leadership and Diversity Chair Academic Conference, whose contributions have since been transformed into an edited book *Diversity in the Workplace: Multidisciplinary and International Perspectives*, we have decided to bring together the papers on gender quotas in the form of this book to bring our discussions to a wider audience. The different chapters illustrate the accelerating and breaking forces in the institutional spread of gender quotas from the standpoint of various disciplines, and provide a balanced and varied insight into this legal phenomenon.

We would like to thank all the writers for their enriching contributions, and our Chair partners Deloitte and L'Oréal for continuing to support our academic endeavours and for having made this project possible. Finally, a warm thanks to Sylvie Boussard for her help and support in coordinating this project.

Stefan Gröschl and Junko Takagi

Introduction:
Gender Quotas in Management

JUNKO TAKAGI AND STEFAN GRÖSCHL

One institutionalized form of combating discrimination towards minority groups and structural inequalities is the implementation of diversity quotas. Diversity quotas exist in various forms in different institutions. The most prevalent perhaps are gender quotas for women candidates to political office which now exist in over 100 countries (Krook, 2007). In the North American context, quotas are more familiar in the form of affirmative action programmes which have been applied most frequently to ethnic minorities in higher education. In recent years, many European countries have also adopted various types of diversity quotas to combat underrepresentation of minority groups in the workplace. For example, in 1987, France implemented a quota law for people with disabilities (PwD) which sets a quota of 6 per cent for firms with 20 or more employees. A similar law exists in Germany where the PwD quota for firms with over 20 employees is 5 per cent. More recently still, a gender quota for women on corporate boards has been introduced in many countries, starting with Norway in 2003 with a minimum target of 40 per cent of either gender, which was attained in 2010. Other countries such as Holland, Spain and France have followed suit, and many others are considering the possibility of applying similar legislation to the gender composition of corporate boards.

While diversity quotas, particularly those focusing on women on corporate boards, seem to be gaining momentum in Europe, it is far from a unanimous trend. Different arguments for and against quotas exist. Proponents of diversity quotas affirm that equal opportunities are not attainable without enforcement of such laws. Opponents suggest that quotas only lead to more stigmatization of minority groups, and will harm their efforts for equality by encouraging the promotion either of underqualified individuals, or of individuals who are perceived to be non-competitive compared with majority members. In recent years, affirmative action programmes in the United States that have been in place for decades have encountered legislative setbacks, with some states retracting from their implementation as a result of discrimination claims by members of the ethnic majority. While the underlying intention of diversity quotas is politico-legal, it is nonetheless important to understand the social and managerial objectives of diversity quotas, the contexts in which they are encouraged (or not), and the arguments that support (or not) their implementation in order to have a better grasp of divergent movements for and against quotas that can be observed.

Diversity quotas are generally perceived as a means to achieving equality through the principle of proportional representation. They are founded on an underlying perception of inequality regarding diversity groups which is manifested in the underrepresentation of certain minority groups in political, social and economic roles. A fundamental assumption of diversity quotas is that people can be counted based on their affiliation to a particular diversity category. Another is that based on these countable diversity categories, groups have a fundamental right to be at least minimally represented in higher education, in the workforce at different levels of the organizational hierarchy, and in politics.

While the above assumptions seem clear at first sight, like most social phenomena, diversity quotas also need to be contextualized in order to understand how they are perceived and their consequent impact. For example, what categories are countable? In the United States, the notion of ethnic origin has been debated over decades, and various forms of categorization have been proposed. In France, the republican principles determine all citizens to be French and does not allow for a distinction based on ethnic origin. This has lead to a heated political debate regarding how to deal with ethnic unrest. The basic notion that we can count people based on their affiliation to a diversity group also raises questions for clarification such as 'how do we ascertain such an affiliation?' Is this the responsibility of the individual to be counted or is it by some less subjective means such as country-of-origin for ethnicity, chronological age when considering the issue of seniors, and medico-legal status for persons with disabilities? What are the legal requirements for a category such as a person with disabilities, and when these requirements are met, can we assume or not that the individual concerned will automatically associate herself with the category? If subjective (self-) and social (other-) identification with a diversity group do not perfectly correspond, what are the implications for the implementation of quotas? Such questions also raise the issue of whether or not it is possible to consider different diversity groups in the same way when discussing quotas. Are quotas for persons with disabilities based on the same premises and do they have the same objectives as gender quotas in the workplace? We believe that there are multiple issues to be discussed and clarified in considering diversity quotas.

The current European debate in diversity quotas, and in particular gender quotas, provides a timely opportunity to assemble scholars from different disciplines and countries to reflect upon the notion of diversity quotas and their applications in different settings. In this book, we focus on the example of gender quotas. Gender is generally recognizable and thus countable. Individuals are able to distinguish themselves as either male or female, and more importantly are categorized as such by socio-legal institutions. There are many examples of inequality of opportunities in management for women and the argument for increasing gender equality is well established in the managerial literature (for example, Fletcher and Ely, 2003; Kanter, 1977; Lorber and Farrell, 1991; Meyerson and Fletcher, 2000). Gender is also a diversity category for which the proportions are equal in society so that it is easier than other diversity categories to compare the issue of representativeness across different contexts.

The history of gender quotas is perhaps most developed in the political science literature where we find discussions around the implementation of gender quotas for women candidates to political office which have been adopted in over 100 countries, the majority of which were introduced over the last 30 years (Krook, 2007). There are four main arguments that have been used to explain this achievement: active lobbying on the part of women (collective mobilization), strategic importance of gender representation as identified by key political players (political elite support), support from international norms (transnational emulation and institutionalization), and consistency with general notions of equality and representation (fit) (Krook, 2007). The latter is elaborated in comparative studies of gender quotas in politics that highlight differences in underlying logics for understanding gender differences. For example, Inhetveen (1999) and Pesonen et al. (2009) describe the logic of 'feminism of equality' that is found in the

Norwegian context and 'feminism of difference' that is found in the German context. The former logic focuses on representativeness while the latter centres around a discourse of competence. The authors argue that the former favours a quota approach (that is, a better fit) while the latter is more critical of quotas (that is, potential issues due to lack of fit). Contextualization and the issue of fit are key factors that explain differences across countries in the implementation and the resulting consequences of gender quotas (see for example Tienari et. al., 2009 regarding gender quotas in Sweden and Finland). In addition, Dahlerup (1998) emphasizes that focusing solely on numbers is not enough to combat inequalities in politics, and emphasizes the need to also examine executive power, and the spread of equality more generally. The need for contextualization of the environment in which gender quotas are considered and adopted, and also the danger of concentrating too much on numbers to the detriment of other measures are sound advice for thinking about gender quotas in management settings.

In the management context, there is less differentiation than in the past between men and women at entry-level positions both in terms of numbers and pay for identical work. However, women are still comparatively scarce in upper-level positions. Fletcher and Ely (2003) explain the underrepresentation of women in management using four frames. One frame describes the problem from the perspective that women lack the necessary competencies and that differences arise due to differences in socialization. The second perspective ascertains that women have different competencies from men which are not legitimate within the system and thus not recognized. The third perspective focuses on systemic discrimination of women due to differential power and opportunity structures between men and women. The fourth approach identifies a cultural bias in favour of social practices created by and for men. Despite the ascendance of women in educational attainment, once employed, they still face obstacles described by all four perspectives so that it is difficult for women to reach the corporate suite (Eagly and Carli, 2007). In this context, many countries are turning to gender quotas on corporate boards to encourage women to top management positions through legal means. A study by Deloitte (2011) shows that since 2003, when a gender quota on corporate boards was first introduced in Norway, the trend has spread gradually through European countries that have either implemented or are considering similar measures. The European Commission's vice-president and European Commissioner for Justice, Viviane Reding, suggests a two-step process to increasing the percentage of women on corporate boards through 1) self-regulation; and 2) legally-binding quotas for publicly traded firms in Europe. This suggests that the trend is likely to continue in the future.

The growing academic interest in women on corporate boards (Burke and Mattis, 2000; Thomson and Graham, 2005; Huse, 2007; Vinnicombe et al., 2008, Fagan et. al., 2012)) focuses mainly on the implementation of legal frameworks in different countries. These studies identify the perceived need for such legislation based on observations of slow progress of women to the senior management level, including the slow increase of women on corporate boards (Daily, Certo and Dalton, 1999; Arken, Bellar and Helms, 2004), and persistence of gender-biases (Bilimoria and Piderit, 1994), including the persistence of 'old boys' networks'. These studies cite the existence of equality legislation, corporate governance frameworks favouring diversity, more senior women, large pay gaps, the presence of work–life balance initiatives and employer of choice initiatives as antecedents for the implementation of a gender quota law for corporate boards. The expected consequences of such legislation are improvement in the quality of board deliberations and overall corporate governance, more socially-oriented decisions, and possible positive impact on firm performance and corporate branding. Arguments in support of more women on corporate boards include improving communication within the firm and with major stakeholders (Milliken and Martins, 1994), understanding diverse markets (Daily, Certo and Dalton, 1999), and new leadership styles (Adler, 1997) and forms of transformational management (Rosener, 1990). Studies have also found that having women on boards create more opportunities for women employees generally (Bilimoria, 2006; Bilimoria and Wheeler, 2000), for example by acting as role models with a positive impact on promotions of women (Beckman and Phillips, 2005).

However, despite equality legislation in many countries, gender biases based on the perception of lack of required competencies, networks and search agents, work–life balance issues and women's perceived lack of motivation prevail and there is a perceived need to further encourage the participation of women particularly in upper-level management. Studies also suggest that it is dangerous to assume that higher minority representation in one sector of society automatically leads to higher representation in other sectors (for example, see Terjesen and Singh, 2008 for gender). In their 43-country study of women on corporate boards, Terjesen and Singh (2008) found correlation between more women in senior management positions and the percentage of women on corporate boards. They also found however, that the longer the tradition of political representation by women, the lower percentage of women on corporate boards, so that they found the highest level of women on corporate boards in emerging democratic countries such as Croatia and Slovenia. As suggested by the political science literature, understanding how gender inequalities are perceived and the context in which gender quotas are applied will help us to better explain such variances in the percentage of women on corporate boards across countries.

In this book we present discussions around the contextualization of gender quotas in different countries. Despite institutionalizing forces pushing (European) countries towards implementing quotas, there are comparative differences in equality logics, the structure of corporate boards, and the overall number of firms that may fall under the legislation. If we take the case of Norway which has already attained its 40 per cent quota, we need to take into consideration its unusual governance practices in order to explain how it was able to close the gender gap on corporate boards so quickly. In Norway, corporate boards are comparatively small with an average of five members (L'Helias, 2010). They also do not set limits on the number of board seats an individual person can hold, so that it is possible for an individual (woman) to hold multiple seats and to even fulfil this activity full time. Compare this to the French situation where board sizes are larger and there is a limit of maximum five seats that any individual can hold. The challenge of filling the estimated 2,700 corporate board seats with women (L'Helias, 2010) in a short time becomes a more daunting task. We look at the question of how gender inequality in the workplace is dealt with in different contexts, and when applicable, how gender quotas have been applied.

In the first part of this book we present case studies and examples of different legislative approaches to gender equality in the workplace and the issue of women on corporate boards. We see that different countries have divergent approaches to addressing gender equality in the workplace due to variation in the social and economic environment of women at work. We have examples of countries that have implemented gender quota laws for corporate boards such as Norway, the Netherlands and Spain. We also have non-European examples from countries that do not have quota laws and that are using other means to achieve gender equality in the workplace, reflecting the impact of different levels of contextualization (that is, country-level vs. continent-level).

We start with Morten Huse's chapter on '"The Golden Skirts": Lessons from Norway about Women on Corporate Boards' which explores who the women on corporate boards in Norway are, how they were recruited, how they behave in the boardroom, and how they contribute to value creation. The author draws tentative lessons about the business case from the Norwegian gender quota law which was the first of its kind and thus the benchmark for all others that follow. Mijntje Lückerath-Rovers's chapter on 'The Feasability of the Dutch Quota Bill' investigates whether the target of 30 per cent women on the Executive and Supervisory Boards of listed Dutch companies is feasible and achievable. Based on the Dutch Female Board Index 2010 that she has created, the author examines what it means for individual companies in the Netherlands if on future vacant seats a woman is appointed.

By way of contrast, there follows a non-European example. Fiona Hurd and Suzette Dyer's chapter 'Legislation and Voluntarism: Two Approaches to Achieving EEO Outcomes for Women in New Zealand' reviews legislative and social changes in New Zealand, details the current employment status of women, and explores why women have yet to achieve employment equity in New Zealand.

Returning to Europe, Patricia Gabaldón's chapter on 'Spain: Driving to Gender Equality' discusses the impact of Spain's quota legislation and policies, and their impact and effect on firms' policies, and the representation of female employees and managers in firms operating in Spain. This finally reinforces the fact that the issues and challenges raised even in countries with gender quota legislation are diverse, justifying the need for case studies such as these and also the importance of taking into account the context in which gender quota laws are applied.

Finally in this part and to emphasize the issue of context, we visit two more countries outside Europe. Stella M. Nkomo, in 'Striving for gender equality in the "New" South Africa: Government and Legislative Initiatives', provides a comprehensive overview of the different policies and interventions (ranging from legislative interventions to novel programmes) that have been put in place to attain gender equality in South Africa since 1994, and discusses the current status of women in various sectors in South Africa. In their chapter on 'Women in India: Their Odyssey towards Equality', Radha Sharma and Shoma Mukherji trace the arduous journey of Indian women towards equality in the workplace and discuss the constitutional provisions for equality of gender and the status of their implementation within the social context in which Indian women grow and join the workforce. The authors throw light on the Women Reservation Bill and its impact on political equality of women along with the current debate regarding the reservation of seats for women in the corporate boards.

In the second part of the book, we present different logics that exist in support (or not) of quota legislation for increasing gender equality in the workplace. Marjan Radjavi begins with a legal perspective on the spread of quota laws in 'Quotas for Securing Gender Justice' and considers quota policies with reference to, on the one hand law, and on the other hand, social practices. She addresses conceptual points from the perspective of international law, and discusses the circulating discourses and practices involved in local organizing on gender justice, and on the efficacy of quotas in two example countries, namely Argentina and Pakistan. Next, Elena Doldor begins to address the question of why we find resistance to quotas in Anglo-Saxon contexts in 'Gender Diversity on UK Boards: Exploring Resistance to Quotas'.

In 'The Construction of Workplace Identities for Women: Some Reflections on the Impact of Female Quotas and Role Models', Junko Takagi and Shora Moteabbed discuss the potential impact of gender quotas for corporate boards on the development of women into top management positions from a role model perspective. They conclude that the impact of having more women on corporate boards may be limited depending on the proportions of female Executive Board members. 'Down for the Count: How Meritocratic Ideology Stigmatizes Quotas in the United States and Some Alternative Paths to Equity' by Maureen Scully addresses the American situation and, like the earlier UK case, identifies meritocratic ideology as an impediment to quota laws and provides suggestions for a more persuasive positioning of quotas.

In the concluding chapter, 'The Gender Issue: Identity and Differences Revisited', Laurent Bibard rediscovers sexual differences to further explore the notion of control and its managerial consequences. This chapter brings us back to the fundamentals of gender differences and their manifestation in the management context among others, incorporating the notion of power and control that is perhaps at the basis of the gender relationship. For us, this chapter takes us to the philosophical origins of the different perspectives discussed in the book regarding gender equality and the means by which this might be achieved. In one sense it is a conclusion, and in another, the starting point of ensuing discussions on gender differences, gender equality and gender quotas.

References

Adler, N.J. (1997). Global leadership: women leaders, *Management International Review*, 37(1), 171–196.

Arken, D.E., Bellar, S.L. and Helms, M.M. (2004). The ultimate glass ceiling revisited: the presence of women on corporate boards, *Journal of Business Ethics*, 50(2), 177–185.

Beckman, C.M. and Phillips, D.J. (2005). Interorganizational determinants of promotion: client leadership and the promotion of women attorneys, *American Sociological Review*, 70(4), 678–701.

Burke, R.J. and M. Mattis (eds) (2000), *Women on Corporate Boards of Directors: International Challenges and Opportunities*. Dordrecht: The Netherlands: Kluwer, pp. 25–40.

Bilimoria, D. (2006), The relationship between women corporate directors and women corporate officers, *Journal of Managerial Issues*, 18(1), 47–62.

Bilimoria, D. and Piderit, S. (1994). Board committee membership: effects of sex-based bias, *Academy of Management Journal*, 37(6), 1453–1477.

Bilimoria, D. and Wheeler, J. (2000). 'Women corporate directors: current research and future directions', in M. Davidson and R. Burke (eds), *Women in Management: Current Research Issues*, Volume II. London: Paul Chapman, pp. 138–163.

Dahlerup, D. (1998) 'Using Quotas to Increase Women's Political Representation', in A. Karam (ed.) *Women in Parliament: Beyond Numbers*. Stockholm: Institute for Democracy and Electoral Assistance (IDEA) and Stockholm University, pp. 91–106.

Daily, C., Certo, T. and Dalton, D. (1999). A decade of corporate women: some progress in the boardroom, none in the executive suite, *Strategic Management Journal*, 20(1), 93–99.

Deloitte (2011) Women in the Boardroom: A Global Perspective. Deloitte Global Services Limited.

Eagly, A. and Carli. L. (2007) Women and the labyrinth of leadership, *Harvard Business Review*, 85(9), 3–71.

Fagan, C., Gonzalez Menendez, M., and Gomez Anson, S. (eds.) (2012) *Women on Corporate Boards and in Top Management: European Trends and Policy*. London: Palgrave Macmillan.

Fletcher, J.K., and Ely, R.J. (2003). 'Introducing gender: overview', in R.J. Ely, E.G. Foldy and M.A. Scully (eds), *Reader in Gender, Work and Organization*. Malden, MA: Blackwell Publishing, pp. 3–9.

Huse, M. (2007). *Boards, Governance and Value Creation: The Human Side of Corporate Governance*. Cambridge, UK: Cambridge University Press.

Inhetveen, K. (1999). Can gender equality be institutionalized? The role of launching values in institutional innovation. *International Sociology*, 14(4), 403–422.

Kanter, R.M. (1977). *Men and Women of the Corporation*. New York: Basic Books.

Krook, M.L. (2007). Candidate gender quotas: a framework for analysis. *European Journal of Political Research*, 46, 367–394.

L'Helias, S. (2010) Women on boards in France, *Directors and Boards*, Third quarter, 31.

Lorber J.L. and Farrell, S.A. (eds) (1991). *The Social Construction of Gender*. Newbury Park, CA: Sage Publications.

Meyerson, D.E. and Fletcher, J.K. (2000). A modest manifesto for shattering the glass ceiling, *Harvard Business Review*, January/February, 127–136.

Milliken, F.J., and Martins, L.L. (1996). Searching for common threads: understanding the multiple effects of diversity in organizational groups, *Academy of Management Review*, 21(2), 402–433.

Pesonen, S., Tienari, J., and Vanhala, S. (2009) The boardroom gender paradox, *Gender in Management: An International Journal*, 24(5), 327–345

Rosener, J. (1990). Ways women lead, *Harvard Business Review*, November–December, 119–125.

Terjesen, S. and Singh, V. (2008). Female presence on corporate boards: a multicountry study of environmental context, *Journal of Business Ethics*, 83(1), 55–63

Thomson, P. and Graham, J. (2005) *A Woman's Place is in the Boardroom: The Business Case*. New York: Palgrave Macmillan.

Tienari, J., Holgersson, C., Merilainen, S. and Hook, P. (2009) Gender, management and market discourse: the case of gender quotas in the Swedish and Finnish media. *Gender, Work and Organization*, 16(4), 501–521.

Vinnicombe, S., Singh, V., Burke, R.J., Bilimoria, D. and Huse, M. (2008) *Women on Corporate Boards of Directors: International Research and Practice*. Cheltenham: Edward Elgar Publishing Ltd.

Quota Systems in Different Cultural Settings

1

The 'Golden Skirts': Lessons from Norway about Women on Corporate Boards of Directors

MORTEN HUSE

Introduction

Norway is considered one of the most progressive countries with regards to increasing the number of women on boards – thanks to it being an early adopter of legislation to force companies to recruit women to the boardroom. To many feminists, this is the boldest move anywhere to breach one of the most durable barriers to gender equality – The Female Factor.

In 2003, amendments to the Public Limited Companies Act in Norway provided for a requirement for a certain minimum proportion of directors from each gender. This has led to a dramatic increase in the number of women on boards of Norwegian companies. Other countries looking to adopt an enforced quota scheme are looking at the results in Norway and plan accordingly.

The role of women in society is changing. This is not only in the public and private sector, but also in the business world. These changes are found in many countries, but the speed and focus may vary. There are various arguments to develop ways to increase the number of women corporate boards of directors. Corporate boards of directors have traditionally been seen as meeting places for societal and business elites. The boards have been considered as arenas where the interests of the 'old boys' network' are promoted, and it has been argued that an invisible glass ceiling is hindering women to get into board and top management positions. Several initiatives for getting women into corporate boards have thus been presented (Vinnicombe et al., 2008).

This chapter concentrates on ways to increase the number of women on corporate boards. And the focus is on lessons learnt from recent developments in Norway. I will present reflections about the results being achieved after a law reform was made with the objective to have 40 per cent of the board members coming from the least represented gender. This has in practice been a law forcing the largest Norwegian corporations to have at least 40 per cent women among the board members. The observations will be about the effectiveness of various programmes or means to increase the number of women on corporate boards, and there will be reflections on consequences for businesses and the individual women becoming board members.

WHY BALANCED GENDER REPRESENTATION?

There are various arguments for increasing the number of women on corporate boards – for example societal arguments, individual career arguments and business case arguments.

The societal case arguments have typically been the starting point for much of the attention to the question, and these are also behind the most far-reaching initiatives to increase the number of women on corporate boards. The societal case arguments are about justice in society, democracy, participation, gender equality and the follow up of various international conventions, for example, UN conventions, human rights and European Union (EU)/ European Economic Area (EEA) conventions. The individual case arguments or the career arguments are often related to the 'glass ceiling' discussions. The business case arguments are about why and how women on corporate boards will improve firm performance. These arguments have particularly been emphasized in contexts where the societal case arguments are not accepted. The main business case arguments are about diversity (that women are different from men), about the use of existing knowledge (that women represent 50 per cent of the knowledge-base in society), about customer relations and understanding customers (that women in many sectors are the main customers), and that men on corporate boards often are too passive.

In the international and national debates the different arguments are often unconsciously mixed. The reasoning and logics behind different initiatives have often suffered from this mixing-up. When an initiative is evaluated it should be done based on the objective for it. If the objective is power balance in society, then the initiative should not only be evaluated based on individual career possibilities or firm performance. These criteria should be considered, but the main evaluation criteria should be societal.

The rest of this chapter is outlined as follows. In the following section we describe the Norwegian case looking at initiatives to increase the number of women directors on corporate boards. This is followed by a section describing the business case for women on boards. The next section describes some results from a study about the 'golden skirts' – the women that have made a living from being independent directors. This is followed by a section that reflects on the quota law discussion in relation to the mainstream recommendation about corporate governance practices. In the final section a summarizing conclusion with recommendation is presented.

Norway – the Societal Case: Initiatives and Innovations to Increase the Number of Women Directors

During recent decades several initiatives and innovations have been made to achieve balanced gender perspectives and to increase the number of women in power positions in society (Vinnicombe et al., 2008). In some countries – like Norway – public policies were made at an early stage to have women represented in the public bureaucracy, governmental committees and on the board in state-owned enterprises. Several political parties also made commitment to have women in leadership position – resulting in a large ratio of women in top political positions in Norway.

International discussions about why and how to increase the number of women on corporate boards can also be traced back more than 30 years. Various initiatives and programmes have been considered. They include political arguments, the development of women networks, the financing and dissemination of research, courses and education for preparing women for board work, mentorship programmes, data registers and other sources of communicating to potential women candidates. Suggestions for setting requirements on the number of women directors through soft as well as hard laws have also been promoted.

The different initiatives have various objectives. Some are directed towards educating or preparing women, some are directed towards motivating those selecting board members, and some initiatives are directed towards facilitating the recruitment process. The effectiveness of the different programmes should be evaluated according to the objective of the specific programme. The effectiveness in relation to increasing the number of women on corporate boards will often be a result of a combination of various programmes (educating programmes, motivating programmes and facilitating programmes). The effectiveness will furthermore depend on various contingencies such as the actors involved and the context within which the programme is developed and executed.

A presentation of boards and corporate governance in Norway is found in Rasmussen and Huse (2011). Norway has a two-tier corporate governance system. However, the executive level is normally not a board, but only one person. Board members are typically non-executives. Norway has also a system where one-third of the board members can be elected by and selected from the employees. Furthermore, Oslo Stock Exchange is dominated by state ownership.

In Figure 1.1 we find an example from Norway illustrating the effectiveness of various programmes to increase the number of women on boards.

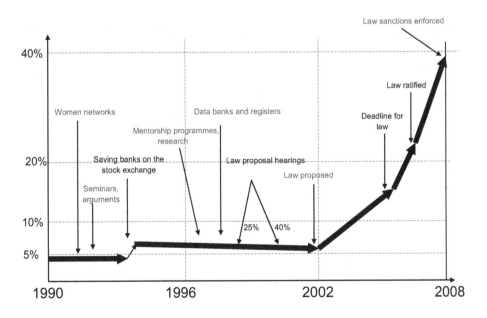

Figure 1.1   Effects of programmes: an illustration from Norway

Figure 1.1 reports the percentage of women on the boards of large corporations in Norway. Figures from 1990 to 1998 are from firms listed on the Oslo Stock Exchange. Figures after 1998 are ASA companies (publicly tradable companies). The ASA form of incorporation was established in Norway in 1998. ASA-incorporated firms are generally the largest companies. The figures reported on women are almost constant, around 5 per cent from 1990 till 2002. No increase took place even though considerable efforts were placed on initiatives such as women networks, seminars and arguments, mentorship programmes, research, data banks and registers on women aspiring to board positions. Two public hearings on law proposals also took place, but no increase in the percentage of women on corporate boards was achieved. The only change displayed before 2002 was around 1994. This change was caused by new types of firms (mainly saving banks) being introduced to the Oslo Stock Exchange.

However, we see an incredible increase from 2002 to 2008 – from 6 per cent to almost 40 per cent. In 2002 a law was proposed by the Norwegian Parliament that all ASA-incorporated firms should have gender balance. Each gender should hold at least 40 per cent of board positions in ASA firms. The ASA firms had a few years to implement this requirement voluntarily – otherwise the law would be ratified and enforced. The enforcement of the law began in the beginning of 2008, but by then all ASA companies (with only very few exceptions) had already met the requirement.

The number of board positions in ASA companies has been reduced from 2007 to 2010 – financial companies were no longer required to have the ASA form of incorporation. Several financial companies thus decided to move from the ASA form of incorporation to the AS form (AS are firms not being publicly tradable). The numbers of board positions held by women and men in this period were 1,061 women/2,067 men in 2007, 1,044 women/1,684 men in 2008, 915 women/1,501 men in 2009 and 906 women/1,419 men in 2010.

The Business Case: Gender Diversity and Board Value Creation

Is the law good for businesses? It is so far impossible to present statistical data about the legal enforcement's consequences on business performance. The research question has until now been if women on corporate boards contribute positively to firm performance – regardless of how women have achieved these positions (Terjesen, Sealy and Singh, 2009). The main business case arguments for women directors are that they bring diversity into the boardroom. Diversity is in this reasoning assumed to be important for board effectiveness. However, we do not even have clear evidence telling that diversity in general – and gender diversity in particular – contributes to board effectiveness. It can be argued that there are no direct relationships between competence and diversity on the one hand, and board effectiveness and value creation on the other (Huse, 2008). Board effectiveness depends on the boards' working style and decision-making culture, and on board leadership (Huse, 2007).

To respond to these research questions we need to clarify what we mean by a board of directors. Do we argue about supervisory or executive boards, or is it about unified boards? And for what kinds of firms? Huse (1994, 2007) identified four different typologies and their respective bodies of theories including:

- aunt boards where nobody considers the board to play any role;
- barbarian boards where independent board members exercise their power;
- clan boards where the board members are protecting their own privileges;
- value-creating boards where board members are involved in developing the company.

The different types of boards will have different working styles, different types of competencies will be emphasized, and value creation will have different interpretations.

Further, what do we mean by diversity? Diversity has something to do with the board members as a group. Diversity and competence are not the same. And what do we mean by good? We may talk about value creation, but it depends on with whom we talk about value creation and what kind of value creation.

When exploring boards we need to understand that there are various actors that work in different arenas. We need to know who the actors are (internal, external or board members), the diversity, knowledge and skills, and who the board members identify themselves with. The arenas may be formal and informal, and not all arenas are open to everybody. The relationships between the various actors are characterized by trust and emotions, and of power and strategizing.

SOME EMPIRICAL STUDIES FROM NORWAY

The few studies that have been done on the contribution of women directors to board or firm effectiveness have given mixed results (Huse, 2008). Some studies conclude that women have made positive contributions, while others conclude that negative or no contributions have been made. A common problem with most of these studies is that they treat women as a homogeneous group and do not take into account that there may be more differences among women and among men, than between men and women in general. It is therefore important to understand to what degree the women joining corporate boards bring to the boardroom different values, knowledge and experiences – or if they behave the same way in the boardroom as men. I will thus present here some of the recent business case studies we have conducted in Norway on women on corporate boards.

- Understanding board diversity. Nielsen and Huse (2010a) and Huse, Nielsen and Hagen (2009) explore how board diversity impacts boards' involvement in different tasks. The conclusion is that there is a need to go beyond the surface-level diversity, for example, insider/outsider ratio, gender, race, educational background, ownership, and so on to deep-level diversity such as real competence, personality, identity and behaviour. Women and men on boards may not be very different. Attributes other than gender may be more important (Huse, Nielsen and Hagen, 2009).
- Importance of values and perceptions. Nielsen and Huse (2010b) show how values, professional experiences and equality perceptions in the boards influence the contributions to strategy. Various processes mediate the relationship between board diversity and women directors, and the boards' involvement in decision-making contribution to strategy.
- How do women differ from men? Huse and Solberg (2006) show how women may differ from men in the boardroom, but it is not gender per se that makes the difference. It depends on the attributes of each individual man or woman. The distinctions

between female, feminine and feminist may visualize that men may also have some characteristics typically attributed to women and vice versa.

- Critical mass. Torchia, Calabro and Huse (2011) and Torchia et al. (2010) show that when women are a minority group on the board they tend to adapt to the majority group. However, when passing a certain threshold (a critical mass) they will not experience this conformity pressure. The will not have any contribution before this threshold is reached. In discussion about boards this threshold is argued to be three persons.

These findings may be summarized in Figure 1.2.

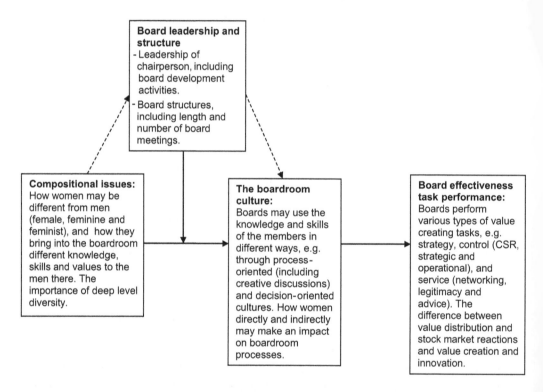

Figure 1.2   Concepts and relationships based on our findings

The figure illustrates that: a) there is a need to go beyond surface-level diversity and understand deep-level diversity; b) there is a need to understand the mediating impact of processes, and how women may impact processes directly and indirectly; c) the processes and the use of knowledge and skills depends on board leadership and structure; and d) women may tend to influence certain aspects of value creation and board tasks more than other aspects. The research findings and the figure illustrate why there is so much ambiguity in research results on the business case for women directors. The reliability of results that do not consider the deeper-level understandings, the mediating and moderating variables on overall firm-level performance measures is questioned.

Who are the Women on Boards – 'Golden Skirts'?

The term 'golden skirts' has received considerable attention in the Norwegian and later also the international press, as well as in research (Seierstad and Opsahl, 2011), and studies have been conducted to explore who the women on boards in Norway are and how they have been selected (Heidenreich, 2010). Critical voices in the international press have been sceptical about the development of an elite group of prominent women that is replacing the 'old boys' network'.

The following tables illustrate that this may be the case.

Table 1.1   ASA multi-board memberships: 2007–2010 (sum)

	Women	**Men**
More than 16 (means more than 4 annually)	8 women	2 men
13–16 positions	13 women	7 men
9–12 positions	27 women	39 men
5–8 positions	107 women	111 men

Table 1.1 shows multi-board memberships for women and men in Norwegian publicly tradable companies (ASA companies). We have summarized the number of board positions during the years 2007, 2008, 2009 and 2010. We found that during these four years 1,309 women held one board position for at least one year in an ASA company in an ASA company. Knowing that only 40 per cent of the board members are women, we should also expect that in absolute figures there should be more men than women having multi-board membership. However, that is not the case. We found that eight women and only two men held more than four positions in ASA companies over the four years, and 21 women and only nine men had, on average, more than three ASA board memberships. One explanation of this situation may be the selection process. As a general criteria for becoming a board member is to have previous board experience, the few women holding such experience are more likely to be offered these positions.

Table 1.2 illustrates how multi-board membership among the gender has changed from 2000 to 2010.

Table 1.2   Gender change in multi-board memberships

	Multi-board directors 2000	**Multi-board directors 2005**	**Multi-board directors 2010**
Women	No women	Some 'golden skirts', family and business women	Professional independent (including the 'golden skirts'), family, officers and business women
Men	'Old boys' network', consultants, investors, lawyers	'Old boys' network', consultants, investors, lawyers	Women have replaced many multi-board men

Multi-board memberships have moved from men to women, and the 'golden skirts' have replaced the 'old boys' networks'. We made an analysis of interlocking directorates among the women with the most board positions. Two women were on three boards together, but they were not on a board with any of the other women. These two women are discussed later. Among the women with an average of more than three board positions, no other women were on more than one board together. Only three women held more than two board positions with the other. This means that within the group of 'golden skirts' there are very limited interlocks and no clear similarity to the 'old boys' network'. Some of the women even indicated that they did not know any of the others.

A framework for understanding board composition is presented in Table 1.3. Based on the recent corporate governance literature we can identify three main types of board positions. The first group is those held by persons having financial and psychological relations to the company leadership, including executive directors, consultants, family and friends and business partners. The second group is those held by persons having financial and psychological relations to the main external stakeholder or ownership groups. These will often be investors, their representatives, family members and friends; sometimes also politicians. Neither of these groups are in the present corporate governance debates and recommendations considered to be independent. The last group of board members will be those that are completely independent – with no relations to either internal nor external actors.

On the other hand, there are people whose career aim is to be a board member as well as those who make a living out of their business but also hold board positions.

Table 1.3   Different types of board members

	Business directors		Professional directors	
	Women	**Men**	**Women**	**Men**
Insider and quasi-insider. Limited replaceable.	Family	Entrepreneur, friend, business relation, majority shareholder	Family, officer	Officer, consultant, lawyer, investor
Stakeholder related directors. Limited replaceable	Investors, their employees and partners. Employee directors	Investors and their employees. Employee directors	Investor, majority shareholder and their partners and employees	Business angels, investor and majority shareholder
Independent directors. Replaceable	Entrepreneur	CEO, 'Old boys' network', expert	'Golden skirts' and those in SMEs	Ex-CEO, 'Old boys' network'

Characteristics of men and women in these six categories are displayed in Table 1.2. In the categories we identify the typical descriptions of the 'old boys' network' as well as the 'golden skirts'. Both 'old boys' networks' and the 'golden skirts' are in the category of independent directors. There are some business directors in Norway who are independent directors, but only one or two of the 30 women holding three or more board positions (based on the 2007–2010 average) are independent business women. The women holding the most board positions in the Norwegian ASA companies are independent professional board members. This is the group of prominent women that we have labelled the 'golden skirts'.

When exploring the transition in Norway based on the gender quota law, we find that the board positions with insider or outsider motivation are hardly replaceable. This means that the transition from men to women has almost only been in the group of independent directors. Few new board members in this period have been recruited among families and friends (Heidenreich, 2010). The men with the most board positions are those being or those representing investors, that is, the 'money sacks'. Interestingly, it is the women (who in practice fill most of the board seats as independent directors) who will make up the largest number of board members on important committees such as the auditing committee, nomination committee and compensation committee. This is a change from the past situation with women only getting positions on the 'least important' committees (Bilimoria and Pederit, 1994).

Who then are the 'golden skirts'? We used the list of the women with the most positions in the period 2007–2010 (Table 1.1). Among the 21 women having on average more than three positions, we found one women who was a major ship owner and was also a board member/chair on her company's subsidiary boards. Two women had strong ties to the main owners of a group of an investment companies, and they were board members on several of them. These two women were also the only women serving on several boards together. The companies they served on changed forms of incorporation in 2010. The remaining 18 were considered to be independent board members. Among them, only three held a main position other than being a board member, but even the main roles held by these three women were taken on while being a multi-board member. In our analyses we thus considered them as professional board members together with the remaining 15. We undertook in-depth portrait interviews with all these women. The formal competencies and qualifications of these women were impressive – with respect to education as well as to practice – but we found that they differed in several ways. As a result of the interviews we categorized them based on a) length experience and b) degree of pragmatism or flexibility in behaviour. This is displayed in Table 1.4.

Table 1.4   Who are the 'golden skirts'?

	Principle- and facts-oriented golden skirts	Pragmatic business-oriented golden skirts
Aspiring golden skirts	'The young, smart and clever – having fact on the fingertips, often having mentors' (around 40 years)	'The ambitious and pragmatic women – using the opportunities given by the law' (50 years +)
Experienced golden skirts	'The iron fists being used to fight – experience from top-level politics' (50 years +)	'The business experienced – being board members before the gender-balance law' (55 years +)

The result is a four square matrix. In our analyses we categorized four women into each of the groups, and two women were classified as in transition, that is, moving in the period with respect to classification. The labels put on the various groups were: a) the 'young, smart and clever'; b) the 'ambitious and pragmatic'; c) the 'iron fists being used to fight';

and d) the 'business experienced'. The 'young, smart and clever' are typically younger than the others, they have 'facts at their fingertips', they have typically been discovered by a mentor, and they emphasize the support of their husbands and his professional network. These women typically have the analytical skills, approaches and competencies of 'McKinsey' consultants. This group would have been larger if we only considered the positions in 2010. They consider themselves as persons bringing knowledge and facts to the board.

The 'ambitious and pragmatic' have the most board memberships. Their backgrounds vary (law, engineering, and so on), but they have limited background in executive business leadership. They typically saw the opportunity to make a living from being a board member as the gender quota law was introduced. They did not wait to be discovered, but actively sought opportunities to be visible and get board positions. The ambition for these women has been more to become a board member rather than to contribute to board behaviour and company performance. However, they typically focus on corporate governance recommendations. There are many women who have similar aspirations, but these are those who have been the most successful.

Norway has a tradition of having women in top positions in politics. The 'iron fists being used to fight' all have a background in top-level politics, often as ministers in the big and heavy industry-related departments in the Norwegian Cabinet. However, it is not enough to have been a minister or a party leader, you also need to bring forth your aspiration for top-level business positions. These women bring their backgrounds from the political arena to the corporate boards. They know the political system. They also know how to use power techniques both inside and outside the boardroom, and they have access to a large network of politicians, business leaders and bureaucrats.

The 'business experienced' 'golden skirts' had considerable business and board experience before the law was introduced, and with the quota law they were the first to be considered for additional positions. The backgrounds of some of these women are really impressive. Their focus on the board is to contribute to value creation, and they feel happy when they see that the company is doing better because of their contribution.

Most of the women, with the exception of those in the 'young, smart and clever' category, have been divorced, are single or without children. Most of the women also find that being a board member fits nicely into their life situation. It is difficult to make a career in business, and many of them describes themselves as good at multi-tasking, and have found that they needed to stow away the 'nice girl' ambition. However, many commented that being a board member is much easier than being a top executive. It is more predictable, and you can more easily plan your time, take days off and combine it with caring for children or grandchildren.

Following these groups over the four year period 2007–2010 we find some development. Some of the women with the highest number of board positions at the beginning of the period are reducing their level of involvement, and there was a woman that did not have any position in 2007 that in 2010 had the most positions on ASA company boards. During this period some women became CEOs of other companies, leading them to reduce their level of other commitments.

The Quota Law Discussion and Codes of Best Practices

The discussion about women on boards in general and the gender quota law in particular has led to an alternative discussion about boards of directors and good corporate governance than the one that has dominated during recent decades. The dominating corporate governance discussion has evolved from the prevention of managerial dominance in large US corporations and how shareholder activism increased in order to protect the interest of shareholders. Recent codes of corporate governance have been adopted by many stock exchanges and they have largely been developed to protect the interest of minority shareholders. A main requirement in this discussion is that board members should be independent. Table 1.5 compares some of the core elements in the dominating codes of best practice with the core elements in the discussion of women directors.

Table 1.5   Comparisons of codes and quota discussions

Corporate governance codes – male/yang	Women quota – female/yin
Independence	Competence
Value distribution	Value creation
Decision-oriented	Process-oriented
Risk aversion and control	Risk willingness and strategy
Short term	Long term
Finance literature	Strategy literature
Shareholder identification	Firm identification

There are various contrasts, and the women on boards discussion challenges many of the corporate governance recommendations, for example, with respect to board member qualifications, the concept of value creation, board decision-making, risk taking, time perspective, academic embedding and the understanding of a firm. Competencies and qualifications of board members are emphasized in the discussion of women directors. Women are not supposed to be board members unless they are truly qualified. The women on board discussion emphasizes value creation in the firm and not only value distribution from the firm. It emphasizes process-oriented decision-making rather than the speed of decision-making. Risk taking and innovation are challenged rather than risk aversion and control, and a long-term rather than a short-term perspective is used. The women on boards discussion is embedded in the strategy and organization behaviour literature, while the code discussion is embedded in finance. And finally there are different underlying understandings of what a firm is. Does a firm exist only to give value to shareholders, or is a firm a distinct institution that plans for long-term sustainability and value creation? The quota law and the women on board discussion may be supported by the lessons from the recent international financial crisis; a renewed attention to long-term sustainability.

Conclusions and Recommendations

The law may have been important in Norway, but there are various learning effects that we should consider before recommending similar laws in other countries and for other types of firms. The Norwegian quota law was directed to large publicly tradable firms (incorporated as ASA). We have, however, now seen a major increase in the number of women directors in other large firms which are not ASA incorporated. There are two main reasons for this increase. The first is that many women are now being very visible as good board members. There is no shortage of highly qualified women for board positions. Highly qualified women are numerous, they are now getting more experience and are becoming more visible.

The second is the imitating or mimicking processes that take place. It has now become a reputation-building initiative to have women on the board. This has been supported by the Norwegian ASA experiences, but may have consequences for firms also in other countries.

I therefore present three general conclusions:

- Conclusion 1. Board diversity may have a positive role in board value creation. We have found that diversity matters. However, we then talk about deep-level and not surface-level diversity. We do also need to explore competence on a deeper level than what typically is the case when making profiles for potential board members. The impacts of diversity in general and gender diversity in particular depend on board processes and board working style and the board leadership.
- Conclusion 2. Different types of value creation. The fiduciary duty of board members is to do what is best for the company, and thus we need to see other aspects of value creation than just shareholder value. Women directors on a general basis have a particular contribution in relation to Corporate Social Responsibility (CSR) and innovation through their strategy involvement.
- Conclusion 3. Women on boards and the Norwegian quota law. Voluntary action did not succeed in increasing the number of women on corporate boards, but it is still too early to make final conclusions about the societal case, the individual case or the business case. However, we can see many positive signs.

It is too early to make a final conclusion about the success of the Norwegian quota law. It was obvious that voluntary actions did succeed in increasing the number of women as board members. When concluding we need to explore societal case effectiveness, the individual case effectiveness and the business case effectiveness. However, we can so far see many positive signs as results of the law, but the real effects will depend on how the law is followed up in the coming years.

References

Bilimoria, D. and Pederit, S.K. (1994). Board committee membership: effects of sex-based bias, *Academy of Management Journal*, 18(1), 47–61.

Heidenreich, V. (2010). Rekruttering til ASA-styrer etter innføring av kvoteringsregelen, (The recruitment to ASA boards after the introduction of the quota rule) *Magma*, 13(7), 56–70.

Huse, M. (1994). Board-management relations in small firms: the paradox of simultaneous independence and interdependence, *Journal of Small Business Economics*, 6(1), 55–72.

Huse, M. (2007). *Boards, Governance and Value Creation: The Human Side of Corporate Governance*. Cambridge: Cambridge University Press.

Huse, M. (2008). 'Women directors and the "black box" of board behaviour', in S. Vinnicombe, V. Singh, R. Burke, D. Billimoria and M. Huse (eds), *Women on Corporate Boards of Directors: International Research and Practice*. Cheltenham: Edward Elgar, pp. 140–151.

Huse, M., Nielsen, S. and Hagen, I.M. (2009). Women and employee elected board members and their contributions to board control tasks, *Journal of Business Ethics*, 89(4), 581–597

Huse, M. and Solberg, A.G. (2006). Gender related boardroom dynamics, *Women in Management Review*, 21(2), 113–130.

Nielsen, S. and Huse, M. (2010a). The contribution of women on boards of directors: going beyond the surface, *Corporate Governance: An International Review*, 18(2), 136–148.

Nielsen, S. and Huse, M. (2010b). Women directors' contribution to board decision-making and strategic performance: the role of equality perceptions, *European Management Review*, 7(1), 16–29.

Rasmussen, J.L and Huse, M. (2011). 'Corporate governance in Norway: women and employee-elected directors' in C. Mallin, *International Corporate Governance*. Cheltenham: Edward Elgar, pp. 121–146

Seierstad, C. and Opsahl, T. (2011). For the few not the many? The effects of affirmative action on presence, prominence, and social capital of women directors in Norway, *Scandinavian Journal of Management*, 27(1), 44–54.

Terjesen, S., Sealy, R. and Singh, V. (2009). Women directors on corporate boards: a review and research agenda, *Corporate Governance: An International Review*, 17(3), 320–337.

Torchia, M., Calabro, A. and Huse, M. (2011). Women directors on corporate boards: from tokenism to critical mass, *Journal of Business Ethics*, 102(2), 581–597.

Torchia, M., Calabro, A., Huse, M. and Brogi, M. (2011). Critical mass theory and women directors' contribution to board strategic tasks, *International Journal of Corporate Board: Role, Duties and Composition*, 6(3), 42–51.

Vinnicombe, S., Singh, V., Burke, R., Bilimoria, D. and Huse, M. (2008). *Women on Corporate Boards of Directors, International Research and Practice*. Cheltenham: Edward Elgar.

2 The Feasibility of the Dutch Quota Bill

MIJNTJE LÜCKERATH-ROVERS

Introduction

In the Netherlands a Bill including quota legislation for Dutch boards was adopted by the Second Chamber on December 9, 2009[1] and sent to the Senate.[2] The Bill introduces provisions to target a balanced distribution of seats between men and women on both the Executive Board (EB) and the Supervisory Boards (SB) of large Dutch corporations. In The Netherlands, the two-tier board structure is predominantly used. This means that the EB and the SB are two separate boards. In order to facilitate international comparison, in the chapter international terminology will be used: the EB members will be referred to as the Executive Directors (EDs) whereas the SB members will be called the Non-Executive Directors (NEDs).

The described Bill applies to both boards. In the proposed article of law a balanced distribution means that at least 30 per cent of the seats on the EB and SB should be occupied by women and at least 30 per cent of the seats by men. To reach this balanced distribution of seats between men and women, companies must take this into account when a) identifying and nominating EDs; b) preparing a profile of the size and composition of the SB; and c) when appointing, recommending and nominating NEDs. Companies subject to the proposed scheme, but who have not reached the desired targets, should explain in the annual report ('comply or explain') why the seats are not evenly distributed, how the company has tried to balance the distribution of seats, and how the company seeks to achieve the balance of seats in the future. No further sanctions are included. The scope of the statutory provision is limited in time. The proposed legislative items are automatically deleted as per 1 January 2016.

For the Dutch listed companies, the required balance of women and men on EBs and SBs as proposed in the Bill appears to be far away (Lückerath-Rovers, 2010). This chapter focuses on the feasibility of the Bill for the Dutch listed companies. For this purpose, we will investigate what the progress in the EBs and SBs should look like. Based on the situation on 31 August 2010 we will examine what it means for the feasibility of the Bill for individual companies if for each vacant seat one woman will be appointed.

---

1   The Dutch House of Representatives, 2009–2010, Parliamentary Paper 31.763, nr. 14.

2   The Dutch Senate, 2008–2010, Paper 31.763, nr. A.

This chapter proceeds as follows. The following will describe the Dutch quota proposal, its implications and the current discussion in the Dutch senate. Next we discuss the current situation regarding the proportion of women on the EBs and the SBs, including some interesting findings of the characteristics (industry, stock exchange segment) of the companies that do have female representation on the board. Then we will see the results of the research on the feasibility of the quota Bill if on vacant seats women will be appointed in the next four years. The final section provides a conclusion.

The Dutch Quota Proposal

THE PATH TOWARDS THE DUTCH QUOTA PROPOSAL

Getting women on to corporate boards has been the subject of heated debate in the Netherlands for some time. Many initiatives have been established since 1996, all with the same goal: to increase the number of women in top positions. In 1996, 'Opportunity in Bedrijf' was set up (with a governmental grant); a foundation with the vision that diversity is of strategic importance and that a balanced business team will perform better. Almost ten years later, in December 2005, the Ministerial Council published its Emancipation policy 2006–2010 and set a number of objectives to support it.[3] These objectives were that more women went to work, that women worked more hours, and that their talents and skills be better utilized. This was considered to be good for women themselves, society and the future. Six main objectives were formulated of which the fifth objective was 'to achieve a proportionate representation of women in decision-making positions'. The specific objective was that the proportion of women in top jobs in the corporate world should increase to 20 per cent by 2010. In November 2006 (a time when a new Dutch administration had to be formed), a letter to 'the lady forming the new administration-Balkenende' was published in one of the largest Dutch Newspapers.[4] This letter was an initiative of the foundation Women on Top. The open letter was signed by more than 1,500 women. Women on Top demanded that the new administration worked on gender balance in corporate governance, science and public administration, with at least 40 per cent men and at least 40 per cent women at the top. Furthermore, the Ambassadors Network (Ambassadeursnetwerk) was set up in 2000 as a result of an initiative of the Ministries of Social Affairs and Employment and Economic Affairs. The Ambassadors Network was an annually changing group of well-known captains of industry such as Ewald Kist (ING) and Gerlach Cerfontaine (Schiphol). Nowadays, it seems that the Ambassadors Network has been merged into Talent to the Top. This initiative, established in May 2007, strives to force Government, business and women themselves to promote female talent to the top on a structural basis. On 30 October, 2007, the Government, together with a large number of corporations, the employers union VNO-NCW, the Social-Economic Council (SER) and the labour union FNV signed a letter of intent to develop the Charter Talent to the Top. The charter was presented in May 2008 and initially signed by 47 companies and government agencies. Although

---

3   The Dutch House of Representatives, 2005–2006, Parliamentary Paper 30.420, nr. 1, Long-term Plan Emancipation 2006–2010.

4   Women on Top (2006), Open letter published in Dutch newspaper *De Volkskrant*, 28 November 2006, p. 12.

none of the goals described above have yet been met, it seems that the 'sense of urgency' has finally reached the top management of organizations. At the beginning of 2011 169 organizations signed the Charter.

In 2008 the Dutch Labour party, the PvdA, filed a motion instructing the Minister of Finance to 'request the Monitoring Committee Corporate Governance Code to include targets for women on boards of directors and supervisory boards' in their recommendations to update the Corporate Governance Code.[5] The motion included a target rate of between 25 and 30 per cent by 2015. On 24 April, 2008, a majority of the Parliament voted in favour of the motion and the motion was therefore adopted. However, the Minister of Finance stated in its response to the motion that any pressure on the Monitoring Committee would affect and harm the self-regulatory character of the Corporate Governance Code. He suggested that the Parliament should decide on legislation if they believe self-regulation is not satisfied in this respect. MP Kalma announced that the PvdA would file for legislation for a statutory obligation if the targets were not included the Corporate Governance Code. Moreover, the FNV trade union believes that at least 40 per cent of the top positions must be occupied by women by 2012. To achieve this, Agnes Jongerius, Chairman of the FNV said that companies and institutions should implement preferential treatment for women.[6] Minister Piet Hein Donner of Social Affairs was not in favour of a legal quota: 'A legal quota for women in senior positions would lead to over-stretched expectations that cannot be fulfilled.'[7]

The Dutch Corporate Governance Code Monitoring Committee (Frijns Committee) presented the revised Dutch Corporate Governance Code on 10 December 2008. The Frijns Committee experienced political, social and media pressure to include in its recommendations a specific target (a percentage) for women on EBs and SBs. On June 4, 2008, the Frijns Committee published their evaluation and recommendations concerning all aspects of the Code. In the report, the Frijns Committee acknowledges the social issues and the need for increased attention to women in top positions, and also highlights the importance of diversity for the independent tasks of the SB. Diversity is defined to include gender, age, expertise and social background. The Committee also argues that companies gain direct benefit from promoting women in top positions since a key success factor for companies is 'attracting and retaining talent'.

Although the Frijns Committee agrees that a structural policy to attract, retain and develop talent in women is important for companies, and also welcomes initiatives designed to stimulate the establishment of best practice in this policy, the Committee opted for a rather vague adaptation of Principle III.3 regarding Expertise and Composition. Companies are encouraged to pursue a mixed board composition, including gender and age. The SB should also include in its report their specific goals with respect to diversity, and explain, if the intended goal has not been reached, how and within what period it expects to achieve this aim. The pursuit of a mixed composition should be reflected in the profile of the SB. The Committee believes that a company itself can best assess how these efforts can be incorporated into the profile, and this is the company's responsibility. This is reflected in the adjustment of the Best Practice Provision III.3.1 regarding the preparation of a profile.

---

5   The Dutch House of Representatives, 2007–2008, Parliamentary Paper 31.083, nr. 17.

6   In Dutch Newspaper *De Volkskrant*, 2 April 2008.

7   Jongerius, A. (2008), interview in Dutch Newspaper *De Volkskrant*, 2 April 2008.

THE QUOTA PROPOSAL

As announced in 2008 by Kalma of the Dutch Labour Party, he indeed initiated the Bill that introduces targets in the Civil Code for the participation of women on the EBs and the SBs of large Dutch companies (Ltds and Plcs). From the proposed section of the law it becomes clear that a balanced distribution means that at least 30 per cent of the seats on the EBs and SBs must be occupied by women and at least 30 per cent of the seats by men. To reach a balanced distribution between men and women, companies must take this into account when a) nominating and appointing EDs; b) preparing a profile of the size and the composition of the SB and; when c) designating, nominating, recommending and appointing NEDs. Companies who are subject to the proposed regulation, but have not reached the desired target, should explain ('comply or explain') in the annual report why the seats are not evenly distributed, how the company has tried to get to the balanced distribution of the seats and how the company intends to realize a balanced distribution of the seats. The scope of the section of the law is limited in time. The proposed sections of law terminates 1 January 2016.

30 PER CENT

According to the Bill, a minimum of 30 per cent women (and men) is required. Since it is not possible to appoint 1.3 women, in practice it is only possible to reach the exact number of 30 per cent when the EB and SB consist of exactly ten persons: when three out of ten are women, makes exactly 30 per cent. But, for example, a SB that consists of four members, and which appoints one woman will only have 25 per cent female directors and therefore should appoint at least two women to reach the minimum requirement of 30 per cent. The female participation in the SB then rises to 50 per cent. Table 2.1 shows for different board sizes the number of women that should be appointed in order to have a minimum of 30 per cent female representation. This is similar to the situation in Norway. The Norwegian quota is usually written as '40 per cent', but this distribution is only recommended for boards with exactly ten members. For boards with fewer than ten members, a scheme is included in the law (see also Table 2.1). For boards with less than ten persons the minimum allowable percentage in Norway is 33 per cent (at a council of nine persons) and the maximum required percentage is 50 per cent (at a council consisting of two, four or six people). Table 2.1 shows that the Bill in the Netherlands is different from Norway only for three board sizes: a board of six directors (two women in the Netherlands is enough, in Norway there have to be three) and nine and ten directors (in the Netherlands two women are sufficient, in Norway there must be four). It should be noted that the Norwegian quota only applies to NEDs and does not apply to the EDs.

Table 2.1   Minimum number of women on Executive Boards and Supervisory Boards of various sizes

Number of members on EB and SB	The Netherlands		Norway	
	Minimum number of women	Actual %	Minimum number of women	Actual %
2	1	50%	1	50%
3	1	33%	1	33%
4	2	50%	2	50%
5	2	40%	2	40%
6	2	33%	3	50%
7	3	43%	3	43%
8	3	38%	3	38%
9	3	33%	4	44%
10	3	30%	4	40%

CRITERIA FOR LARGE COMPANIES

The target provisions only apply to larger Ltds and PLCs. Ltds and PLCs are not subject to the proposed statutory provision, if in accordance with art. 2:397 paragraph 1 Civil Code they meet two of the following three requirements:

- the value of the assets according to its balance sheet does not exceed €17,500,000;
- net sales for the financial year does not exceed €35,000,000;
- the average number of employees for the financial year is less than 250.

Based on these criteria we estimated how many companies in the Netherlands would fall under this proposal. In the database Reach information is stored of more than 2.2 million Dutch companies that are registered in the Chambers of Commerce. Unfortunately, information on the number of employees is insufficiently reliable. For many companies the number of employees is either not known or the number 'one' is given, especially for holding companies. Companies are exempted from the quota law if they stay under two of the criteria, thus, companies must comply with the target if they *do* meet two of the criteria. Table 2.2 shows the number of companies in the Netherlands that meet the search criteria. Of the more than 2.2 million companies registered with the Chamber of Commerce, over one million are registered as a Ltd or a Plc. Furthermore. 5,136 of these Ltds and PLC shave a balance sheet total that exceeds 17.5 million and 11,406 have a turnover in excess of 35 million. Both criteria combined provide a number of at least 4,541 companies that fall under the quota proposal.

Table 2.2   Estimated number of companies in the Kalma group

	Number of companies that meet the criteria
All organizations registered	2,220,802
– of which Ltd/Plc	1,027,865
a) total assets exceeds 17.5 million	5,136
b) value turnover> 35 million	11,406
Combined a) and b)	4,541

CURRENT DISCUSSION IN THE SENATE

During the discussion of the quota in the Senate on 2 February 2010, the VVD (Dutch Liberal Party) argued that the target of 30 per cent in some sectors is too low, while in others it might be too high. The VVD therefore wonders if there shouldn't be a link between the supply of women in a sector.[8] In addition, VVD opens the discussion on the scope of this subject, since the settlement is only applicable for larger companies and not for other forms such as foundations, associations and cooperatives (where especially a lot of women work, think of healthcare and education, according to the VVD). The VVD therefore doubts the feasibility of the quota, partly because of the lack of a penalty and thinks that repealing the provisions in 2016 (when the target should be achieved) is too optimistic. They also refer to the self-regulation on this theme through the Dutch Corporate Governance Code and the poor compliance of the 'comply and explain' principle in general, The Christian Union and the SGP (Reformed Political Party) wonder what is actually meant in paragraph 2 of the proposed Article 166 'as much as possible the balanced distribution between men and women must be taking into account' and ask for an explicit explanation of this statement.[9] 'How does a company sufficiently take into account the intended distribution and when does one fail in this duty?' Recently, professors in Corporate Law, Assink, Kroeze and Verbrugh (2010), argued that they are in favour of the quota; just to break through the now still often subjective selection process for new candidates. They argue that a somewhat subjective assessment of personal qualities ('we want the best candidate, male or female') is strongly influenced by the similarity that current EDs and NEDs experience with a nominee (including their gender).

Current Situation at Listed Companies in the Netherlands

The Bill in the Netherlands is estimated to apply to more than 4,500 Ltds and PLCs Little is known regarding the precise number of women on the EB and SB of those companies. Therefore, the research in this chapter is based on female representation at Dutch listed companies included in the Dutch Female Board Index 2010 (Lückerath-Rovers, 2010). The Female Board Index is an annual report on female representation in the boardroom

---

8   The Dutch Senate. 2009–2010, Paper 31.763, nr. B.

9   The Dutch Senate. 2009–2010, Paper 31.763, nr. B.

and has been published since 2007. Table 2.3 shows the percentages of the 99 companies in the Index of 2010[10] that have female representation in their boards, as of 2007.

Table 2.3   Companies with female directors from 2007 to 2010 (n=99)

	2010 # and % all companies	2009 # and % all companies	2008 # and % all companies	2007 # and % all companies
Companies with female directors*	39 (39.4%)	39 (39.4%)	34 (34.3%)	31 (31.3%)
Companies with no female directors	60 (60.6%)	60 (60.6%)	65 (65.7%)	68 (68.7%)
Companies with female EDs	9 (9.1%)	8 (8.1%)	7 (7.1%)	7 (7.1%)
Companies with at least one female NED	36 (36.4%)	36 (36.4%)	31 (31.3%)	28 (28.3%)

*   The sum of companies with female EDs (nine) and companies with female NEDS (36) does not add to the number of companies with female directors (39). While six companies with a female ED also have one or more female NEDs.

Since December 2007 the number of companies with female directors has increased slightly, from 31 companies (31 per cent) in 2007 to 39 companies (39 per cent) in 2010. However, the last reported period 2009–2010 has contributed nothing to this slight increase. The majority still does not have a woman appointed to either the EB or the SB, (60 companies; 61 per cent). The number of companies with a female ED is only nine (9.1 per cent). an increase of two additional companies as of 2007. The number of companies with at least one female NED increased from 28 in 2007 to 36 in 2010 (36.4 per cent). Figure 2.1 illustrates the development as from 2007 for the 99 companies in the sample.

Whereas Figure 2.1 shows the number of companies with female directors, Figure 2.2 shows the number of female directors in 2010 as a percentage of all directors. Of the 749 directors only 61 are female (8.1 per cent). This is the weighted average of 52 female NEDs (10.7 per cent) and nine female EDs (3.4 per cent).

Table 2.4 shows the number of female directors from 2007 till 2010. In four years time, the total number of female directors in the 99 companies in the sample increased from 44 in 2007 (5.9 per cent) to 61 in 2010 (8.1 per cent). The largest increase appeared in 2009, when a net increase of 11 directors was observed. This is caused by the fact that in 2009 both the number of appointments was relatively higher (14) as the number of resignation was lower (three). In 2010 the number of appointments was lower (eight) as the number of resignations was higher (six).

---

10   Each year the number of companies in the Female Board Index changes due to de-listings, takeovers and newly listed firms. The numbers shown here only include the 99 companies that were include in the 2010 Index to prevent any bias occurring from the companies (with or without women on the boards) that left the exchange.

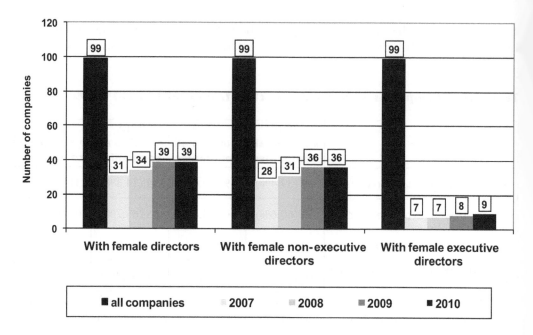

Figure 2.1   Companies with female directors since 2007
Source: Female Board Index 2010, Lückerath-Rovers, 2010.

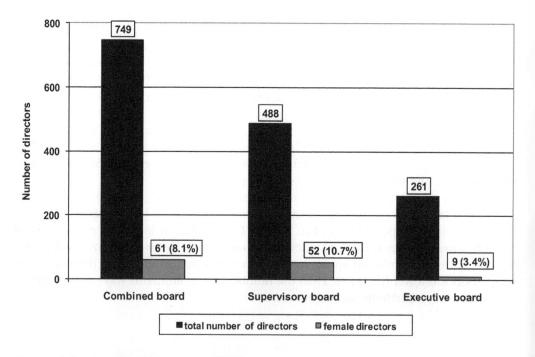

Figure 2.2   Female directors in 2010
Source: Female Board Index 2010, Lückerath-Rovers, 2010.

Table 2.4   Female directors from 2007 to 2010 within 99 listed companies

99 Dutch listed companies	2010		2009		2008		2007	
	#	%	#	%	#	%	#	%
total number of directors	749		766		747		748	
– of which female directors	61	8.1%	59	7.7%	48	6.4%	44	5.9%
total EDs	261		269		267		262	
– of which female EDs	9	3.4%	8	3.0%	7	2.6%	7	2.7%
total NEDs	488		497		480		486	
– of which female NEDs	52	10.7%	51	10.3%	41	8.5%	37	7.6%

The 61 board seats occupied by women are taken by 53 different women (see 0). Some women have multiple board seats. The maximum number of positions among the women is four: Marike van LierLels is appointed to four SBs (with KPN, TKH, USG People and Reed Elsevier). One woman director has three board seats: Pamela Boumeester with Delta Lloyd, Ordina and Heijmans). Three women directors have two board seats (Tineke Bahlmann, Annemiek Siderius-Fentener van Vlissingen and Herna Verhagenat respectively with Nedap and ING, Draka and Heineken, and Nutreco and SNS Reaal). The remaining 48 women directors all have one board position, including the nine female EDs. Table 2.5 shows the breakdown of the number of functions by different people. The 749 board positions are taken by 667 different people. On average each person takes 1.12 positions, this is only marginally higher for female directors (1.17) than for male directors (1.12).

Table 2.5   Number of board seats taken by different male and female directors

	Total board seats	# Individuals	1	2	3	4
Total number of directors	749	668				
Male directors	688	615	558	42	14	1
Female directors	61	53	48	3	1	1

The 99 companies are divided into nine industries according to the Industry Classification Benchmark (ICB) as used by Euronext. The breakdown of the number of companies with female directors per industry is given in Table 2.6. Besides the Telecom sector, the industry with relatively most companies with women on the board are the financials (seven out of 13 companies have one or more female directors), followed by 'oil and gas' and 'basic materials'.

Table 2.6   Female directors in different industries

		All companies	Companies with female directors		All directors	Female directors	
		N	n	%	n	n	%
0001	Oil and gas	2	1	50.0%	22	1	4.5%
1000	Basic materials	4	2	50.0%	36	3	8.3%
2000	Industrials	31	13	41.9%	224	17	7.6%
3000	Consumer goods	13	5	38.5%	97	8	8.2%
4000	Healthcare	6	1	16.7%	43	2	4.7%
5000	Consumer services	13	6	46.2%	99	11	11.1%
6000	Telecom	1	1	100.0%	11	3	27.3%
8000	Financials	13	7	53.8%	125	12	9.6%
9000	Technology	16	3	18.8%	92	4	4.3%
	Total	**99**	**39**	**39.4%**	**749**	**61**	**8.1%**

The 99 companies are also categorized by their trading segment on the Amsterdam Euronext. The segments are based on the three share indices (AEX, AMX and AscX) and a category 'other' shares. The AEX index includes a maximum of 25 of the most actively traded securities on the Amsterdam exchange, normally the 25 shares with the highest trading volume (the large caps). This is followed by the AMX index (25 midcap shares) and the AScX-index (max 25 small caps). While this study excludes non-Dutch companies, the sub-samples shown below do not include all 25 companies for each index. Table 2.7 shows firstly the breakdown of the number of companies within each segment and the number of companies with female directors and secondly the same for the number of directors per segment. The 21 AEX companies in the sample most frequently have female directors appointed to the EB and/or SB. Sixteen AEX companies have one or more female directors appointed to the board; six AEX companies (2009:5) have a female ED and 14 AEX companies (2009:15) have a female NED on the SB. Five AEX companies do not have female directors on either the EB or SB. These companies are BAM, Boskalis. DSM, SBM Offshore and Wereldhave. Eleven of the 22 AMX companies in the sample have female directors appointed; no AMX company has a female ED and the 11 AMX companies (39 per cent) together have 13 female NEDs.

Secondly, Table 2.7 shows the relative proportion of female directors within each Euronext trading segment. The AEX companies have the largest percentage of female directors, of the 237 board seats within AEX companies 33 are occupied by a woman (14 per cent). Six of the nine female EDs are appointed with an AEX company and 27 of the 52 female NEDs are appointed to a SB of an AEX company. The least female directors are found in the category 'other', the percentage of female directors is only 4.4 per cent (nine female directors) and 81.6% of the companies has no female directors on either one of the boards.

Table 2.7   Female directors and Euronext segment

	All companies	Companies with female directors		All directors	Female Directors	
	N	n	%	n	n	%
AEX	21	16	76.2%	237	33	13.9%
AMX	22	11	50.0%	192	13	6.8%
AScX	18	5	27.8%	117	6	5.1%
Other	38	7	18.4%	203	9	4.4%
All companies/directors	**99**	**39**	**39.4%**	**749**	**61**	**8.1%**

The desired balance in the Bill is still far from being met. The Female Board Index 2010 shows that on August 31, 2010 only 3.4 per cent of the 261 EDs and 10.7 per cent of the 488 NEDs of the 99 listed companies was a woman. Figure 2.3 demonstrates the current growth of the percentage of female EDs and NEDs and also shows what the growth should be like, if the 30 per cent should be achieved at January 2016. At the current growth rate, the percentage female NEDs at 1 January 2016 (end of 2015) would be 15.7 per cent and for female EDs 5.4 per cent. At the current growth rate, the 30 per cent will be achieved in 2030 for the female NEDs and 2077 for the female EDs.

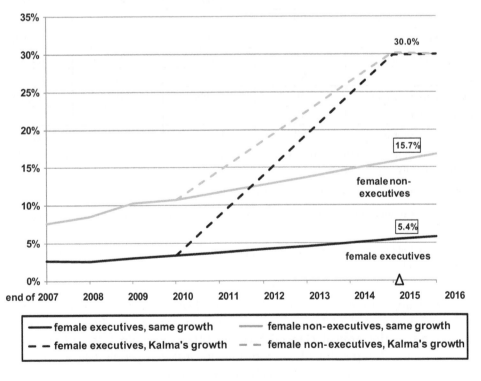

Figure 2.3   The Female Board Index in relation to Kalma's amendment of law
Source: Female Board Index 2010, Lückerath-Rovers, 2010.

Research Design and Results

The research builds upon the data of the listed companies that are part of the Dutch Female Board Index 2010 (Lückerath-Rovers, 2010).The data included in the Female Board Index is extended with the current term of all EDs and NEDs by August 31, 2010 Next, for each ED and NED it was firstly determined when his or her current appointment ends, and, secondly, whether this is a definite termination or whether reappointment is possible. The end of each appointment period is therefore divided into a) a hard end (the maximum of 12 years is reached, reappointment is not possible) and b) a soft end (reappointment possible). It should be noted that the maximum term of 12 years (three times four years) only applies to the NEDs in the Dutch Corporate Governance Code and therefore is defined as a 'hard stop'. For EDs the Corporate Governance Code requires that EDs can be appointed for a maximum period of four years, but subsequently there is no limit on the number of reappointments.

Table 2.8 shows the difference between the current situation (as described in the previous section) and the minimum required by the Dutch Quota Bill as per January 2016.

Table 2.8   Required impact of Dutch Quota Bill on 99 listed companies

	Current situation 31 August 2010		Required situation January 2016	
	n =	**%**	**n =**	**%**
Number of companies	99		99	
Women on EB	9	9.1%	77[1]	77.8%
Women on SB	36	36.4%	85[2]	85.8%
Number of EDs	261		261	
Of which are women:	9	3.4%	100[3]	38.3%
Number of NEDs	488		488	
Of which are women:	52	10.7%	176[4]	36.1%

1   This is the number of listed companies that fall under the Bill (85) minus the number of companies with an EB of only one person (8).

2   The number of companies that fall under the Bill. (85).

3   The number of female EDs that should be appointed as per January 2016 with the 85 companies that fall under the Bill.

4   The number of female NEDs that should be appointed as per January 2016 with the 85 companies that fall under the Bill.

The current appointment periods of EDs and NEDs was determined by the rotation schedule of the EB and/or SB using information from corporate websites, annual reports and minutes of the Annual General Meeting (AGM). Certain EDs and/or NEDs still have a permanent appointment. In addition, for a dozen people whose current term was not available via the above information and furthermore were appointed before the commencement of the Code, we also assumed a permanent appointment. A total of 100 people have a permanent appointment, the majority are EDs (94 per cent) and male

(98 per cent). Of 649 persons the current term ends in the period 2010–2016. Especially in the four-year block 2011–2015 the appointments terminate relatively steady: about 15 per cent of the appointment periods end annually for EDs and approximately 24 per cent for NEDs.

Of each listed company the minimum number of women that should be appointed to the EB and SB in order to meet the target of 30 per cent by January 1, 2016 was calculated. Here the current size of the EB and the SB was held constant for the years 2011–2016. Not all listed companies have to comply with the Bill because they meet two or more of the criteria of Art. 2:397 paragraph 1 Civil Code and thus qualify for exemption. Six meet all three criteria for exemption from the Bill; eight companies meet two criteria for exemption. For the other 85 listed companies the Bill will apply.

RESULTS

In total until 2016, there are 599 (re)appointments of NEDs (male and female) and 199 of EDs. To reach the intended effect of the Bill, 241 appointments (including reappointments) of a NED should be assigned to a woman (40 per cent) and 111 appointment moments (including reappointments) of EDs (56 per cent). This means that of all appointments in the coming years approximately one out of two should be assigned to a woman, and when the desired percentage is achieved, it may revert to one out of three. At first glance, based on the number of possible appointments of women directors in the period 2011–2016, in general a 30 per cent share of women in 2016 seems achievable. For each individual firm it is investigated how quickly it can meet the 30 per cent target of women on both EBs and SBs. Table 2.9 shows the division of the 99 companies based on board size, and consequently the number of women directors they have to appoint.

Table 2.9   Number of companies per different board sizes

Size EB	Number of women	Number of companies	Size SB	Number of women	Number of companies
1	0	17	1	0	1
2 of 3	1	58	2 of 3	1	24
4.5 of 6	2	24	4.5 of 6	2	53
7–10	3	0	7–10	3	19
—	—	—	11	4	2
		99			**99**

Of the 85 companies that fall under the Bill, 58 (68 per cent) can meet the target for the EB and 83 (98 per cent) can meet the target for the SB. Of all 99 companies, 64 (65 per cent) can meet the target for the EB and 97 (98 per cent) can meet the target for the SB. The companies that are unable to meet the target have too many directors with a permanent appointment and will only meet it if these contracts are terminated. This is particularly true for EDs. Of the companies that can meet the target, all can reach this by 2014. This means that the rather rigid method in this study (as soon as possible a vacant place is occupied by a woman) can be somewhat loosened to still have the intended result in 2016.

Table 2.10 and Figure 2.4 summarize the percentage of women directors based on the appointments at individual companies. The 99 companies are presented in two groups: 85 companies that must comply and 14 that are exempted. Table 2.10 shows the development of the average proportion of women on the EBs and SBs in these two groups. For the 85 companies that are covered by the Bill the maximum possible proportion of women on the EB and SB is, respectively, 30.3 per cent and 40.3 per cent. These are the average rates of all 85 companies. Figure 2.4 shows the average of all 99 companies in the sample.

Table 2.10   Possible development of the average percentage of women on the Executive Board and Supervisory Board in 99 listed companies

	N	2010	2011	2012	2013	2014	2015
EB							
Exempt companies	14	2.4%	4.8%	8.3%	19.0%	19.0%	19.0%
Companies covered by the Bill	85	2.5%	11.1%	19.7%	27.3%	30.3%	30.3%
SB							
Exempt companies	14	3.2%	22.9%	38.0%	43.3%	43.3%	43.3%
Companies covered by the Bill	85	8.9%	25.4%	35.5%	39.7%	40.3%	40.3%

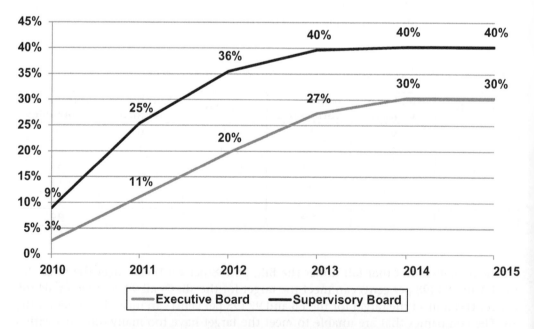

Figure 2.4   Possible development of the average percentage of women on the Executive Board and Supervisory Board in 99 listed companies

Concluding Remarks

Although the Bill applies to all large Ltds and Plcs, this chapter only examined the feasibility of the Bill for listed companies. This chapter describes that the number of companies covered by the Bill will approximately be 4,500 Ltds and Plcs. Of this group of companies, too little information is known to make an estimation of the number of required appointments for female directors. Furthermore, they are not obliged by a maximum term of four years or the disclosure of a rotation schedule. The analysis of the 99 listed companies in the Dutch Female Board Index 2010, however, gives some insight into the feasibility of the target for these companies. Of these 99 companies, 85 companies should meet the target number as listed in the Bill. Based on the number of appointments made in the period 2011–2016, it can be conclude that most of the listed companies can meet the target for the NEDs before 2014, but only if the currently appointed EDs and NEDs are not automatically reappointed. It will be more complicated to meet the target for female EDs. This is caused both by the currently low number of female EDs (and thus a bigger increase is necessary) and the bigger number of permanent appointments of EDs.

Although, the introduction of a legal quota has many pros and cons, the Dutch Corporate Governance Code states that the reappointment of directors cannot be an automatism and must be carried out after careful considerations. Here, one must also take the profile into consideration, of which it was earlier indicated that (especially) the SB aims for a diverse distribution in terms of gender and age. This seems not to apply for EDs for that matter; with respect to the EDs the Dutch Corporate Governance Code states that it is common practice to reappoint EDs if they have fulfilled their function properly.

Looking forward: in 2010 a new Dutch administration was installed. The right wing parties have a small majority (51 per cent) in the Second Chamber. These right wing parties are planning to abolish all preferential treatment of grant programmes to have more female representation in the labour force or in higher management positions. Most likely the quota proposal, which was approved by the Second Chamber in 2009, would not have been approved in the current Second Chamber. However, the quota proposal is now still to be voted on by the Senate. The discussion has come to a standstill while a new Senate will be elected in May 2011. As it seems today (March 2011), the left wing parties will have a small majority (52 per cent) in the Senate and they might be in favour of the quota law proposal. On the other hand, it might also be the case that a right wing-oriented Second Chamber is not likely to be able to cooperate with a left wing-oriented Senate, and this might lead ultimately to new elections. In short, with respect to the quota proposal the end of the discussion is not to be expected any time soon. The Dutch Female Board Index will be published in September 2011, maybe this year the threat of the quota legislation has finally impacted the number of women directors?

References

Assink. B.F., Kroeze, M.J. and Verbrugh, M. (2010). Kroniek van het vennootschapsrecht. (Chronicle of Dutch corporate law), *Nederlands Juristen Blad*, (15), 998–1007.

Lückerath-Rovers, M. (2010). *The Dutch Female Board Index 2010*. Rotterdam, Erasmus. Institute Monitoring and Compliance.

3 Legislation and Voluntarism: Two Approaches to Achieving Equal Employment Opportunity Outcomes for Women in New Zealand

FIONA HURD AND SUZETTE DYER

Introduction

Equal Employment Opportunity (EEO) in the New Zealand context is deemed both a philosophy and a practice aimed at eliminating discrimination in paid employment (Mintrom and True, 2004). Mintrom and True (2004) hold that through implementing non-discriminatory policies and practices throughout all phases of the employment process, EEO practices can address human rights concerns and provide pragmatic solutions to a number of business issues. Access to and participation in paid employment is deemed a fundamental and inalienable human right under the International Labour Organization (ILO) Convention 100, 1951, and the United Nations Convention of the Elimination of all Forms of Discrimination Against Women, 1979, ratified in New Zealand in 1983 and 1985 respectively. These conventions link meaningful paid employment to active citizen engagement and participation in social, political and economic aspects of their lives, as well as upholding the rights for equal remuneration between men and women (Ministry of Women's Affairs, 2002a). Mintrom and True suggest that EEO policies and practices have the potential to realise the human rights of all New Zealand citizens by enabling access to meaningful paid employment based on individual interest and ability. In the New Zealand context, EEO practices are also offered as a solution to facilitate the achievement of the State's obligations under the Treaty of Waitangi (www.eeotrust.org.nz). The Treaty of Waitangi requires political action to ensure Maori (New Zealand indigenous people) are treated fairly in all aspects of New Zealand society. More recently, EEO is recognized to be a mechanism to introduce anti-discriminatory employment practices to address the human rights of an increasingly diverse workforce. Specifically, demographic changes within the New Zealand population and workforce show more women entering and remaining within paid employment, an aging population and increased ethnic diversity resulting from immigration policy changes.

A number of New Zealand advocates of EEO (for example, Ministry of Women's Affairs www.mwa.govt.nz; National Equal Opportunity Network www.neon.org.nz; The Equal Employment Opportunity Trust www.eeotrust.org.nz; The Human Rights Commission www.hrc.govt.nz), offer EEO as a solution to a number of pragmatic business concerns. For example, embedding EEO philosophy and practice in the recruitment, selection and hiring decision-making processes is believed to widen the talent pool available to firms and increase the likelihood of employing a workforce that demographically resembles the diversity within the community. A workforce that reflects community diversity is proffered to lead to a number of positive organizational outcomes. Importantly, a diverse workforce is believed to lead to heightened staff engagement, lower turnover, improved public image and reputation, and improved customer service. Combined, these positive organizational outcomes ought to lead to improved organizational performance (Mintrom and True, 2004). In turn, the aggregate outcome of increased organizational performance will lead to national economic growth.

New Zealand operates two systems for implementing EEO. The first is a legislative framework that obliges public sector employers to address EEO; the second is a voluntary framework for private sector employers. Women, Maori, ethnic minorities and people with disabilities were identified as four groups experiencing differentiated educational and employment outcomes in New Zealand. While EEO practices initially were introduced to address the employment outcomes for these groups, the focus has expanded to include issues relating to age, sexuality and religion. In this chapter we concentrate on the EEO outcomes for New Zealand women. To do so, we review the legislative and voluntary EEO frameworks that concurrently operate in the New Zealand context. We then detail the educational and employment outcomes of New Zealand women. We discuss the gendered educational and employment outcomes in relation to the three themes of the timing of the implementation of EEO in New Zealand, the limitations of the current EEO framework, and the impact of the gendered structure of paid and unpaid work on EEO outcomes. We conclude that in the current environment, ideal EEO outcomes are unlikely to be achieved, and that New Zealand women will likely continue to experience vertical and horizontal segregation in employment, and earn significantly less than their male counterparts for some time to come.

Anti-discrimination and Minimum Employment Standards Legislation

In New Zealand, the minimum standards of employment and the fair treatment for all are set out in the Equal Pay Act 1972, the Parental Leave Act 1987, the New Zealand Bill of Rights Act 1990, the Human Rights Act 1993 and the Employment Relations Act 2000. The Human Rights Act 1993 sets out 13 grounds of unlawful discrimination that include age (from 16 years), race, colour and ethnicity, disability, employment status (unemployed, or in receipt of a welfare payment), ethical, religious and political beliefs (including not holding any), family status (including parental status, and being related to a particular person), marital status (including single, divorced, being in a particular marital arrangement, or living in the nature of marriage), sex (including pregnancy and childbirth) and sexual orientation.

Paid parental leave has been available only since 2002 with the passing of the Parental Leave and Employment Protection (Paid Parental Leave) Amendment Act 2002 and more recently, the Parental Leave and Employment Protection (Paid Parental Leave for Self-Employed Persons) Amendment Act 2006. Government-paid parental leave is available to eligible parents of newborn babies and adopted babies; specifically full wage recovery not exceeding $NZ440 per week (at the time of writing, www.ird.govt.nz) for 14 weeks with provision for unpaid parental leave for up to 52 weeks (inclusive). In addition, there is some Government financial assistance with the cost of early childhood care and targeted assistance for low-income working families. Most recently, the Employment Relations (Flexible Working Arrangements) Amendment Act 2007 enables eligible employees to request flexible work hours to enable them to balance their work and family commitments.

The Legislative Framework for Equal Employment Opportunity in New Zealand

In 1984, the Government Employing Authorities issued a statement on equal employment opportunities, marking the development of EEO initiatives in New Zealand (State Services Commission, 1995). In this statement, employing Government organizations became obliged to implement EEO and were required to monitor and review existing policies and to implement procedures to detect direct and indirect forms of discrimination. The Government Employing Authorities Statement was the first to formally recognize employers' legal obligation to provide anti-discriminatory employment practices in accordance with the New Zealand Human Rights Commission Act 1977 and the ratification of the ILO Convention 100, 1951, the United Nations Convention on the Elimination of all forms of Discrimination Against Women 1979, and the United Nations Declaration of Human Rights 1948 (Mintrom and True, 2004). This 1984 statement specifically addressed the employment opportunities and outcomes for women, Maori, ethnic minorities and people with disabilities. Following this statement, a number of laws were passed that required Government employing organizations to address EEO. Of interest in this chapter are the State Owned Enterprise Act 1986, the State Sector Act 1988, the Local Government Act 2002, the Employment Equity Act 1990 (repealed) and the Employment Contracts Act 1991 (repealed).

State Owned Enterprises Act 1986, State Sector Act 1988, Local Government Act 2002: The first two Acts required State Owned Enterprises and public sector employers respectively to be 'good employers'. To achieve this, chief executive officers were required to establish and maintain EEO polices with the aim of eliminating discrimination in employment for the four targeted groups, to advertise all vacancies and to make all employment decisions based on qualifications and experience. These Acts also required the State Services Commissioner to report on EEO progress in Government employing organizations. The passing of the Local Government Act 2002 extended these obligations to local government bodies, required local governments to report on the demographic outcomes of local-level elections, as well as design annual EEO programmes for local-level government employees (Mintrom and True, 2004).

The Employment Equity Act 1990 (repealed): In 1985, a claim was made under the Equal Pay Act that compared clerical workers' skills, responsibilities and effort with male occupations (Ministry of Women's Affairs, 2002a). This claim was declined, leading to a working group investigating employment equity in New Zealand (Wilson, 1988). One outcome of this report was the Employment Equity Act 1990. This Act established processes to promote EEO within all public sector organizations and within private sector organizations of 100 or more employees. The Act provided the mechanisms to make pay equity claims between male-dominated and female-dominated occupations; a process which would be facilitated by the industrial relations framework in New Zealand, at that time characterized by multi-employer collective bargaining (Ministry of Women's Affairs, 2002a). The passing of the Employment Equity Act also effectively was a formal recognition of the slow progress towards achieving desired EEO outcomes within the private sector; thus, extending the legislative framework to the private sector (Commission forEmployment Equity, 1991). The Commission for Employment Equity (1991) also recognized that to enact EEO practices required more than a legislative framework, but must also be viewed as a 'systemic and structural change [programme of action], which aims to promote good employment practices and policies which prevent discrimination' (p. 2).

The Employment Contracts Act 1991 (repealed): The Employment Equity Act was repealed within three months of enactment by the incoming 1990 National-led Government which promptly introduced the Employment Contracts Act 1991. The Employment Contracts Act introduced enterprise-based wage bargaining, thus making pay equity claims between male-dominated and female-dominated organizations or industrial sectors no longer possible (Ministry of Women's Affairs, 2002a). Moreover, the Employment Contracts Act relinquished private sector employers from the obligations of EEO, who instead would be encouraged to voluntarily implement EEO policies and practices. With the focus on voluntary uptake in the private sector, EEO became constructed as a 'management practice that minimizes the potential for employers to be found guilty of discrimination' (Mintrom and True, 2004, p. 27). Thus, since the repealing of the Employment Equity Act, EEO legislation covers only public sector employment, accounting for approximately 20 per cent of the New Zealand labour force. The remaining 80 per cent of private sector employees are covered by the voluntary uptake and implementation of EEO policies and programmes (Mintrom and True, 2004).

The Voluntary Framework for Equal Employment Opportunity in New Zealand

To support private sector organizations to develop EEO programmes and good management practices, and hence, move beyond the minimum anti-discrimination legislation, the National-led Government provided funding to establish the Equal Employment Opportunity Trust (EEO Trust) (Mintrom and True, 2004), officially opening in 1992 with a founding membership of 30 private sector organizations (www.eeotrust.org. nz). Continued funding would be provided by fee-paying private sector membership. The EEO Trust defines 'equal employment opportunity' as a:

means [to] eliminating barriers to ensure that all employees are considered for the employment of their choice and have the chance to perform to their maximum potential. Through EEO and effective diversity management, employers can make the most of New Zealand's increasingly diverse workforce.

(http://www.eeotrust.org.nz/equal/index.cfm)

The EEO Trust promotes equality in employment as a practical solution to ensuring organizations can attract and retain well-qualified staff. The EEO Trust proposes that good management practices will result in enhanced employee retention and satisfaction, enhanced public image and reputation, and improved business performance. The Trust places an emphasis on assisting organizations to develop good human resource management practices that enable hiring, training, development and promotion decisions to be based on individual merit, as the preferred means to reduce discriminatory staffing decisions. Currently 400 employing organizations hold EEO Trust membership (www.eeotrust.org.nz).

Along with providing information and advice, the EEO Trust also conducts self-reporting survey-research with member organizations, and to a lesser extent, some non-member organizations. In 1998, the EEO Trust introduced the two-yearly Diversity Surveys and the inaugural Work and Family Award. The Diversity Surveys track the adoption and success of EEO programmes. The Work and Family Award was designed to recognize the efforts of applicant organizations towards achieving work–life balance and, since 2007, the extent to which applicants recognize and support their diverse workforce.

More recently, the National Equal Opportunity Network (NEON) was established. This organization works closely with the EEO Trust and the Human Rights Commission to promote best practice within New Zealand. This organization offers similar support, information and services to private and public sector employers as the EEO Trust (www. neon.org.nz). NEON, the EEO Trust and the Human Rights Commission draw upon the foundation document 'Framework for the Future Equal Opportunities in New Zealand' (Mintrom and True, 2004), produced for the Equal Employment Opportunities Unit of the Human Rights Commission. This report sets the contemporary foundation for EEO direction in New Zealand.

While successive New Zealand governments have stated an interest in improving the employment outcomes for four target groups (women, Maori, ethnic minorities and disabled people) since 1984, in the next section we focus on and detail the employment outcomes of women in New Zealand.

What have New Zealand Women Achieved Since 1984?

New Zealand women have made significant inroads in education and paid employment. These improvements in women's position in society have manifest in New Zealand being ranked fifth in the Global Gender Gap Report since 2007 (Hausmann, Tyson and Zahisi, 2010). On the face of it, gaining such an outstanding ranking gives the impression that gender equality is being addressed in New Zealand. Unfortunately, between the 2009 and 2010 Global Gender Gap Reports, New Zealand women actually lost some of the previous equality gains (Hausmann, Tyson and Zahisi, 2010, 2009). Moreover, New

Zealand women continue to experience discrimination in the workforce, in politics, and in the home. Significant gendered horizontal and vertical employment segregation and pay disparity continue to this day.

WOMEN'S EDUCATIONAL ACHIEVEMENTS

Women and girls have made significant gains in educational participation and achievement in New Zealand over the past three decades. This trend of greater involvement in higher education by women compared to men is evident in the proportion of the population aged between 25 and 64 years with upper secondary- and tertiary-level qualifications. For example, in 2009, for the two age brackets of 25–34 and 35–44 years, the proportion of women with tertiary-level qualifications was 32.2 and 25.7 per cent respectively, compared to men in these two age brackets of 26.2 and 22.7 per cent respectively. In the 45–54 year age bracket, the proportion of women and men with tertiary-level qualifications is near equal, at 18.4 and 18.9 per cent respectively. It is only in the age bracket 55–64 years that the proportion of men with tertiary-level qualifications is significantly higher than that of women, at 17.2 and 12.8 per cent respectively (Ministry of Social Development, 2010). Between 1994 and 2009, women's tertiary-level enrolment has been higher than men (Ministry of Social Development, 2010). Near gender equality is evident in certificate-level tertiary enrolments figures. However, women outnumber men in overall tertiary education enrolment figures (13.7 per cent and 11 per cent respectively), and women are significantly more likely to be enrolled in bachelor degree programmes compared to men (4.4 per cent and 2.8 per cent respectively).

Even though more women than men are engaging in tertiary study at the bachelor level, stereotypical gender differences remain in terms of the degrees women and men are graduating with (Ministry of Women's Affairs, 2010a). For example, in 2006, women graduates still predominated in the areas of nursing; teacher education, curriculum and education studies; human welfare studies and services; and radiography. The same year, women graduates were significantly underrepresented in the five fields of mechanical and industrial engineering and technology; electrical and electronic engineering and technology; civil engineering; physics and astronomy; and computer science (see Table 3.1).

Table 3.1   The five most and least common narrow fields of specialization for domestic female bachelors degree graduates in 2006

Most Common			Least Common		
Field of study (narrow level)	Number of female graduates	% of graduates in this field who are female	Field of study (narrow level)	Number of female graduates	% of graduates in this field who are female
Nursing	1,290	94%	Mechanical and industrial engineering and technology	260	9%
Teacher education	2,100	87%	Electrical and electronic engineering and technology	410	11%
Curriculum and education studies	930	86%	Civil engineering	240	14%
Human welfare studies	110	83%	Physics and astronomy	90	15%
Radiography	110	83%	Computer science	540	16%
All fields	13,060	62%	All fields	13,060	62%

Note: Students can be counted in more than one field.

Source: Ministry of Women's Affairs (2010b). Analysis of Graduate Income Data 2002–2007 by Broad Field of Study. Working paper by the Ministry of Women's Affairs http://www.mwa.govt.nz/news-and-pubs/publications/graduate-income-data.

Table 3.2 compares the five most common degrees held by men and women. Teaching and education, and nursing remain the two most common degrees held by women. The next three most common degrees held by women in order of ranking include studies in human society, business and management, and law. The five most common degrees held by men in order are business and management, sales and marketing, law, studies in human society and information systems. Significantly, more women are graduating with business and management, and law degrees than men however this has not translated into the workforce, with men still predominating the two occupational categories of managers and lawyers.

Table 3.2   The five most common narrow fields of study for women and men graduating with a bachelor's degree in 2006

Women			Men		
Field of study (narrow level)	Number of graduates	% of females	Field of study (narrow level)	Number of graduates	% of all males
Teacher education	1,820	13.9%	Business and management	830	10.5%
Nursing	1,220	9.3%	Sales and marketing	560	7.1%
Studies in human society	1,060	8.1%	Law	500	6.3%
Business and management	980	7.5%	Studies in human society	490	6.2%
Law	810	6.2%	Information systems	490	6.2%
All fields	13,060	100%	All Fields	7,890	100%

Note: Students can be counted in more than one field.

Source: Ministry of Women's Affairs (2010b). Analysis of Graduate Income Data 2002–2007 by Broad Field of Study. Working paper by the Ministry of Women's Affairs. http://www.mwa.govt.nz/news-and-pubs/publications/graduate-income-data.

In contrast to tertiary-level study, women are still significantly underrepresented in trades training in New Zealand as illustrated in Table 3.3. Trade training comes under the umbrella of the 'Modern Apprenticeship Programmes'. These programmes are coordinated, managed and administered by respective Industry Training Organizations (ITOs). In 2008, women comprised 9.4 per cent of all modern apprentice enrolments (Ministry of Women's Affairs, 2010a). Out of the 25 possible modern apprenticeship programmes available in New Zealand, women outnumbered men in only three areas: hairdressing (99.3 per cent women), public sector training (77.3 per cent women) and retail training (53.2 per cent). Men continue to dominate in the trades training of building, engineering, motor trades, electrotechnology and horticulture (Ministry of Women's Affairs, 2010a).

Table 3.3   Participation in modern apprenticeships, by most popular Industry Training Organizations, and gender

Women	Number	% of all female modern apprenticeships	% female in Industry Training Organization
New Zealand Horticulture ITO Inc.	217	19.0	26.0
Agriculture ITO Inc.	159	13.9	23.1
Hospitality Standards Institute	157	13.8	39.1
Public Sector Training Organization	126	11.1	77.3
New Zealand Association of hairdressing Inc.	84	7.4	93.3

Men	Number	% of all male Modern Apprentices	% of males in the Industry Training Organization
Building and Construction ITO Inc.	1,981	18.0	99.8
New Zealand Engineering, Food and Manufacturing ITO Inc.	1,817	16.5	96.5
New Zealand Motor ITO Inc.	1,677	15.2	97.1
Electrotechnology ITO Inc.	790	7.2	98.3
New Zealand Horticulture ITO Inc.	619	5.6	74.0

Source: Ministry of Women's Affairs (2010a). Indicators for Change 2009 Tracking the progress of New Zealand women labour force participation rate, by gender, 1998–2008, p. 25. Available from http://www.mwa.govt.nz/news-and-pubs/publications/indicators-for-change-2009-1/indicators-for-change-2009-pdf.

WOMEN'S POSITION IN PAID EMPLOYMENT

Women's labour force participation rate to December 2010 was recorded at 62 per cent (Department of Labour, 2010), with nearly 60 per cent concentrated within the four (of ten) industrial categories of health care and social assistance (18 per cent), wholesale and retail (15 per cent), education and training (13 per cent) and other business services (12 per cent). Similarly, the three occupational categories of professionals, clerical and administration, and community and personal services account for 60.7 per cent of all working women (Department of Labour, 2010). These narrow occupational and industrial fields that women dominate are estimated to contribute to between 20 and 40 per cent of the gendered pay gap in New Zealand (Dixon, 2000).

WOMEN'S LEADERSHIP ROLES

During the 1980s, the New Zealand Government made an international commitment to achieve gender parity in leadership roles in government appointed bodies by 2010 (Human Rights Commission, 2008). While significant gains have been made towards achieving this goal and the 1984 mandate requiring government employing organizations to redress discriminatory employment practices, gender equality in leadership or governance roles has not yet been realized in either the public or private sector.

Women in parliament: The New Zealand Government was the first to concede to the pressure from the women's suffragette movement and made legislative changes enabling women to vote in 1893; and in 1919 women gained the legal right to stand for parliamentary elections. The first woman to be elected to Parliament was in 1933, and to date, only 106 women have held a seat in Parliament (Ministry of Women's Affairs, 2010a). Following the 2008 general election, New Zealand women gained 34 per cent of the seats in Parliament (compared with 32 per cent in the 2005 election), and made up 30 per cent of Cabinet Ministers (Ministry of Women's Affairs, 2010a). Local body elections in 2007 resulted in 29 per cent of women gaining city, regional and district councillors (including mayors and chairs) (Ministry of Women's Affairs, 2010a).

Women in public sector leadership roles and statutory board memberships: As of December 2009, women held only 17 per cent (six of 25) public sector chief executives positions (down from 27 per cent in 2005), and 38 per cent of senior management positions in the State sector (up from 36 per cent in 2005) (Ministry of Women's Affairs, 2010c). More significant achievements have been gained in public sector statutory board membership in the same period, 41.5 per cent of ministerial appointments to statutory boards were women (down from 42 per cent in 2008, Human Rights Commission, 2008). Of those appointments, women still predominate on statutory boards of health (53.7 per cent) and social welfare (47.1 per cent), as well as comprising 51.9 per cent of school board trustees (Ministry of Women's Affairs, 2010a). In 2010, 34 per cent of national union executive members, 41 per cent of school principals (yet 72 per cent of teachers) and 22.45 per cent senior positions in universities (up from 19.19 per cent in 2008) were held by women (Human Rights Commission, 2010).

Women in the judiciary: Even though more women than men graduate with law degrees, this has not translated to equal status within the legal profession and their progression in the judiciary remains slow. Currently, the Chief Justice is a woman and, as of March 2010, 28 per cent of all judges were women, with women comprising 18.24 per cent of legal partnerships (Ministry of Women's Affairs, 2010c). While women represented 61 per cent of bar admissions in 2006, they only accounted for 41 per cent of those receiving practicing certificates, 19 per cent of those achieving principality and 35 per cent of those gaining sole barrister status (New Zealand Law Society, 2006).

Women's private sector leadership roles: In their 1994 benchmark survey, McGregor, Thomson and Dewe reported that New Zealand women were underrepresented at every level of management. In her follow-up study, McGregor (2002) found little progress, and while women comprised 27.1 per cent of total management positions, they continued to be concentrated in the lower managerial levels, with little advancement to senior ranks. Women's progression to senior management and directorships continues to be slow. In 2010, women comprised 9.32 per cent of board members of the top 100 companies listed on the New Zealand Stock Exchange, 6.82 per cent of directorships on the New Zealand Alternative Market and 11.54 per cent of newspaper editors (a decrease from 14.81 per cent in 2008) (Human Rights Commission, 2010).

To redress private sector underrepresentation in senior leadership positions, the Ministry of Women's Affairs is committed to work jointly with the private sector, including the Institute of New Zealand Directors, Business New Zealand and business leaders to develop initiatives to promote women to senior levels. These initiatives include 'promoting the business case for more women on boards, identifying board ready women and investigating non-legislative mechanisms, such as corporate governance guidelines requiring companies to set gender diversity objectives' (Ministry of Women's Affairs, 2010c, p. 9). This voluntarist approach is supported by Business New Zealand chief executive, Phil O'Reilly, who argues against legislative quota systems such as those that have been introduced in countries such as France, Norway and the Netherlands (Johnston, 2010).

HOURS OF PAID EMPLOYMENT

Of those engaged in paid employment in December 2010, 77.5 per cent worked full time and 22.5 per cent worked part time (or less than 30 hours per week). Women accounted for 46.7 per cent of the total workforce; however, they made up 39.5 per cent of the full-time workforce (Statistics New Zealand, 2011b, Table Reference HLF025AA), and just over 72.5 per cent of the part-time work-force (Statistics New Zealand, 2011a, Table Reference HLF030AA). Not all part-time workers choose this status in the labour market. A comparison of Statistics New Zealand (2011a and b) Tables HLF025AA and HLF030AA reveals that of the part-time workforce, 20 per cent of women and nearly 27 per cent of men were looking for more hours, and 4.5 per cent of part-time working women and 7.6 per cent of part-time working men were looking for full-time employment.

UNPAID WORK

Women continue to perform the majority of unpaid work in New Zealand. The 1998/99 Time Use Survey reveals that on average women spend 4.8 hours per day on unpaid work, and 2.2 hours on paid work; in contrast, men spend 4.8 hours on paid work, and 2.8 hours on unpaid work (Statistics New Zealand, 2001. However, part-time women workers, unemployed women and women not in the labour market spend more total hours on paid and unpaid work than their male counterparts. Only full-time women workers have similar working hours to their male counterparts. This Time Use Survey was repeated in 2009/2010, and results are currently unavailable (Ministry of Women's Affairs, 2010a). More recently, the 2006 census recorded a number of unpaid activities, including taking care of children and the elderly. These statistics reveal that in all areas, women do more unpaid work than men on average, regardless of their employment status (for example, employed full time, part time, unemployed or not in the labour market) (Statistics New Zealand, 2006).

WORKING MOTHERS

One of the enduring trends since the 1970s is the growth in the number of working mothers. A comparative study of the 2001 and 2006 New Zealand Census data showed growth in full-time work for working mothers between 2001 and 2006, with the corresponding decline of their unemployment rate reflecting economic growth experienced between the two census dates (Ministry of Women's Affairs, 2009). However, the comparative report also revealed that women with dependent children are most likely to work part time, older mothers have a higher participation rate than younger mothers, while mothers with school-aged children, partnered mothers, and mothers with post-secondary school qualifications are more likely to be in paid employment. Solo-mothers, mothers with young children, and mothers with three or more children are least likely to be in the labour force. Unsurprisingly, women who engage in fewer paid hours report higher levels of work–life balance satisfaction (Ministry of Women's Affairs, 2010a).

The return to paid employment of mothers is supported in the recent 'Babies and Bosses' report (OECD, 2008). In this report, the authors claim that working mothers help reduce child poverty, and that governments ought to ease the transition back to paid employment, for example, by providing tax incentives and child care subsidies, synchronizing school and work hours, and enabling more flexible work arrangements. In New Zealand, however, women's engagement in paid employment does not always result in child (or adult) poverty reduction. This is because of the low-wage rates associated with much of women's paid work (as will be illustrated below). Moreover, the authors of 'Babies and Bosses' make special mention of government initiatives that support low-income families as providing incentives for women to remain outside of paid employment (OECD, 2008). In saying so, the authors discount unpaid work performed in the home and primarily carried out by women as unproductive activities that do not add value to the nation or the economy, reinforcing attachment to the labour market as the preferred means to take care of self and family. New Zealand's 'Working for Families' (www.ird.govt.nz) is such an initiative where the Government provides targeted financial assistance to low-income working families. However, the recent 'Welfare Reform' agenda in New Zealand resembles the Organization for Economic Co-operation and Development (OECD) preference for entry in to the labour market as the preferred means for taking care of the self and family with their renewed interest in encouraging beneficiaries and in particular solo-mothers to re-enter paid employment (Bennett and Collins, 2011).

GENDERED PAY RATES

Despite the passing of the Equal Pay Act 1972, and women's increased participation rate in employment, their higher tertiary-level qualification rates compared to men, and their (slow) progression into non-traditional occupations and senior levels in organizations, significant gender pay gaps continue. On first job placement, New Zealand women earn less than their male counterparts and the pay gap continues to grow in the first five years of paid employment (Ministry of Women's Affairs, 2010b). For example, young women with tertiary qualifications such as certificates, diplomas and bachelor's degrees, earn on average 10 per cent less than their male counter parts in the first year of employment; this grows to a difference of nearly 18 per cent within the first five years. Women with higher-level tertiary qualifications such as postgraduate certificates and diplomas, and honours, master's and doctoral degrees, begin their working life with a gendered income gap of 6 per cent, which widens to nearly 18 per cent in the first five years (Ministry of Women's Affairs, 2010b). These gendered gaps differ between occupations and industries.

Average and medium hourly, weekly and annual incomes remain significantly lower for women than men (Statistics New Zealand, table builder, www.stats.govt.nz). Women in male-dominated industries tend to earn on average more than women in female-dominated industries, and men in female-dominated industries typically earn on average more than the women in those industries, but less than men in male-dominated industries. In 2007, women's average weekly income was $NZ626, and their average hourly earnings were $NZ19.54, compared to men's of $NZ946.00 and $NZ23.21 respectively. Significantly, in 2007, women's weekly average earnings were still lower than the 1998 average weekly earnings of men of $NZ681. As expected, women predominate in the lower total income bracket levels, while men predominate in the higher total income brackets (Statistics New Zealand, 2006 Census Data, www.stats.govt.nz).

Discussion

Despite significant interest in addressing gendered employment outcomes, New Zealand women have made slow progress. There are a number of explanations for this slow progress; however, due to space constraints, we limit our discussion to exploring three significant issues. These are (1) the timing of the implementation of EEO in New Zealand; (2) the shortcomings of the current EEO framework; and (3) the gendered structure of paid and unpaid work.

THE TIMING OF THE IMPLEMENTATION OF EQUAL EMPLOYMENT OPPORTUNITY IN NEW ZEALAND

The 1984 Government Employing Authorities statement and ensuing interest in equal employment opportunities throughout the 1990s (State Services Commission, 1995) coincided with the implementation of the structural adjustment programme in New Zealand based on neo-liberal principles (Brook Cowen, 1997; Kelsey, 1995; Pawson et al., 1996; Roper, 1993). These principles assume that free-market mechanisms are the most efficient method for managing marketplace activity and for achieving distributive justice. Any State interference in controlling the market, it is argued, is harmful to society because this will result in wasteful use of scarce resources and inequitable distribution of market gains (wages, profits, goods and services) required to meet individual welfare needs (Cheyne, O'Brien and Belgrave, 2000). The role of the State in promoting social wellbeing then, is to set rules governing property rights and to facilitate individual freedom of choice (Brook Cowen, 1997). Within such a framework, neo-liberals assert that social justice is achieved by individuals making informed choices. Any disparities in outcomes are deemed to occur as a result of individuals making poor choices, and such disparate outcomes are viewed as incentives for those individuals to make better choices to improve themselves and their own position in life (Cheyne, O'Brien and Belgrave, 2000). In line with these assumptions, the implementation of neo-liberalism within the New Zealand context throughout the 1980s and 1990s involved public sector reforms, the privatization of state assets and social spending reforms (Pawson et al., 1996).

Integral to these public sector reforms were the State Owned Enterprise Act 1986, the State Sector Act 1988 and the Public Finance Act 1989. Combined, these Acts required employing public sector organizations to trade as efficiently as private sector employing organizations in accordance with narrowly defined economic efficiency imperatives. These Acts also enabled state assets (for example, the national telecommunications and power networks) to be corporatized and then privatized (Boston et al., 1996; Cheyne, O'Brien and Belgrave, 2000; Pawson et al., 1996). Public sector reform and the privatization of state assets resulted in significant downsizing and restructuring of public sector employment. Immediately prior to public sector reform, the six largest government agencies employed more than 66,000 workers. By 1994, only 25,000 workers remained (Pawson et al., 1996), and by 2001 state sector employment was reduced to approximately 37 per cent of 1985 figures (Mintrom and True, 2004). Thus, EEO initiatives were expected to be implemented and achieved within a framework that required public sector managers to adopt managerialist restructuring agendas that had the aim of transforming the public sector to reflect private sector firms, and in particular, to implement managerial discretion in decision-making (Boston et al., 1996). Moreover, Mintrom and True (2004) point out, EEO considerations were not embedded in the ensuing redundancy decisions.

LIMITATIONS TO CURRENT EQUAL EMPLOYMENT OPPORTUNITY FRAMEWORK

Mintrom and True (2004) suggest that the current EEO legislative and voluntarist framework has a number of limitations that need to be redressed if the human rights ideals and business case benefits are to be realized. First, they argue that to be effective, EEO must have a legislative framework that defines discrimination, sets out positive processes enabling the establishment of organizational-level EEO initiatives, and is adequately resourced to ensure systematic monitoring, enforcement and penalization for organizations that do not achieve stated EEO goals. To date, the legal framework merely defines discrimination and requires public sector employers to address EEO initiatives, while the private sector is invited to consider EEO as a solution to achieve performance targets.

Second, Mintrom and True recognize individuals' need to have access to a variety of education and training options before horizontal and vertical segregation in employment can be eliminated. As discussed above, although New Zealand women are gaining tertiary-level qualifications at a rate higher than their male counterparts, many women remain concentrated in traditionally female educational programmes and are significantly underrepresented in trades training. Based upon the current gendered educational and training outcomes, it is unlikely that the ideals of EEO across industrial or occupational sectors will materialize any time soon.

Third, Mintrom and True also suggest that New Zealand's employment relations framework needs to be reviewed to address gendered employment outcomes. The limitation of the employment relations framework is particularly evident in relation to continued pay inequities. Gendered pay gaps continue despite the passing of the Equal Pay Act 1972, New Zealand's ratification of the ILO Convention 100 and the CEDAW Convention, and a series of Government reports investigating the gendered pay gap (Ministry of Women's Affairs, 2002a; 2002b; 2002c; Statistics New Zealand, 1999). Moreover, in 1999, the Committee for CEDAW expressed concern over New Zealand's persistent pay gap, and recommended that 'further efforts by government, including considering development of a strategy for equal pay for work of comparable value' (cited in Ministry of Women's Affairs, 2002a, p. 15). Indeed, the Employment Equity Act 1990 (repealed in 1991) provided such mechanisms to make pay parity claims. Under the current employment framework, however, these mechanisms no longer exist (Ministry of Women's Affairs, 2002a).

Finally, as with any change initiative, Mintrom and True conclude that to be truly successful, the adoption of EEO will require strong organizational leadership, intra-organizational networks that actively promote EEO initiatives, and, in this instance, the normative adoption of the human rights values as well as the business case that underpin EEO.

THE GENDERED STRUCTURE OF PAID AND UNPAID WORK

The introduction of maternity leave, parental leave, paid parental leave, the creation of more part-time employment and improved child care facilities, has enabled more New Zealand women to return to paid employment after having children (NACEW, 2008). However, as discussed earlier, women, and in particular mothers, dominate the part-time workforce and many of these jobs are not linked to career paths (Statistics New Zealand, 2011a; NACEW, 2008). Women also continue to perform the majority of unpaid work in the home and community.

In contrast, men dominate the full-time workforce and are more likely than women to work overtime. New Zealand fathers of young children work on average 48 hours per week (Callister, 2005). Within the New Zealand context, the long work-hours culture and the male work norm partly explain why so few women make senior levels within the organizational context; *and those who do, are more likely to* delay marriage and children, or to choose to remain childless (International Labour Organization, 2004). The male work norm is characterized by an uninterrupted working life and a good worker is assumed to prioritize paid employment over all other aspects of life (Bunkle and Lynch, 1992). This male work norm *continues to be embedded in* male-dominated occupations and industries and upwardly mobile career paths (Bunkle and Lynch, 1992; Olsson and Pringle, 2004; Statistics New Zealand, 2006; Wilson, 1993).

Despite the efforts of the EEO Trust and the Department of Labour (www.dol.govt.nz) to raise work–life balance issues in the public forum, and the passing of the Employment Relations (Flexible Working Arrangements) Amendment Act 2007, there is very little change in the paid and unpaid gendered division of labour in New Zealand. Until more men are empowered to reduce their working hours and simultaneously increase their unpaid contribution to the family, it is unlikely that the ideals of EEO will be achieved in this country. Indeed, the gendered pay gap serves to reinforce the gendered structure of paid and unpaid work. Therefore, resolving gendered pay inequities must be embedded in any discussion that sets out to address employment segregation.

Conclusion

The political economy of New Zealand remains entrenched in a liberal philosophy strongly committed to tenets of atomized individualism and self-help. These same philosophical tenets are synonymous with the particular legal and voluntarist framework of EEO currently existing in New Zealand. For example, both neo-liberalism and EEO share a philosophical commitment to individualism and the primacy of paid employment. Neo-liberalism places importance on individuals to make good choices about their life, EEO facilitates the realization of individual choices by advocating non-discriminatory employment practices with an emphasis on individual merit. Issues not related to the job are to be ignored in employment decisions, so too, neo-liberal philosophy deems the private sphere beyond the scope of government intervention. Yet, a number of structural factors explain why women have been slow to achieve similar employment status as men since EEO was first discussed and introduced in New Zealand. Women's low incomes, continued gendered education outcomes and their high contribution to unpaid work help reinforce the current inequitable employment outcomes. Yet, these factors remain beyond the scope of EEO discourse as it is framed in the New Zealand context. These structural issues reinforce gender roles in the private and public spheres, and until both men and women are empowered to adjust their working days, contribute equitably in the work of the home as well as in the paid public sphere, and achieve pay parity, we believe it is unlikely that the goals of EEO will be achieved. Until these structural issues are addressed, EEO merely provides the appearance of offering a liberal solution to a fundamentally neo-liberal problem, that of exacerbating social inequalities.

References

Bennett, A. and Collins, C. (2011). Govt to Mount Full-scale Welfare Reform, 23 February, *The New Zealand herald.co.nz*. Retrieved on 24 February 2011 from http://www.nzherald.co.nz/nz/news/article.cfm?c_id=1&objectid=10708128.

Boston, J., Martin, J., Pallot, J. and Walsh, P. (1996). *Public Management: The New Zealand Model.* Oxford: Oxford University Press.

Brook Cowen, P. (1997). 'Neo-liberalism', in R. Miller (ed.), *New Zealand Politics in Transition.* Auckland, NZ: Oxford University Press, pp. 341–349.

Bunkle, P. and Lynch, J. (1992). 'What's wrong with the new right?', in C. Briar, R. Munford and M. Nash (eds), *Superwoman Where Are You? Social Policy and Women's Experience.* Palmerston North, NZ: Dunmore Press, pp. 23–40.

Callister, P. (2005). *The Changing Gender Distribution of Paid and Unpaid Work in New Zealand.* Paper presented to the Workshop on Labour Force Participation and Economic Growth, Wellington, NZ, 14–15 April.

Cheyne, C., O'Brien, M. and Belgrave, M. (2000). *Social Policy in Aotearoa New Zealand*, 2nd edition. Auckland, NZ: Oxford University Press.

Commission for Employment Equity (1991). *In to the '90s: Equal Employment Opportunities in New Zealand.* Wellington, NZ: Industrial Relations Services, Department of Labour.

Department of Labour (2010). Female Labour Market Factsheet – December 2010. Retrieved on 5 January 2011 from http://www.dol.govt.nz/publications/lmr/quick-facts/female-fig05.asp.

Dixon, S. (2000). *Pay Inequality Between Men and Women in New Zealand.* Occasional Paper 35(2). Labour Market Policy Group, Department of Labour.

Hausmann, R., Tyson, L. and Zahisi, S. (2009). *The Global Gender Gap Report.* Geneva: World Economic Forum.

Hausmann, R., Tyson, L. and Zahisi, S. (2010). *The Global Gender Gap Report.* Geneva: World Economic Forum.

Human Rights Commission (2008). *New Zealand Census of Women's Participation.* Wellington, NZ: Human Rights Commission.

Human Rights Commission (2010). *New Zealand Census of Women's Participation.* Wellington, NZ: Human Rights Commission. Retrieved on 10 February 2011 from http://www.hrc.co.nz/hrc_new/hrc/cms/files/documents/05-Nov-2010_09-29-40_HRC_Womens_Census_2010_WEB.pdf.

International Labour Organization (2004). Breaking through the Glass Ceiling – Women in Management, Update 2004, International Labour Organization, Geneva. Retrieved on 21 October 2007 from http://www.ilo.org/wcmsp5/groups/public/---dgreports/---dcomm/documents/publication/kd00110.pdf.

Johnston, M. (2010). Women lose boardroom gains: report, 8 November, *The New Zealand Herald*, p. A3

Kelsey, J. (1995). *The New Zealand Experiment: A World Model for Structural Adjustment?* Auckland, NZ: Auckland University Press.

McGregor, J. (2002). *Rhetoric or Reality: A Progress Report on the Rise of Women's Power in New Zealand.* Working Paper Series 02/1.

McGregor, J., Thomson, M. and Dewe, P. (1994). *Women in Management in New Zealand: A Benchmark Survey.* Working Paper Series, University of Western Sydney Nepean Faculty of Commerce.

Ministry of Social Development (2010). *The Social Report, Te Purongo Oranga Tangata.* Wellington, NZ: Ministry of Social Development. Retrieved on 10 January 2011 from http://www.socialreport.msd.govt.nz.

Ministry of Women's Affairs (2002a). *Next Steps Towards Pay Equity: A Discussion Document*, July. Wellington, NZ: Ministry of Women's Affairs.

Ministry of Women's Affairs (2002b). *Mahi Orite, utu Tokeke: Pay Equity for Women*, September a. Wellington, NZ: Ministry of Women's Affairs.

Ministry of Women's Affairs (2002c). *Next Steps Towards Pay Equity: A Background Paper on Equal Pay for Equal Worth*, September b. Wellington, NZ: Ministry of Women's Affairs.

Ministry of Women's Affairs (2009). *Mothers' Labour Force Participation*, December Wellington, NZ: Ministry of Women's Affairs, December. Retrieved on 4 March 2011 from http://www.mwa.govt.nz/news-and-pubs/publications/mothers-labour-force-participation#overall-participation-rate-of.

Ministry of Women's Affairs (2010a). *Indicators for Change 2009: Tracking the Progress of New Zealand Women Labour Force Participation Rate, by Gender*, February. Wellington, NZ: Ministry of Women's Affairs. Retrieved on 15 December 2010 from http://www.mwa.govt.nz/news-and-pubs/publications/indicators-for-change-2009-1/indicators-for-change-2009-pdf.

Ministry of Women's Affairs (2010b). *Analysis of Graduate Income Data 2002–2007 by Broad Field of Study*, March. Working paper by the Ministry of Women's Affairs, Wellington, NZ. Retrieved on 15 March 2011 from http://www.mwa.govt.nz/news-and-pubs/publications/graduate-income-data.

Ministry of Women's Affairs (2010c). *The Status of Women in New Zealand 2009: The Seventh Report on New Zealand's Progress on Implementing the United Nations Convention on the Elimination of All Forms of Discrimination Against Women*. Wellington, NZ: Ministry of Women's Affairs.

Mintrom, M., and True, J. (2004). *Framework for the Future Equal Employment Opportunities in New Zealand: Report Produced for the Equal Employment Opportunities Unit of the Human Rights Commission, as Part of the Equal Employments Opportunities Framework*. Wellington, NZ: The Human Rights Commission. Retrieved on 2 January 2011 from http://www.hrc.co.nz/eeo/.

NACEW (2008). *Critical Issues for New Zealand Women's Employment: Now and in the Future*. Wellington, NZ: Department of Labour.

New Zealand Law Society Annual Report (2006). Retrieved on 6 November 2007 from http://www.nz-lawsoc.org.nz/hmcontact.asp.

OECD Observer (2008). *Policy Brief: Babies and Bosses: Balancing Work–Family life*, July. Retrieved on 3 March 2009 from http://www.oecd.org.

Olsson, S. and Pringle, J.K. (2004). Women executives: public and private sectors as sites of advancement? *Women in Management Review*, 19(1), 29–39.

Pawson and colleagues (1996). 'The State and Social Policy', in R. Le Heron and E. Pawson (eds), *Changing Places: New Zealand in the Nineties*. Auckland, NZ: Longman Paul, pp. 210–246.

Roper, B. (1993). 'The End of the "Golden weather": New Zealand's Economic Crisis', in B. Roper and C. Rudd (eds), *State and Economy in New Zealand*. Auckland, NZ: Oxford University Press, pp. 1–25.

State Services Commission (1995). *EEO: 1984–1994 and Beyond*. Wellington, NZ: State Services Commission.

State Services Commission (1997). *EEO Policy to 2010: Future Directions of EEO in the New Zealand Public Sector Service*. Wellington, NZ: State Services Commission.

Statistics New Zealand (1999). *Exploring the Gap: An Exploration of the Difference in Income Received from Wages and Salaries by Women and Men in Full-time Employment*, July. Wellington, NZ: Statistics New Zealand.

Statistics New Zealand (2001). *Around the Clock: Findings from the Time Use Survey 1989/1990*. Wellington, NZ: Statistics New Zealand.

Statistics New Zealand (2006). *Report of New Zealand Population Census, 2006* Wellington, NZ: Statistics New Zealand. www.stts.govt.nz

Statistics New Zealand (2011a). *Employed Part-Time by Sex by Wanting Hours Change* (Annual–Dec): Table reference: HLF030AA. Retrieved on 3 March 2011 from www.stats.govt.nz infoshare.

Statistics New Zealand (2011b). *Employed Persons, Full and Part-Time Status by Sex* (Annual–Dec):
Table reference: HLF025AA. Retrieved on 3 March 2011 from www.stats.govt.nz infoshare.

Wilson, M. (1988). *Towards Employment Equity: Report of the Working Group on Equal Employment Opportunities and Equal pay*. Report of the New Zealand Department of Labour.

Wilson, M. (1993). 'Women and the Law', in Women's Electoral Lobby (ed.), *Walking Backwards into the Future: A Collection of Essays Commissioned by Women's Electoral Lobby*. Hamilton, NZ: Women's Electoral Lobby.

List of Acts

Equal Pay Act, 1972

The Human Rights Commission Act, 1977

State Owned Enterprises Act, 1986

State Sector Act, 1988

Public Finance Act, 1989

New Zealand Bill of Rights, 1990

Employment Equity Act, 1990 (repealed)

Employment Contracts Act, 1991 (repealed)

The Human Rights Act, 1993

The Employment Relations Act, 2000

The Parental Leave Act, 1987

Local Government Act, 2002

The Parental Leave and Employment Protection (Paid Parental Leave) Amendment Act, 2002

The Parental Leave and Employment Protection (Paid Parental Leave for Self Employed persons) Amendment Act, 2006

The Employment Relations (Flexible Working Arrangements) Amendment Act, 2007

List of Websites

The Ministry of Women's Affairs www.mwa.goct.nz

Ministry of Social Development www.msd.govt.nz

Statistics New Zealand www.stats.govt.nz

The Human Rights Commission www.hrc.co.nz

Equal Opportunity Trust www.eeotrus.org.nz

National Employment Equality Network www.neon.org.nz

OECD www.oecd.org

The Inland Revenue Department www.ird.govt.nz

4 Spain: The Drive for Gender Equality

PATRICIA GABALDÓN

Introduction

Over the past decade there has been an increased effort to research the gender of top executives and boards of directors of companies. The ratio of women over men reaching top positions is still very low in many countries, though it has been increasing in some developed countries. Governments, like in Sweden and Norway, are one step ahead and have introduced regulations in order to improve equal opportunities; setting quotas on the gender composition of boards of directors of private firms. Besides this debate, focus has been on good corporate governance and good diversity management. If diversity means more women as top executives or members of boards of directors, we can assume a positive effect on shareholder value and firm performance. This has not been proved yet, but this might be a strong argument for having more women in top management positions. Many of the previous studies on gender diversity on the boards of directors of companies show that in many cases, well-managed diversity is a variable that positively influences empirically the performance of the company because it contributes to the view of the board and different leadership styles.

Internationally, the European Commission, through various legislative directives and provisions of the Treaty (European Commission for Employment, Social Affairs, Equal Opportunities) has improved the momentum of women's leadership in business by promoting equal treatment between men and women, by, in particular: access to employment, equal pay, maternity leave or paternity leave, social security and so on (see European Commission (2010 and 2000); 'Strategy for Equality Between Women and Men 2010–2015', and 'Equal Treatment EU laws, 2000').

Spain has had two relevant initiatives for legislation-based action to foster women's promotion to higher positions and promoting quotas: the new Code for Corporate Governance (CNMV, 2006, 2010) and the Equality Law of March 2007.

In 2007, the Spanish stock exchange regulator, the Securities Markets Commission (Comisión Nacional del Mercado de Valores, CNMV) issued its third Corporate Governance Code (Informe Comisión Conthe). As a result of this requirement, Spanish-listed companies are required to present a report of good governance, including their board structure, standards and practices to the CNMV (2006). The Code establishes the content of the Corporate Governance Report (Informe de Gobierno Corporativo) that all companies listed in the Spanish Stock Exchange[1] are required to file every year. The Conthe Code contains recommendations for all areas of corporate governance and requires companies to either comply or explain all cases in which they are not in compliance with the report's recommendations.

The second step taken by the Spanish Government in the realm of gender diversity has been the Constitutional Act 3/2007 of 22 March for effective equality between women and men, known as the Equality Law (Ley de Igualdad). This law includes the requirement for companies with more than 250 employees to develop gender equality plans as well as specific measures to counteract work–life imbalance.

One of the most controversial aspects of the law is the section that refers to women on corporate boards. According to Article 75, 'Companies obliged to present unabridged financial statements of income will endeavour to include a sufficient number of women on their boards of directors to reach a balanced presence of women and men within eight years of the entry into effect of this act' (Equality Law, 2007, p. 483), balanced presence being defined by the law as 40/60 of either sex from the enactment of this Act in 2007, that is, until it becomes effective in 2015. In addition, the implementation of equality plans in companies of more than 250 employees has yielded the result that 3,397 companies already have a Plan for Equality and 1,895 companies have at least one woman on their boards of directors (Informa D&B, 2009/2010).

Women in the Spanish Labour Market

Over the last few years, Spain has taken significant steps to foster higher women/men ratios in business, including legislation, incentives and support for private initiatives and public awareness. As a result of most of these initiatives, in 2010 women constituted 51 per cent of the Spanish workforce, and held 32.47 per cent of managerial positions (INE, 2010). However the biggest challenge still lies at the top management level, specifically at board level, where women represent only 7.6 per cent of members in Spanish listed companies.

One of the most used excuses for the lower presence of women on corporate boards is a potential lower qualification than men. According to the figures available for Spain, as it can be seen in Figure 4.1, this situation has changed already and the presence of women in tertiary and post-tertiary education is slightly higher than the presence of men. However, based on current data, around ten years from now, the qualification excuse will no longer be viable.

The female employment rate in Spain in 2008 was 54 per cent of the working population as can be seen in Table 4.1, almost six points below the EU–15 data. This might look a big gap, but it was 11 percentage points in 2002, so we can confirm the incorporation of women into the Spanish labour force, and we can also confirm that the gap is closer to European standards. The most difficult part is when analyzing the unemployment rates, as the female Spanish unemployment rate is double the figures in the EU–15 both in 2002 and 2008.

---

1   The IBEX35 is a capitalization weighted index comprising the 35 most liquid Spanish stock traded in the Spanish continuous market. It is the official reference index for the four Spanish stock markets of the Spanish stock market interconnection system.

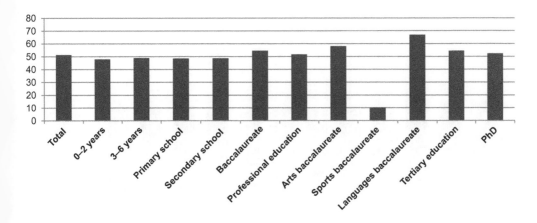

Figure 4.1   Level of education: percentage of women to total students: 2007/2008
Source: Author, based on INE statistics.

Table 4.1   Female employment and unemployment rates (%)

	Employment rates		Unemployment rates	
	2002	**2008**	**2002**	**2008**
EU–15	55.6	60.4	8.5	9.0
EU–25	54.7	59.4	9.7	9.0
EU–27	54.4	59.1	9.7	8.9
Eurozone	53.1	58.8	9.5	9.6
Spain	44.4	54.9	15.7	18.4

Source: Eurostat.

Fifty-one per cent of the total labour force in Spain is female, but the majority of those women are inactive or non-working. During the twenty-first century, the 'inactive' female population has decreased from 63 per cent to 60 per cent at the end of 2010. This said, of the remaining 40 per cent that were working or looking for a job in 2001, 56 per cent were unemployed and by 2010 this figure decreased to 45 per cent. Reflecting on these figures, we come to the conclusion that, of the total number of working-age women, just 14 per cent were working in 2001 and in 2010 this number is still around 20 per cent, which from any point of view can be considered a huge quantity.

The total number of working women in 2001 was 6.1 million, and in 2010 this number increased by 25 per cent, achieving the number of 8.1 million (see Figure 4.2 for more details). The active population has increased in this period by 30 per cent, from 7.2 million to 10.2 million women. Consequentially, the level of unemployment among women has increased by 48 per cent (from 1.1 million in 2001 to 2.1 million nine years later). Putting all these figures together we can conclude that the economic development and growth of the Spanish economy has promoted the incorporation of women into the labour force, and has especially increased as the new female generations join the labour market, but the economy has not been able to create enough jobs for all these newcomers, and the unemployment figures have doubled in almost ten years.

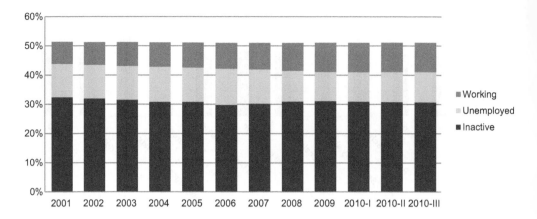

Figure 4.2   Female labour market in Spain (percentage total)
Source: Author, based on INE statistics.

The need for an adequate work–life balance is one of the most traditional reasons for women not to join the labour force, and even when they do join, implementing this is a big challenge for the family. If we take a look at the changes in the use of time of men and women in Spain since 1993, we can confirm some changes (see Table 4.2). During any day, women devoted, in 1993, 5.28 hours per day more than men to doing any kind of housework. This difference has been reduced to 3.39 hours in 2006, with a decreasing rate over the 13 years, but remains very significant. Men dedicate more time to work and leisure than women, both in 1993 and in 2006, but the difference is not as big as the difference as the time dedicated to housework by women.

In the case of women, the time used to do housework has decreased by almost two hours per day in the past 13 years, but this was accompanied by an increase in the time devoted to work and a very remarkable decrease in time to spare (almost an hour per day). Anyway, there is not a big difference between men and women, as males have also seen the time dedicated to work increasing and to leisure decreasing by almost the same amount. However, the time dedicated to housework by men has been almost stable in this period, averaging between two and three hours per day. Again, this figure is around four hours less than women.

Table 4.2   Male and female uses of time in Spain

	1993	1996	2001	2006	Change 1993–2006
Women					
Personal needs	10.08	10.35	10.34	10.27	**0.19**
Housework	7.58	7.35	7.22	5.59	**1.59**
Education	0.37	0.18	0.29	0.31	**0.06**
Work	1.01	1.23	1.52	2.31	**1.30**
Leisure	8.00	8.47	9.17	7.07	**0.53**

Men					
Personal needs	10.35	10.52	10.34	10.33	**0.02**
Housework	2.30	3.05	3.10	2.20	**0.10**
Education	0.52	0.26	0.44	0.28	**0.24**
Work	3.22	3.10	3.28	4.28	**1.06**
Leisure	9.16	10.15	9.59	8.19	**0.57**

Source: Own preparation, using the 'Uses of time' by the Instituto de la Mujer.

Note: The data might not total 24 hours, as the secondary activities are also included in the estimation.

We do not have specific data for working women, not even for executive women, but, very probably this trend would not be that much different from the reality we have seen in the previous paragraphs.

Taking all the above figures into consideration, we can conclude that the integration of women in executive boards of companies is not that successful. Comparing figures from 2000 and 2009 in Table 4.3, it can be seen that women only represented 31 per cent of the total number of directors (both private and public) in 2000 and this figure is less than 25 per cent in 2009. However, women are very well represented in the body of women legislators, even better than in 2000, and directors in the public sector, holding 35 per cent of roles in 2009, but are under-represented in the role of private corporate directors, where just 23.8 per cent are women (although this rate is increasing over the period). It is very relevant to say that 45 per cent of firms without workers are run by women in 2009. This might be a sign of the need for work–life conciliation among women, as we will see later on in this chapter.

Table 4.3   Female executives in Spain

	% women 2000	% women 2009
Total working population	36.87	40.85
Corporate directors and directors of public administration	31.07	24.7
Women legislators and directors in the public sector	25.58	35.5
Corporate directors (firms with more than ten workers)	15.45	23.8
Management (firms less than ten workers)	23.8	30.3
Management (firms without workers)	47.59	45.7

Source: Survey on Spain's active population, INE 1998–2007.

Let us take a final look at the Spanish female labour market by taking into consideration the salary gap between men and women. In 1995, the sectors with the smallest difference between male and female salaries were those with a strong union presence such as mining, metallurgy, machinery and similar professions, and the gap in these was as much as 20 per cent. Fortunately, these gaps have decreased over the following 13 year period by an average of 33 per cent. Some industries, such as construction, have a difference in salaries of just 8.6 per cent. However, looking at the figures at the top of the list – directors in companies with ten or more employees – although the gap has decreased by 33 per cent, there is still a difference of more than 20 per cent. If we transfer this into an average salary in any of these positions, we might be talking about a remarkable absolute difference in salaries.

Table 4.4   Salary gap in Spain: differences between male and female salaries

	1995	2005	2006	2007	2008	Change 1995–2008
Occupation	32.85	27.49	26.33	25.62	21.87	-33%
Directors in companies with ten or more employees	33.10	35.69	34.65	33.82	24.58	-26%
Professions associated with second and third year university and related	27.71	25.60	25.44	26.08	18.53	-33%
Professions associated with university first cycle and related	27.69	22.73	20.43	18.84	11.65	-58%
Technicians and support professionals	20.62	29.07	27.37	25.15	22.47	9%
Administrative employers	29.08	29.32	29.89	29.95	25.39	-13%
Hospitality, restaurants and other personal services	23.51	25.21	21.57	20.19	16.20	-31%
Security services	22.53	—	17.98	..	14.43	-36%
Shop assistants and other services in commerce	37.65	23.78	22.07	22.93	22.99	-39%
Construction, except machine operators	—	18.13	14.40	16.49	8.69	-52%
Mining, metallurgy, machinery and similar professions	20.24	18.94	13.50	14.14	10.15	-50%
Graphic arts industries, textiles and clothing, in food processing, furniture makers, artisans and other similar professions	30.48	25.78	26.26	25.29	28.04	-8%
Operators in industrial facilities, fixed machinery, fitters and assemblers	37.48	34.32	31.90	31.82	31.05	-17%
Drivers and operators of mobile machines	34.05	23.41	22.95	22.22	23.92	-30%
Non-qualified workers in services (excluding transport)	38.93	29.42	28.60	30.10	27.84	-28%

Source: INE, Encuesta de Estructura Salarial, and own calculations.

Women on Spanish Corporate Boards

The percentage of female employees in private companies according to the Global Gender Gap 2010 in Spain is 48 per cent. However, as this study explains, as in almost all countries, there is a clear pattern across the levels of positions and female employees 'tend to be concentrated in entry or middle-level positions'. Only Norway shows more than 40 per cent of board director-level positions held by women and this is a result of a mandate that requires this as a minimum quota of each gender on the boards of public companies. This shows the importance of quotas and how they can change the traditional pattern of males controlling top positions in corporations.

Some studies have researched the presence of women in the 1,000 biggest firms in Spain and the results are not that different: only 6.61 per cent of the board members of these firms are women (Escot, Gimeno and Mateos de Cabo, 2007). This research shows that there are two types of firms that are mainly integrating those women: family firms and cooperatives. In the case of family firms, this is usually because of the flexibility women can get, and in the case of cooperatives it is a result of the strict internal democracy of the organization that gives equality a top priority. Additionally, in these types of firms women are not in these positions as independent members of the board – they are usually executive board members or family board members, with a level of power that progressively increases. The same research states that the size of the board and the firm are key variables for the presence of women on boards. Firstly, the bigger the board, the easier it is to include female members, and secondly, the bigger the company, the lesser the presence of women in these corporate boards. Furthermore, there are generally more women holding board-level positions in services firms than industrial and technological firms.

Focusing on the most important listed companies, IBEX 35 companies in Spain are legally obliged to provide information on issues of corporate governance (Transparency Law 26/2003 of July 17). Similarly, listed companies on the stock market provide their information publicly for the same reason. In the area of the boards of directors, notes that only 4 per cent are executive directors compared to 96 per cent external, according to the Corporate Governance Report (IAGC) of 2009 published by the CNMV. Within IBEX 35 companies, according to the latest figures available from the Corporate Governance Reports, there are 503 directors, of whom 51 are women – 10 per cent of them are directors, a figure which has decreased slightly compared to 2009, when the number of directors was less and the women councillors the same (10 per cent). However if we look at these figures in detail the reality is still very uneven in the largest Spanish companies.

In 2010, women comprised 10 per cent of the total number of board members in IBEX 35 corporations (see Table 4.5). This figure is far from the ratio proposed by the Equality Law. We have to say that there was a big jump from 2006 to 2007, which means that the implementation of the Conthe Code and the Equality Law was achieving its goal – doubling the presence of women on boards – but these figures have not changed that much since then. The truth is that more women are joining Spanish corporate boards (18 more) but more men are joining them also, so the relative female presence has not increased that much (see Figure 4.3 to see the evolution of this figure).

Table 4.5   Women holding presidencies and board positions in IBEX 35 companies

	2004	2005	2006	2007	2008	2009	2010
Men and women							
Board (total)	503	478	463	506	507	506	503
President	37	37	35	35	35	35	35
Vicepresident	39	40	41	53	55	51	51
Member of the board	417	388	379	413	409	413	410
Secretary of the board	10	13	8	5	8	7	7
Number of women							
Board (total)	13	10	16	33	43	52	51
President	2	0	1	1	1	1	0
Vicepresident	1	1	1	2	4	4	4
Member of the board	12	9	14	31	38	46	46
Secretary of the board	0	0	0	0	0	1	1
% women							
Board (total)	2.58	2.09	3.46	6.43	8.48	10.28	10.14
President	5.41	0	2.86	2.86	2.86	2.86	0.00
Vicepresident	2.56	2.50	2.44	3.77	7.27	7.84	7.84
Member of the board	2.88	2.32	3.69	7.51	9.29	11.14	11.22
Secretary of the board	0	0	0	0	0	14.29	14.29

Source: IAGC and Corporate Governance Reports.

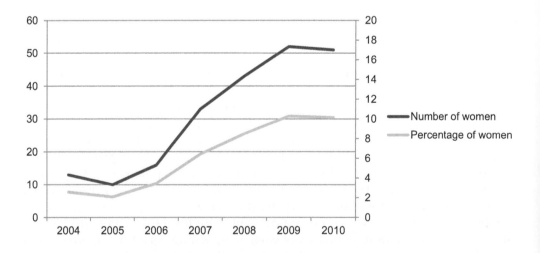

Figure 4.3   Presence of women on corporate boards: 2004–2010

Source: IAGC and Corporate Governance Reports.

If we go deeper into the information provided by their Corporate Governance Reports, we can see that:

- Most companies that do not meet the criterion of gender diversity proposed by the Code of Corporate Governance in 2007, have not changed their position in subsequent years, and the number of women remains the same. In 2001, among IBEX 35 companies there are six companies where there are no women on the governing body even after the actions recommended by the Unified Code to correct this situation.
- The maximum representation of women on boards of directors of these companies is 27 per cent achieved in a board composed of ten directors, of which three are women (Red Electrica Española), 17 percentage points higher than the average for IBEX 35 companies.
- In 2009, the boards of 27 companies – 79.4 per cent of IBEX-35 companies – have the presence of a woman, a figure higher than in previous years, although its growth rate is the lowest in the period under review. In 2010, 11 companies increased the number of directors, and only one introduced new female presence as a result of this expansion (triggering an increase of four advisors and two women). Only one company (Enagas) replaced a male board member with a woman. Female board members are usually independent members or proprietary (in the case of family firms). Only BBVA and Santander have female board members that come from the executive director positions.

There is a general consensus in studies carried out in recent years that work–life balance hinders womens' progression towards senior corporate positions, followed by a lack of awareness and social stereotypes (Cruzado and Velasco, 2005; Singh and Vinnicombe, 2006; Gomez Ansón, 2005). As a result, a number of public and private campaigns have been launched in Spain to tackle these specific issues and to eliminate inequality. These can be divided in two categories: legislation and private actions.

The Equality Law mentioned before was one of the most important actions and it includes the requirement for companies with more than 250 employees to develop gender equality plans as well as specific measures to counteract work–life imbalance. The problem is that this proposal is just that: it recommends but it does not oblige. However, as one of the statements of the Equality Law gives advantages in public contracts to companies fulfilling this requirement, it is clear that companies wanting to work with public administration would have more incentive to fulfil this requirement. The Equality Law launch started an intense debate on whether Article 75 was promoting or harming the inclusion of women on corporate boards, as promoting women to board-level positions may be viewed as fulfilling a quota rather than recognizing their individual merits (Matute, Paul and Sanmartín, 2007).

In addition to the Equality Law and other Government initiatives, private measures and public campaigns have also been developed over the past years, looking to foster greater awareness of women's issues. Those policies focus especially on work–life balance, however, more and more of those actions are looking for more equal access and establishment of women in the labour market (decreasing the wage gap and diminishing the glass ceiling.)

The low percentage of women on Spanish firms' boards over time makes us reflect on women's likelihood of appointment to the board of directors. It is reasonable to assume that, taking into account the different types of directors: internal (executive) and external (proprietary, independent, and so on), the fact that most female board members are external advisors could be the result of a lack of women in senior management (preamble CUBG Recommendation 15), which is a problem if the ultimate goal of the regulations, recommendations and laws, both at European and national level, is to achieve effective equality for women as a key economic development of society.

There is therefore an urgent need to examine the current state of the boards of directors of listed companies, to check objectives are being met, providing a basis on which to predict the future behaviour of other Spanish companies. Strategies that set quotas, targets and other affirmative policies to increase the percentage of female employees have been the subject of debate for a long time. On the one hand we have those who think these policies may create negative perceptions regarding the advancement of women and, on the other hand, we have those who think that this is the quickest and perhaps only way to reach critical mass in female representation.

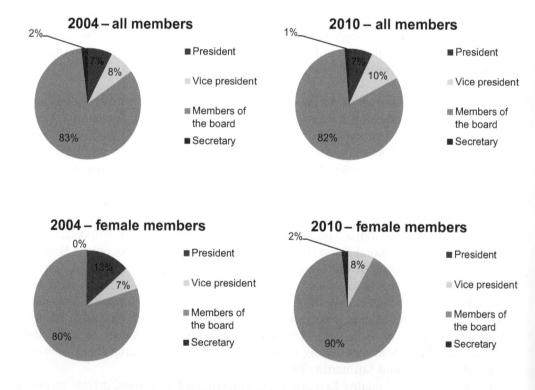

Figure 4.4   Board membership of IBEX 35 companies, 2009
Source: IAGC and Corporate Governance Reports.

Since 2005, we have seen an increase of more than 6 percentage points in the relative weight of women on the boards of directors, the presence of female directors in executive positions remains unchanged (see Figure 4.4).

Notwithstanding the very positive trend that we have seen over the last few years, the numbers are still low and the progress slow. Female directors only represented 7.6 per cent of all directors in 2008 and 44.6 per cent of all companies still do not have a single female director. The implementation of gender equality policies in companies with more than 250 workers has been pretty successful with 3,397 corporations having one and 1,895 firms with at least a woman on the corporate board (Informa D&B 2009/2010). According to the International Business Report (IBR) of Grant Thornton, women in director-level positions are 21 per cent of the total, a figure slightly higher than the 17 per cent from 2007. Nevertheless, only two out of ten director-level positions are held by women and 36 per cent of Spanish businesses don't have any women in their top management team. On the other hand, 47.6 per cent of the self-employed in Spain are women.

Some Food for Thought

The goal of this chapter is to evaluate the influence of the proportion of women on corporate boards in Spanish listed firms. We have seen a theoretical and empirical motivation for dealing with this issue of diversity in corporate governance. The presence of women in top management positions in still low in many countries, though it has been increasing over time. In countries such as Sweden or Norway the gender composition of boards is regulated by law in order to improve equal opportunities. If it could be shown statistically that more females in top positions or women on boards of directors have positive effects on firm performance, this may be a strong argument for having more women on boards, but there is no such clear evidence thus far.

An important question for understanding the effect of increased female participation in corporate leadership is whether such differences are fundamental variances between men and women or just because the board is diverse. In this scenario, now the question is: is the impact of legislation (quotas) enough to correct the trend in the near future? Many barriers may fall when women enter top positions in management, as when representation increases, women may build their own networks, helping each other to become more integrated and promoted within networks (Croson and Gneezy, 2008).

In the case of Spain, the presence of females in top positions has increased during the past years, and it has definitely been reinforced by the introduction of the Conthe Code and the Equality Law (see De Anca, 2008 for more detail). However, there is still a long way to go as female integration in corporate boards in Spain is still far from the figures of Norway or Finland. There are several ways of becoming a member of the board: being part of the family that owns the firm; being promoted from from a top executive position in the company; having been an independent member of the board, elected because of expertise in a certain field. Independent directors may be perceived as trustworthy. All of these types of members have increased over the last decade in Spain, but there is still room for many more women as, since 2007, the trend has not changed that much.

It is important for all institutions, companies, nominating committees, women's associations and specialist headhunters to make a conscious and determined effort to draw attention to those women who have achieved board-level status and promote this to other women. It is not about lowering standards or compromising financial knowledge, but diversifying skills, experiences and enrichment requirements for businesses. If this does not happen, educated and experienced women will be marginalized, and the economy may lose interested, very talented and highly qualified workers (Adams and Ferreira, 2004).

Effort is required to push more women into executive board-level positions. This applies to both women who have demonstrated leadership and management skills as well as those who, although they have not proved it yet, have high potential to succeed. These workers are already in the company and it is part of the firm's role to detect a 'pipeline' of female candidates. It would be more difficult to wait until a position arises than to identify a spontaneous generation of female colleagues who could match the requirements of the role. However, there is light at the end of the tunnel, as there might be some generational changes in the future. Recent research has shown that, for women, there is an inverse relationship between the percentage of women on boards and the average age of the board (Carter, Simkins and Simpson, 2002).

Measures to balance work and life, as well as other private programmes such as mentoring, training and so on might provide the impetus required for women to join corporate boards. This cannot be seen as an exclusively female right as these proposals have to apply to both men and women in order to change the traditional role of women in firms. Quotas might provide an initial push, but we shouldn't lose sight of women holding top positions in corporations in the future as, supported by these initiatives, men and women can become equally integrated in these roles.

This is just the tip of the iceberg, and the final message should be that the presence of women on boards has to be reinforced, not only to create more equality per se, but as a way of making corporate governance better for the firm and more inclusive.

References

Adams, R. and Ferreira, D. (2004). *Diversity and Incentives in Teams: Evidence from Corporate Boards.* Working Paper, Federal Reserve Bank of New York.

Carter, D.A. Simkins, B.J., and Simpson, W.G., (2002). *Corporate Governance, Board Diversity, and Firm Value.* Working paper, Oklahoma State University.

CNMV (2006). *Código Unificado de Gobierno Corporativo* (http://www.cnmv.es/index.htm.)

CNMV (2010). Informe Anual de Gobierno Corporativo.

Croson, R. and Gneezy, U. (2008), Gender differences in preferences, *Journal of Economic Literature,* 47(2), 1–27.

Cruzado, M. and Velasco, A. (eds) (2005). *¿Vives o Trabajas? Flexibilidad Laboral y Equibrio Personal. (Do you live or do you work? Labour flexibility and personal equilibrium).* Madrid: LID Editorial.

De Anca (2008). 'Women on corporate boards of directors in Spanish listed companies' in, *Women on Corporate Boards of Directors: International Research and Practice* by Vinnicombe, S., Singh, V. and Burke, R.J. (2008), Cheltenham: Edward Edgar Publishing.

Escot L., Gimeno R. and Mateos de Cabo R. (2007). ¿Dónde están las consejeras?: un análisis de la ausencia de mujeres en los Consejos de Administración de las mayores empresas españolas (Where are the female directors? Analysis of the absence of female in the corporate boards of the biggest Spanish companies). *Comunicación del X Encuentro de Economía Aplicada (Communications of the X Conference on Applied Economics).*

European Commission (2000). *Directive 2000/78/EC of 27 November 2000, establishing a general framework for equal treatment in employment and occupation.* Available online: http://eur-lex. europa.eu/LexUriServ/LexUriServ.do?uri=CELEX:32000L0078:EN:HTML

European Comission (2010). *Strategy for equality between women and men 2010–2015.* Available online: http://eur-lex.europa.eu/LexUriServ/LexUriServ.do?uri=COM:2010:0491:FIN:EN:HTML

Gomez Ansón, S. (2005). Diversidad de género en los consejos de administración de las sociedades cotizadas y cajas de ahorro españolas (Gender diversity in corporate boards of Spanish listed companies and savings banks boards. Research paper by the Fundacion de Estudios Financieros), *Papeles de la Fundación* (12). Madrid: Fundación de Estudios Financieros.

INE (Instituto Nacional de Estadística) (2008). *Encuesta de población activa 2009 (Active population survey 2009).* http://www.ine.es/.

Informa D&B (2009/2010). *Las mujeres en los consejos de administración de las empresas españolas. Estudio comparativo 2009/2010 (Women on Spanish corporate boards. A comparative study, 2009/2010).*

Matute, Paul and Sanmartín (2007). *Informe ICSA de retribución de la mujer directiva en España (ICSA Report on remuneration of female directors in Spain).* ICSA Recursos Humanos.

Singh, V. and Vinnicombe, S. (2006). *The Female FTSE Report 2006.* Cranfield, UK: Cranfield University.

The Equality Law (2007). *Ley Orgánica Para la Igualdad Efectiva de Mujeres y Hombres 121/000092.* Madrid: Boletín Oficial de las Cortes Generales (92–17), 467–509. http://www.mtas.es/igualdad/legislacion/EqualityAct3-2007.pdf.

5 Striving for Gender Equality in the 'New' South Africa: Government and Legislative Initiatives

STELLA M. NKOMO

Introduction

South Africa became a democratic nation in 1994 after years of a repressive system of racial segregation known as apartheid. From the outset, gender equality has been one of the key principles of the new democracy. On 27 April 2011, South Africa celebrated 17 years of democracy. A poignant question is how much progress has been made towards gender equality in a context where the Government has made it a key priority in the transformation of South Africa? The purpose of this chapter is to interrogate this question by providing a historical overview of the absence of gender equality during apartheid and the effects of new dispensation legislative interventions to achieve equality. The chapter concludes with a discussion of the prospects for gender equality in the post-transition period.

Gender Equality under Apartheid

While racial discrimination and oppression in South Africa has colonial origins, the official establishment of the apartheid system of legal racial segregation was ushered in with the election of the National Party in 1948. Apartheid was a system of interconnected social, political and economic structures that systematically oppressed blacks and privileged whites. It is incommensurable to use the term gender equality when discussing the status of women under apartheid. Much of what has been written about apartheid has focused on its racialization of South African society. Yet, historically women of all races were subjected to patriarchal laws that entrenched a subordinate status relative to men. Women were generally defined as minors with few political and economic rights. South African women were effectively relegated to second-class citizenship as they were under the social and even legal control of their fathers or husbands. The infamous section 11(3) (b) of the Black Administration Act of 1927 officially gave married black women the legal status of children. Thus, before apartheid, the colonial administration through what Nhlapo (1995) refers to as 'defensive customary law' officially sanctioned African customs once more fluid and context driven into rigid laws that entrenched the subordinate status of African women. In the white community, women were refused the vote until 1930. Examining patriarchy alone overlooks the ways in which gender and race intersected to create different forms of patriarchy towards the women of South Africa. In other words, the meshing of apartheid with patriarchy accentuated the subjugation of African, coloured and Indian women.

The plight of African women was directly connected to the control of the movement of African men. Control was exercised as early as 1923 with the Native Areas Act. This Act and subsequent laws separated African family members from one another. In the case of African women, they were more restricted from entering urban areas than African men. Entrance was dependent upon the qualifications of their 'guardians' (that is, husbands), qualifications often impossible to meet (Bernstein, 1985). As a result, African women who had been deemed superfluous appendages were largely confined to living apart from their husbands in impoverished rural Bantustans. There was little hope of employment in these desolate and barren spaces.

The repression of African women was intensified when African women became subject to the strict influx control measures of the Natives Abolition of Passes and Coordination of Documents Act which was passed in 1952. The curious name of this act did not abolish passes (that is, documents that controlled the movement of African men) but consolidated them into a single reference book which contained information on identity, employment, place of legal residence, payment of taxes, and, if applicable, permission to be in the urban area. Despite a heroic resistance campaign waged by women of all races, the Act became applicable to African women in 1963 and made it an offence not to carry the book and for an employer to employ anyone who did not possess it. This law and the Bantu Laws Amendment Act of 1964 resulted in the majority of African women regulated to a life of dire poverty and unemployment.

African women were also severely disadvantaged when they were able to find employment. A race and gender hierarchy prevailed in the South African workplace (Booysen, 1999; Booysen, 2007; Booysen and Nkomo, 2010) which ensured African women would occupy poorly paid unskilled jobs, primarily domestic work that kept them away from their children and families. While white women acquired some privileges due to their race, they mainly worked in typically female jobs in the workplace (for example, secretary, nurse and so on). The few African, Indian or coloured women who gained access to professional female jobs (for example, nurses) were only allowed to work in their respective communities and were paid only about a third of what a white nurse would earn (Bernstein, 1985). During apartheid, the best and highest paid jobs in the economy including management positions were exclusively reserved for white men. Black men were primarily employed in unskilled jobs (Booysen, 2007) or if they did on rare occasions hold supervisory jobs, they were only allowed to supervise other blacks. The confinement of African, Indian and coloured men to low paying jobs further exacerbated the status of the African, Indian and coloured women as their husbands were unable to adequately support their families (Bernstein, 1985).

Post-Apartheid Gender Equality Legislation

This section details gender equality legislation enacted since 1994. The scope and number of laws reflect the level of commitment to gender equality at the time. The Government placed considerable emphasis on promoting gender equality throughout South African society (Mathur-Helm, 2005). This was not a new commitment but was in keeping with the African National Congress's long-standing commitment to building a non-sexist society resulting from the influence of women in the struggle for equality. African women participated in political campaigns but did not initially have the right to vote within the African National Congress (ANC) until the founding of the ANC Women's League in 1943. It was the founding of the multi-racial Federation of South African Women during the struggle to resist the pass laws that led to the writing of the 'Women's Charter' at its first conference in 1954. The formation of the Federation was based on the observation that the existing male-dominated political organizations were unlikely to meet women's specific needs for equality (Wells, 1993).

The Women's Charter (Federation of South African Women, 1954, p. 1) called for the following:

> We resolve to struggle for the removal of laws and customs that deny African women the right to own, inherit or alienate property. We resolve to work for a change in the laws of marriage such as are found amongst our African, Malay and Indian people, which have the effect of placing wives in the position of legal subjection to husbands, and giving husbands the power to dispose of wives' property and earnings, and dictate to them in all matters affecting them and their children.

The Charter also specified a number of requirements for gender equality in South Africa including the right to vote, representation in government, employment opportunities, equal pay, compulsory education for every child, free movement and participation in all structures of society. The Women's Charter was incorporated into the African National Congress Freedom Charter in 1955 signalling the party's official endorsement of gender equality and non-sexism. The strong presence and leadership of women during the struggle to end apartheid foreshadowed their active participation in the new government. The result is evident in the many legal and structural interventions introduced in the early days of the transition to democracy (Geisler, 2000). Women had a direct effect on the content of the new South African constitution through the formation of the Women's National Coalition. In 1992, the ANC Women's League initiated the formation of the Women's National Coalition which consisted of 105 diverse organizations covering political parties, rural women's organizations, religious and professional associations (Geisler, 2000). The coalition issued a 'Women's Charter for Effective Equality' that was to inform the bill of rights in the constitution. As a result, the principle of gender equality is enshrined in the South African constitution making it one of the most gender sensitive in the world.

The South African Constitution adopted in 1996 is the supreme law of the country. It provides the foundation for understanding the national legal framework mandating gender equality. Equality and human rights are core values articulated in the Constitution. Its founding provisions are found in Chapter 1 (p. 3) and are stated as:

> *The Republic of South Africa is one, sovereign, democratic state founded on the following values: (a) human dignity, the achievement of equality and the advancement of human rights and freedoms; (b) non-racialism and non-sexism; (c) supremacy of the constitution and the rule of law; (d) universal adult suffrage, a national common voters roll, regular elections and a multi-party system of democratic government, to ensure accountability, responsiveness and openness.*

Within Chapter 2, Clause 9 (p. 7) specific reference is made to non-discrimination on the basis of gender:

> *The state may not unfairly discriminate directly or indirectly against anyone on one or more grounds, including race, gender, sex, pregnancy, marital status, ethnic or social origin, colour, sexual orientation, age, disability, religion, conscience, belief, culture, language and birth.*

It does however allow for discrimination if it is fair and aimed towards improving the status of disadvantaged individuals. It is important to stress that the Constitution is based on the notion of substantive rather than formal equality (that is, equality of outcome rather than equality of opportunity). Thus, it supports the idea that equality might require differential treatments of groups and interventions for improving the status of women.

To ensure proper monitoring of the gender equality clause, the new Government established a Commission for Gender Equality. The function of the Commission for Gender

> *to promote gender equality and to advise and make recommendations to Parliament or any other legislature with regard to any laws or proposed legislation which affects gender equality and the status of women' is contained in Section 187 (Constitution of South Africa, 1996). A difficult issue was the role of customary law in a constitutional democracy. It was resolved that if there is a contradiction between gender equality and customary law, the constitution takes precedence.*

The second significant piece of legislation in respect to gender equality is the Employment Equity Act promulgated in 1998. The goal of the Employment Equity Act is to achieve employment equity by a) promoting equal opportunity and fair treatment in employment through the elimination of unfair discrimination; and b) implementing affirmative action to redress the disadvantages in employment experienced by designated groups (Africans, coloureds, Indians, persons with disabilities and women), in order to ensure their equitable representation in all occupational categories and levels in the workplace (Employment Equity Act, 1998). Thus, the act has two intentions. One is to ensure equal opportunity and non-discrimination. The other intention is to redress demographic disparities in the workplace. This is reflected in Section 42 of the Act which reads, 'The demographic profiles of the national and regional economically active population should be reflected in the employment areas of designated employers. This reflection will show that the workplace is redressed and equality together with a diverse and representative workforce is achieved' (Employment Equity Act, 1998). While it stands to eliminate unfair discrimination at the workplace, it provides for fair discrimination to ensure that Africans, coloureds, Indians, women and people with disabilities are equitably represented at all occupational levels (Department of Labour, 2010).

Thirdly, the Promotion of Equality and Prevention of Unfair Discrimination Act was adopted in 2000 and provides a framework to tackle unfair discrimination on any grounds, including harassment and hate speech. Its goal is to support transformation of South African society. The Act included a provision for the establishment of Equality Courts at every magistrate's court to hear any case of discrimination. Finally, a number of additional laws have been adopted to improve the status and women and to ensure protection against oppression. These laws are summarized in Table 5.1 and cover areas ranging from violence against women and rights within customary marriages.

Table 5.1   South African gender legislation

Law	Year adopted	Purpose
Domestic Violence Act (replaced the Prevention of Family Violence Act of section 19)	1998	Broadens the definition of domestic violence to include not only married women and children, but unmarried women who are involved in relationships or living with their partners, people in same-sex relationships, mothers and their sons, and other people who share a living space.
Recognition of Customary Marriages Act	1998	Provides for the recognition of customary marriages, specifies the requirements for a valid customary marriage and regulates the registration of customary marriages. It sets out some of the consequences of such a marriage and gives spouses in a customary marriage equal status and capacity.
The Maintenance Act	1998	Provision of stronger measures for women to acquire maintenance for children. Maintenance may be automatically deducted from a person's salary. If maintenance is not paid, a magistrate can seize property belonging to the person who is supposed to pay.
Choice on Termination of Pregnancy Act	1996	Recognize women's reproductive health rights and right to an abortion.
Criminal Law (Sexual Offences) Amendment Act	2007	Modifies the definition of consent and the evidential requirements for proving rape (including abolition of the cautionary rule against complainants' evidence and providing that no negative inference can be drawn from a delay in reporting rape). Subsequent amendments specify minimum sentences for rape and instructions for how police investigations must be conducted in cases involving rape.

Government Structures and Gender Equality

The Government under the leadership of former President Thabo Mbeki established The Office on the Status of Women (OSW) in the Presidency to drive gender equality, particularly in government structures. The OSW developed South Africa's National Policy Framework for Women's Empowerment and Gender Equality (NGPF) under the direction of the Presidency in accordance with its jurisdiction over the national gender programme as guided by the vision of equal and inalienable rights of all men and women enshrined in the Bill Rights of the South African Constitution. The main purpose of the NGPF was to establish a clear vision and framework to guide the process of developing laws, policies, procedures and practices that would ensure equal rights and opportunities for women and men in all spheres and structures of Government as well as in the workplace, the community and the family. The resulting policy document was approved and adopted by the Cabinet in 2000. In terms of scope, the NGPF applies to all Government departments, provincial administrations, local structures, state-owned enterprises and other public entities. It also provided an important framework for all organizations and institutions in South Africa. The vision for gender equality stated in the NGPF is that of a society in which women and men realize their full potential and participate as equal partners in creating a just and prosperous society for all. The key principles underpinning the national vision of gender equality are:

- equality between men and women;
- recognition of differences and inequalities among women;
- women's rights are human rights;
- customary, cultural and religious practices are subject to the right to equality;
- public and private are not separable spheres of life;
- entitlement to the right of integrity and security of person;
- affirmative action programmes for women;
- economic empowerment for women;
- mainstreaming gender equality;
- partnerships between Government and civil society.

To give effect to the NGPF, Government created a national gender mainstreaming system comprised of a comprehensive network of structures, mechanisms and processes was developed to enable institutions to work towards gender equality (Gouws, 2004). Gender focal persons were placed within every Government department and municipality to coordinate gender sensitive planning and programme implementation. More recently, the current President, Jacob Zuma, established a Ministry on Women, Children and Persons with Disabilities within the national and provincial executive. Standing committees were also established on the Quality of Life and Status of Women in national and provincial legislatures.

In addition to Governmental interventions, the Government also endorsed several regional and international protocols including the Southern African Development Community (SADEC) Gender and Development Protocol that requires members to provide for the empowerment of women, to eliminate discrimination and to achieve gender equality and equity through the development and implementation of gender responsive legislation, policies, programmes and projects. South Africa is also a signatory to the Convention for the Elimination of All Forms of Discrimination Against Women (CEDAW), the Beijing Platform for Action, the Protocol to the African Commission on Human People's Rights on the Rights of Women in Africa and the United Nations Millennium Declaration.

The ANC also set quotas for the representation of women in political leadership. A target of 50–50 representation was set for 2015 in accordance with SADEC Protocol on

Gender and Development. To achieve this target, the ANC, which is the dominant political party, implemented a quota system requiring 1:1 ratio of male to female candidates on election lists.

In addition to all of the above measures, the Government has instituted charters for certain industry sectors to empower historically disadvantaged groups in South Africa. These charters emanate from the Black Economic Empowerment Act of 2003 (BEE) and subsequent amendments in 2004 and 2007. BEE is a strategy to increase black ownership of businesses and accelerate black representation in management. As part of this umbrella strategy for transformation, specific targets (not quotas) for the empowerment of women were set in a mechanism known as industry charters. For example, the Broad-Based Socio-Economic Empowerment Charter for the South African Mining Industry of 2004 required each mining and minerals company with 50 employees or more to have a plan to reach 10 per cent women representation within five years. The charters also include requirements in terms of ownership, human resource development, housing and facilities, and community development. To do business with the Government, companies must submit their BEE scorecard that indicates performance in a number of areas including employment equity.

Progress towards Gender Equality

Just how much progress has been made towards gender equality given the scope and quantity of measures that have been put in place since 1994? Statistics on the representation of women in various sectors of South African society indicate that overall greater progress has been made in the government sector than in the private sector. For example, according to the Commission on Gender Equality, the overall representation of women is 178 (45 per cent) out of 400 members of the lower house of Parliament. In the upper house, women constitute 29.6 per cent of the 54 members. Within the South African Government, women hold 42 per cent of ministerial positions and 39 per cent of deputy minister posts. This is in stark contrast to South Africa's classification during the apartheid Government when the total number of women in Parliament never exceeded eight and was often lower (Republic of South Africa, 1994). South Africa has moved from the bottom of the global classification of women in political leadership to one of the top three in the world. Globally, South Africa ranks third after Rwanda and Switzerland in terms of the representation of women in Parliament.

When we turn to the private sector, the picture is much less representative. Each year the Commission on Employment Equity publishes a report that describes the state of equality in South African organizations (both private and public including Government) covered by the Employment Equity Act. These organizations are required to file a report annually showing the status of different race and gender groups in different job categories. The 2010 report indicates that generally whites and white males in particular continue to dominate management positions in the private sector but not in Government and state-owned enterprises (that is, former parastatals). Representation of various groups in terms of race and gender in the latter sectors is more closely aligned to their economically active population than in the private sector (see Figures 5.1 to 5.4).

African males hold 32.2 per cent of top management posts in Government followed by African women at 17.5 per cent. The picture for private sector top management positions is quite different. White males hold 62.9 per cent of private sector positions and also 46.0 per cent of top posts in the educational sector followed by white women with African, coloured and Indian women holding the lowest percentages of the various race and gender groups. A similar profile exists for senior management. African males again have the highest representation in senior management positions in Government followed by African females, white men and white women. In general, African, coloured and Indian females are grossly underrepresented in senior management positions in Government, especially at local government level. Senior management positions in the private sector are dominated by whites, particularly white men at 53.4 per cent. White women have a higher representation (16.9 per cent) compared to African, coloured and Indian women who together hold less than 8 per cent of senior management positions.

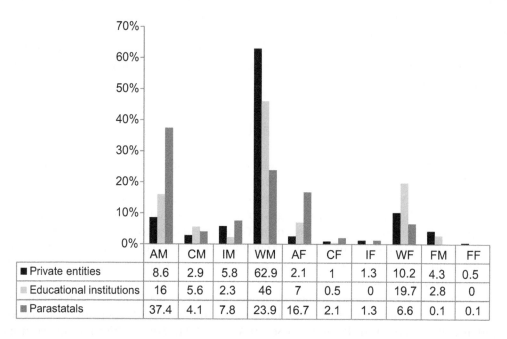

	AM	CM	IM	WM	AF	CF	IF	WF	FM	FF
■ Private entities	8.6	2.9	5.8	62.9	2.1	1	1.3	10.2	4.3	0.5
▨ Educational institutions	16	5.6	2.3	46	7	0.5	0	19.7	2.8	0
■ Parastatals	37.4	4.1	7.8	23.9	16.7	2.1	1.3	6.6	0.1	0.1

Figure 5.1   Workforce population distribution for top management (private sector employers)

Source: Department of Labour (2009–2010, p. 10). South Africa 10th CEE Annual Report.

Overall, the 2010 Employment Equity Report indicates slow progress towards race and gender equality. The greatest gains for both racial/ethnic men and women have been in government. This change is reflective of the reality that political power shifted to the black majority in 1994, and it is the one sector where government can more effectively create change in employment practices. However, economic power still largely resides in the private sector that is white-male dominated (Booysen, 2007). This coupled with South Africa's initial reluctance to take a punitive approach to employment equity and affirmative may explain the slow progress. Additionally, private sector organizations have been less than fully cooperative in filing the annual reports although the percentage filing reports has increased in the last two years (Department of Labour, 2010).

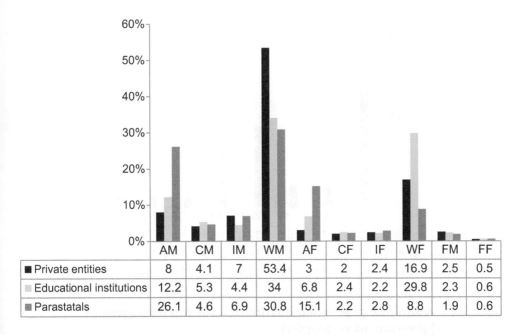

	AM	CM	IM	WM	AF	CF	IF	WF	FM	FF
■ Private entities	8	4.1	7	53.4	3	2	2.4	16.9	2.5	0.5
▨ Educational institutions	12.2	5.3	4.4	34	6.8	2.4	2.2	29.8	2.3	0.6
■ Parastatals	26.1	4.6	6.9	30.8	15.1	2.2	2.8	8.8	1.9	0.6

Figure 5.2   Workforce population distribution for senior management (private sector employers)

Source: Department of Labour (2009–2010, p. 13). South Africa 10th CEE Annual Report.

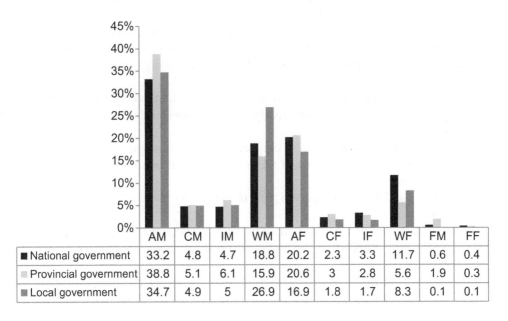

	AM	CM	IM	WM	AF	CF	IF	WF	FM	FF
■ National government	33.2	4.8	4.7	18.8	20.2	2.3	3.3	11.7	0.6	0.4
▨ Provincial government	38.8	5.1	6.1	15.9	20.6	3	2.8	5.6	1.9	0.3
■ Local government	34.7	4.9	5	26.9	16.9	1.8	1.7	8.3	0.1	0.1

Figure 5.3   Workforce population distribution for senior management (government employers)

Source: Department of Labour (2009–2010). South Africa 10th CEE Annual Report.

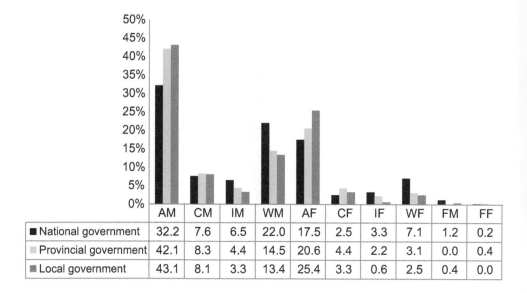

	AM	CM	IM	WM	AF	CF	IF	WF	FM	FF
■ National government	32.2	7.6	6.5	22.0	17.5	2.5	3.3	7.1	1.2	0.2
▨ Provincial government	42.1	8.3	4.4	14.5	20.6	4.4	2.2	3.1	0.0	0.4
■ Local government	43.1	8.1	3.3	13.4	25.4	3.3	0.6	2.5	0.4	0.0

Figure 5.4   Workforce population distribution for top management (government employers)

Source: Department of Labour (2009–2010, p. 10). South Africa 10th CEE Annual Report.

A source providing a more detailed picture of the extent of gender equality in private sector organizations is the South African Business Women Association's annual census. The census which has been conducted annually since 2004 collects data from 339 companies listed on the Johannesburg Stock Exchange (JSE) as well as Government and state-owned enterprises. The 2011 census reflects the following (see Figures 5.5 to 5.7):

- The direct comparison of men versus women reveals men overwhelmingly dominate CEO/MD positions and Directorship in Johannesburg Stock Exchange-listed companies.
- Although women comprise 45.1 per cent of the employed population, women constitute less than 10 per cent of CEOs and chair of boards of listed entities and state-owned enterprises.
- Percentages for CEOS, chairperson and directorships have all marginally dropped since 2010.
- The percentage of women as executive managers has increased modestly to 21.6 and very slowly since 2004 when the first census indicated women held 14.7 per cent of the positions.
- South Africa is faring better than international counterparts (that is, United States, New Zealand, Canada, Australia and the United Kingdom) in terms of women in executive management.
- Only 37 companies have 25 per cent or more director and executive manager positions held by women.

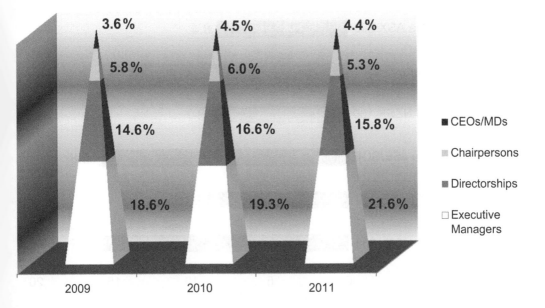

Figure 5.5   Census trend pyramids
Source: Business Women's Association of South Africa (2011, p. 24). BWA South Africa Women in Leadership Census.

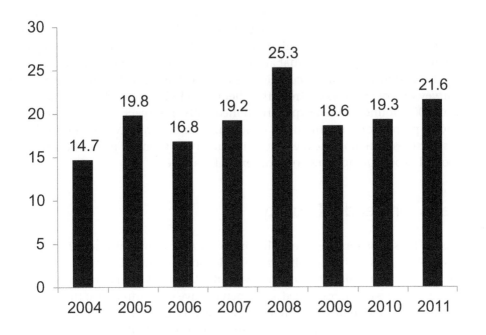

Figure 5.6   Percentage of female executive managers: 2004–2011
Source: Business Women's Association of South Africa. BWA South Africa Women in Leadership Census Reports 2004–2011.

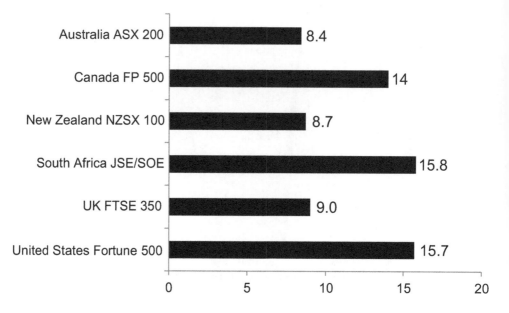

Figure 5.7   Percentage of board directors who are women (South Africa vs. international counterparts)

Source: Business Women's Association of South Africa (2011, p. 29). BWA South Africa Women in Leadership Census.

There is little doubt the post-1994 period has resulted in marked changes in the representation of previously disadvantaged people in some of the upper tiers of organizations – positions from which they were totally excluded during apartheid. However, it is critical to point out that at the lower levels of the labour market women are still concentrated in particular occupations and sectors and these tend to have low pay. In her survey of women workers from the chemical, clothing, textile and retain sectors, Benjamin (2008) found women experienced inequality in respect to pay, job grading, job descriptions, promotions, treatment by male management and involvement in decision-making structures. A majority experienced inequality in terms of promotion and 40 per cent reported experiencing some form of sexual harassment.

Prospects for Gender Equality

What are the prospects for gender equality in South African organizations? Interrogating this question requires first describing the broader social political context within which the question of gender equality resides today. South Africa has been heralded as one of the only cases in which women organized as women to have some input into the negotiations that established a new political system as part of a transition to democracy (Waylen, 2007). Typically, getting women's emancipation on to the front burner in a sustainable manner in new democracies after a struggle against authoritarianism has proved difficult in many countries (Baldez, 2002; 2003). While the South African experience has been different, a number of feminist scholars are concerned as to whether gender equality gains will continue in the current post-transition period (Seidman, 2003; Waylen, 2007).

For example, Waylen (2007) identifies a number of factors that have circumscribed the space for significant gender equality outcomes. A major factor is the decrease in women's organizing that has reduced large-scale advocacy on gender issues. Previous women's alliances like the Women's National Coalition of 1992 that exerted significant influence during the construction of the constitution have declined as many of its leaders have moved into national government. A corollary factor is the recent muting of women's voices within ANC structures (Waylen, 2007, p. 539). The grassroots participation in ANC as well as previous space for dissent has been minimized because of its rather hierarchical and centralized governance structures (Waylen, 2007). Some scholars argue the replacement of the Government's initial economic policy of redistribution to one of fiscally conservative growth has impeded significant socio-economic changes. Without radical socio-economic changes poverty will continue to adversely affect women, particularly poor women (Waylen, 2007). Very recently the Women's League of the ANC expressed their disappointment about the invisibility of attention to women's empowerment in the new economic growth path for South Africa unveiled in President Jacob Zuma's 2009 State of the Nation address (Mbanjwa, 2011). At the same time, the Commission for Gender Equality has called for an overhaul of the Employment Equity Act because of the slow progression of black women into executive management (Speckman, 2011).

Another worrisome factor scholars point to is the limited progress of the national gender machinery. Waylen (2007) points to the lack of resources and staff and the problems of bureaucratic resistance the OSW encountered in carrying out its responsibilities for gender equality. Similarly, the Commission on Gender Equality has struggled to be successful in spite of limited resources, internal leadership challenges and lack of sustained support from women's organizations (Waylen, 2007; Seidman, 2003).

Perhaps the most significant contextual factor mitigating concerted attention to gender equality is two co-existing societal discourses. One is the overwhelming discourse of dissatisfaction with progress towards racial equality expressed most often by the Government and majority black population. Although addressing racial inequality was a major promise of the new Government during its 1994 campaign, there was space for including gender inequality (Seidman, 2003). The growing dissatisfaction with the slow pace of eradicating racial inequality seems to have dampened attention to gender equality.

The contradictory ways in which attention to racial inequality trumps gender inequality is illustrated by recent discourse emanating from the Black Management Forum (BMF). The forum called for white women to be excluded from the Employment Equity Act of 1998 because statistics suggest organizations are favouring them for management positions in the private sector at the expense of qualified blacks. On the occasion of the election of a black woman as the new President of a large business association, Business Unity of South Africa, the BMF called her selection a blow to transformation (Donnelly, 2010). The subtext of the discourse is that racial transformation should give precedence to addressing the inequality of black men in South African organizations.

The other discourse is one I label 'apartheid fatigue' – white South Africans who view issues of inequality as things in the past because blacks enjoy political power. Thus, there is extensive debate about the need for a continued focus on redress (Habib and Bentley, 2008). A number of studies have shown that white South African attitudes towards affirmative action and preferential treatment are largely negative (for example Wambugu, 2005; Oosthuizen and Naidoo, 2010). Conservative white groups hold the view that affirmative action and BEE initiatives erode the rights of non-African groups (Habib and Bentley, 2008). Apartheid fatigue draws upon Ahmed's 'equity fatigue' notion – an impatience with the continued focused on equity because of a belief that inequity and inequality are things of the past (Ahmed, 2007). Segments of the white population appear to be unable or unwilling to recognize the continued effects of historical apartheid on the status of black men and women of all races (Steyn and Kelly, 2009; Nkomo, 2011). In sum, the current South African political and social context suggests the climate for gender equality is not the same as it was in the immediate post-apartheid period. This perhaps partially contributes to understanding why changes in the representation of women in management and leadership positions in the corporate sector have remained rather stagnant in the last few years. However, it is also important to look at factors that have been identified through empirical research on the status of women in management in South Africa.

The research focusing on gender equality in organizations is rather sparse. However, it does shed some light on individual and organizational level impediments to gender equality in the workplace (Ely and Padavic, 2007). There has been some research focusing on the glass-ceiling phenomenon in South Africa. The factors identified echo those reported in the extant literature on the phenomenon: gender stereotyping, male-dominated organizational cultures and tension between work and family responsibilities. Lloyd and Mey (2007) found that male respondents in their study attributed the shortage of women in managerial positions to a lack of commitment and drive among women. In a recent study of gender impediments to the South African executive suite, April, Dreyer and Blass (2007) cited the prevalence in modern South African society of roles allocated on the basis of gender. Booysen and Nkomo (2010) tested the think male, think manager hypothesis among a group of 562 managers and confirmed the hypothesis for black and white men but not for black and white women. Black and white men were less likely to attribute successful managerial characteristics to women and this was the case more so for black men than white men. Similar results were reported by Menon and Kotze (2007, p. 84) who conducted a study of human resource integration in the South African military. Some of the interviewees in their study reported 'traditional black men who are used to being respected at home by their wives, find it difficult to work under women'.

Organizational-level factors also contribute to gender inequality in organizations. Organizational culture has also been identified as a major obstacle to women's equality in South African organizations. Mathur-Helm (2006) noted that the women in her study felt left out within a male-dominated organization culture, and found it hard to develop a sense of belonging in the organizational system. It also seems that there is a preference for same gender subordinate–supervisor dyads. Milner et al. (2007) examined the impact of gender on the quality of relationships between leaders and subordinates. They found South African males experience more positive leader–member exchange relationships under male supervision, whereas females experienced more positive leader–member exchange relationships under female supervision.

A final factor is the approaches organizations have adopted in response to employment equity legislation. A recent study of diversity management practices in 12 South African organizations found that the majority had a compliance orientation that reduced issues of equality to a focus on numbers (Steyn and Kelly, 2009). That is, in most organizations the level of meaningful engagement with diversity was variable and, even in the best cases, lacking in deep transformative potential. In only a very small number of cases were there an integration of diversity into core business operations with attention to the importance and value of working with diversity successfully. The research also pointed to the relative silence on gender inequality in the 12 organizations. Authors of the report concluded, 'Unfair discrimination on the basis of gender seemed more flagrant than on the basis of race; gender discrimination was normalised within organisational practices while racial discrimination was publicly accepted as taboo' (Steyn and Kelly, 2009, p. 17). The results of this study confirm findings from a study conducted by the Commission on Gender Equity on the promotion and protection of gender equality in the private sector. Their study revealed that most companies are ignorant of national and regional treaties and commitments to gender equality; and that companies typically lacked a focused gender equality strategy or women's empowerment programmes (Hicks, 2009, p. 5). Steyn and Kelly (2009) and Hicks (2009) echo what was reported by Stott and Shunmugam (2002, p. 9) in their study of gender equality in the private sector that concluded, 'Gender equality was largely seen as an affirmative action issue which must be addressed because of legislative requisites. Though some companies were committed to mainstreaming gender equality and accelerating employment equity, few had been able to adequately integrate an approach that addressed race and gender inequalities simultaneously.'

Conclusion

Gender equality in the workplace is not a finished project in South Africa. The challenges of achieving gender equality in a country where attention to women's empowerment and equality formed part of the transformation to a democratic society at the outset suggest just how difficult it is to remove deeply rooted attitudes and structures of gender equality embedded in patriarchy and racism. Legislation and structures of the state have not been able to deeply penetrate the spaces where gender inequality is enacted and sustained in everyday practices, perceptions, attitudes and behaviours (Acker, 2006). The proportional gender representation employed by the African National Congress did result in significant representation of women in national government structures (Paxton, Kunovich and Hughes, 2007). However, this has not been replicated in the workplace and the broader society. Tinker (2004) has argued that quotas for women in elected legislators rarely result in dramatic changes since the women elected must be party loyalists as party loyalty effectively curbs their power and authority. It is also possible that the level of gender representation attained in the ruling party may have created an illusion of gender egalitarianism masking gender inequalities or minimizing its urgency (Benschop and Doorewaard, 1998).

Current discourses in South Africa about equality and transformation provides insight into the current resurgence of racial inequality as the prime inequality to be erased. What is not stated is that the discourse is inflected with patriarchical assumptions. It appears talk about the lack of racial equality is mostly about the plight of African men. From a Foucauldian perspective, this discourse reflects the political power base of African men in the national Government despite the discourse of women's empowerment (Doolin, 2003; Kelan, 2009). At the same time, the apartheid fatigue discourse impedes progress towards both racial and gender equality as some whites believe issues of discrimination and injustice are things of the past. Consequently, there is little need for disruptive redress interventions.

Another conclusion from the South African experience is that quota representation of women in legislative structures does not always translate into the authority and power to change dominant power relations and remove inequality regimes in institutions (Acker, 2006). Nor has the focus for gender equality been evenly directed. Some believe those responsible for the Employment Equity Act have tended to focus on the upper end of the labour market (that is, managerial and professional positions) rather than ensuring equality for women and men lower down in the occupational structure (Budlender, 2011).

There are a few positive signs for the prospects for gender equality as South Africa enters its seventeenth year of democracy. The growing level of frustration among women with progress on gender equality may lead to a new mobilization of women's voices. At the same time, the Department of Labour appears to be embracing a more punitive approach towards organizations that do not comply with the requirements of equality legislation. There is also a litigation stance emerging in the Commission on Gender Equity to ensure the state delivers on its commitment to gender equality. At the same time, the South African Parliament will soon be debating Gender Equality Bill that may institutionalize gender quotas more broadly (Ministry for Women, Children and People with Disabilities). Whether these developments will translate into gains in gender equality in the workplace will only be determined by time.

References

Acker, J. (2006). Gender, class and race in organizations, *Gender & Society*, 20(4), 441–464.

Ahmed, S. (2007). The language of diversity. *Ethnic and Racial Studies*, 30(7), 235–256.

April, K., Dreyer, S. and Blass, E. (2007). Gender impediments to the South African executive boardroom. *South African Journal of Labour Relations*, 31(2), 51–67.

Baldez, L. (2002). *Why Women Protest: Women's Movements in Chile*. Cambridge, UK: Cambridge University Press.

Baldez, L. (2003). Women's movement and democratic transition in Chile, Brazil, East Germany and Poland. *Comparative Politics*, 35(3), 252–272.

Benjamin, N. (2008). From policy to programme: an empirical assessment of responses to HIV/AIDS in the workplace. Cape Town: Labour Research Service.

Benschop, Y. and Doorewaard, H. (1998). Covered by equality: the gender subtext of organizations. *Organization Studies*, 19(5), 787–805.

Bernstein, H. (1985). *For their Triumphs and for their Tears: Women in Apartheid South Africa*. London: International Defense and Aid Fund for Southern Africa, p. 48.

Booysen, L. (1999). A review of the challenges facing black and white women managers in South Africa. *Southern African Business Review*, 3(2), 15–26.

Booysen, L. (2007). Societal power shifts and changing social identities in South Africa: workplace implications. *South African Journal of Economic and Management Science*, 10(1), 1–20.

Booysen, L. and Nkomo, S.M. (2010). Gender role stereotypes and requisite management characteristics: the case of South Africa. *Gender in Management: An International Journal*, 25(4), 1754–2413.

Budlender, D. (2011). *Gender Equality and Social Dialogue in South Africa*. Geneva: Industrial and Employment Relations Department and Bureau for Gender Equality, International Labour Office.

Department of Labour (2010). *10th CEE Annual Report*. Johannesburg, South Africa.

Donnelly, L. (2010). *The Mail and Gardian*, May 13. Retrieved on 21 March 2011, from Busa versus BMF: http://www.mg.co.za/article/2010-05-13-busa-versus-bmf.

Doolin, B. (2003). Narratives of change: discourse, technology and organization. *Organization*, 10(4), 751–770.

Ely, R. and Padavic, I. (2007). A feminist analysis of organizational research on sex differences. *Academy of Management Review*, 32(4), 1121–1143.

Geisler, G. (2000). Parliament is another terrain of struggle: women, men and politics in South Africa. *The Journal of Modern African Studies*, 38(4), 605–630.

Gouws, A. (2004). The politics of state structures: citizenship and the national machinery for women in South Africa. *Feminist Africa*, 3(3), 1–12.

Habib, A. and Bentley, K. (2008). *Racial Redress and Citizenship in South Africa*. Pretoria: HRSC Press.

Hicks, J. (2009). *Gender Equality in South Africa: Progress and Challenges*. Johannesburg: Commission for Gender Equality.

Kelan, E.K. (2009). Gender fatigue: the ideological dilemma of gender neutrality and discrimination in organizations. *Canadian Journal of Administrative Sciences*, 26(3), 197–210.

Lloyd, H.R. and Mey, M.R. (2007). Gender differences in perceptions of workplace progression: an automotive industry case study, *Southern Africa Business Review*, 11(3), 95–120.

Mathur-Helm, B. (2005). Equal opportunity and affirmative action for South African women: a benefit or barrier. *Women in Management Review*, 20(1), 56–71.

Mathur-Helm, B. (2006). Women and the glass ceiling in South African banks: an illusion or reality? *Women in Management Review*, 21(4), 311–326.

Mbanjwa, X. (2011). Women's league Lekgotla sets out plan for female empowerment, 22 February, *The New Age*. Retrieved on 21 March 2011 from http://www.thenewage.co.za/110-52-1007-53-Women%E2%80%99s_League_lekgotla_sets_out_plan_for_female_empower-ment.

Menon, S.T. and Kotze, E. 2007, Human resource integration in the South African military: a view from the trenches. *Human Resource Management*, 46(1), 71–94.

Milner, K., Katch, L.A., Fisher, J. and Notrica, V. (2007). Gender and the quality of leader-member exchange: findings from a South African organisation. *South African Journal of Psychology*, 37(2), 316–329.

Ministry for Women, Children and People with Disabilities (2011). *Green Paper: Towards a Gender Equality Bill* (draft). Retrieved on 4 July 2011 from www.pmg.org.za.

Nhlapo, T. (1995). 'African customary law in the interim constitution', in S. Liebenberg, *The Constitution South Africa from a Gender Perspective*. Cape Town: David Phillip, pp. 157–166.

Nkomo, S. M. (2011). *The Challenges of Moving from the Letter of the Law to the Spirit of the Law*. Unpublished manuscript.

Oosthuizen, R. M. and Naidoo, V. (2010). Attitudes towards and experience of employment equity. *SA Journal of Industrial Psychology/SA*, 36(1), Art. #836, 9 pages. DOI: 10.4102/sajip.v36i1.836

Paxton, P., Kunovich, S. and Hughes, M. M. (2007). Gender in politics. *The Annual Review of Sociology*, 33(1), 263–284.

Republic of South Africa (1994). *Beijing Conference Report: The 1994 Country Report on the Status of South African Women*. Cape Town.

Seidman, G.W. (2003). Institutional dilemmas: representation versus mobilization in the South African Gender Commission. *Feminist Studies*, 29(3), 541–563.

Speckman, A. (2011). Law 'is failing to advance' black women. *The Star*, 28 March, p. 17.

Steyn, M. and Kelly, C. (2009). *Widening Circles: Case Studies in Transformation*. Cape Town: Incudisa.

Stott, L. and Shunmugam, N. (2002). 'Business and gender equality: lessons from South Africa', in K. Madden and M. Friedman (eds) *In Focus Series (No. 4)*. London, International Business Leader Forum, pp. 2–15.

Tinker, I. (2004). Quotas for women in elected legislators: do they really empower women? *Women' Studies International Forum*, 27(5–6), 531–546.

Wambugu, J. N. (2005). When tables turn: Discursive constructions of whites as victims of affirmative action in a post-apartheid South Africa. *Psychology in Society*, 31, 57–70.

Waylen, G. (2007). Women's mobilization and gender outcomes in transitions to democracy: the case of South Africa. *Comparative Political Studies*, 40(5), 521–546.

Wells, J. C. (1993). *We now demand! The History of Women's Resistance to Pass Laws in South Africa*. Johannesburg, Witwatersrand University Press.

CHAPTER

6 *Women in India: Their Odyssey towards Equality*

RADHA R. SHARMA AND SHOMA MUKHERJI

Introduction

WOMEN ON CORPORATE BOARDS IN INDIA: CURRENT SCENARIO

On the occasion of the International Women's Day on 8 March 2011, Mr Murli Deora, Minister for Corporate Affairs, Government of India, declared that a provision for reserving one seat for a woman director in all company boards with five or more directors would be included in the Companies Bill to be tabled in Parliament in the near future. While a majority of the industry leaders agree that there is a need for greater representation of women on their company boards, a large number of them are averse to a mandatory provision. If media reports are relied upon, there has been a mixed response to the inclusion of women on the company boards, especially from private sector industry in India.

The status of women on company boards is evident from a study under the aegis of the Associated Chambers of Commerce and Industry of India (ASSOCHAM) in 2010. The survey of 100 companies listed on the Bombay Stock Exchange (BSE) revealed that of the 1112 directors on the respective boards, only 59 were women. The scenario is not very different internationally as can be observed from the comparative data of women representation on corporate boards in six countries, presented in Table 6.1.

Table 6.1 Comparative percentage of women on corporate boards in six countries

Country	Female representation on boards
India	5.3 %
Canada	15 %
USA	14.5 %
UK	12.2 %
Hong Kong	8.9 %
Australia	8.3%

Source: Standard Chartered Bank: Women on Corporate Boards in India 2010 report.

Disparity of women representation on corporate boards is a global issue but to raise the representation of Indian women in company boards closer to the international level, focused and concerted efforts are needed. Corporate India requires giving serious thought to inclusion of gender diversity on the company board if the objective of the proposed Companies Bill (India) is to be achieved. Except for a few companies in sectors like finance, banking, insurance and IT there has been lack of planned initiatives for female talent management for the board-level role. With transparent processes, comprehensive training and grooming more and more women can get the opportunity to be inducted into the corporate boards. But it is not only private companies which lack initiatives; even the public sector companies have not done much to promote women participation in their boards. The conclusions of the ASSOCHAM study find support in a review of top 20 Indian companies listed in Fortune 500, India (see Table 6.2). There are a total of 250 board members in these companies of whom only 11 (4.4 per cent) are women. Further, eight of them are government officers who have been nominated to the boards by the Government.

Table 6.2   Gender diversity in top 20 Indian companies among Fortune 500 companies

	Company	Total directors	Female directors	Percentage of female directors
1	Indian Oil Corporation	16	2	12.5
2	Reliance Industries	13	0	0
3	State Bank of India	14	1	7.14
4	Bharat Petroleum	10	0	0
5	Hindustan Petroleum	9	0	0
6	Oil & Natural Gas Corporation	13	2	15.38
7	Tata Steel	7	0	0
8	Tata Motors	14	0	0
9	Hindalco Industries	11	1	9.09
10	ICICI Bank	12	1	8.33
11	Coal India	13	1	7.69
12	NTPC	19	0	0
13	Larsen & Toubro	18	1	5.56
14	BhartiAirtel	16	0	0
15	SAIL	13	0	0
16	EssarOil	11	1	9.09
17	BHEL	12	1	8.33
18	MRPL	10	0	0
19	Mahindra & Mahindra	12	0	0
20	BSNL	7	0	0
	Total	**250**	**11**	**4.4**

Source: Fortune 500 India, December 2010 and respective company website.

A study carried out by WLL and KPMG (2009) found that corporate India is waking up to the benefits of including women in top management as they have the important attributes of compassion, sensitivity, conflict resolution capabilities and good time management.

The authors have conducted a secondary research of women in top leadership and board-level roles from corporate India to study their views about the empowerment of women and to explore how they have been able to resolve the issue of work–life balance. The findings are presented in Table 6.3.

Table 6.3   Women in leadership roles in corporate India

	Name	Company	Position	Importance of woman power	Work–life balance
1	Akhila Srinivasan	Shriram Life Insurance	MD	Can be change agent and help women to realize potential	Time and energy management
2	Chanda Kochhar	ICICI Bank	MD and CEO	Inspiration for women	Believe it can be done
3	Chitra Ramkrishna	National Stock Exchange	Jt. MD	Helps you to empower others	Good time management
4	Kalpana Morparia	JP Morgan, India	CEO	Ability to make a difference	Work is life
5	Kaku Nakhate	Merrill Lynch	President and Country Head	Helps firm to change and achieve common goals	Strong collaborations at work and home
6	Kiran M. Shaw	Biocon	Chairperson, MD	Can be change makers and impact society	Take quarterly break and develop a hobby
7	Lalita Gupte	Nokia, Alstom, ICICI Venture Fund	Board Member	Communicates a woman has a place in business leadership	Same efficiency in running home and office
8	Leena Nair	Hindustan Unilever	Executive Director –HR	Influencing change and making a difference	Engage family in career path
10	MadhabiPuri Bach	ICICI Securities	MD and CEO	Make a difference in others' lives	Enjoy work and get family support
11	Mallika Srinavasan	Tractors and Farm Equipment	Director	Unified impact on society	Flexible and open mind
12	Manisha Girotra	UBS India	CEO and Country Head	Inspiring a handful of women is rewarding	Live in the moment
13	Meher Pudumjee	Thermax Ltd	Chairperson	Making a difference and being good human being	Delegate
14	Naina L. Kidwai	HSBC	Country Head, Member, APAC Board	Have to be powerful to think what it is like	Enjoy what you do

	Name	Company	Position	Importance of woman power	Work–life balance
15	Preetha Reddy	Apollo Hospitals	MD	Enables you to make a difference	Make it seamless
16	Roopa Kudva	CRISIL	MD and CEO	Enables you to make a difference	Enjoy both work and non-work life
17	Sangeta Talwar	National Dairy Development Board	MD	Empower others to achieve and excel	Engage with life every moment
18	Schauna Chauhan	Parle Agro	CEO	Good feeling	Productive time management
19	Shikha Sharma	Axis Bank	MD and CEO	Enables you to make a difference	Treat family, work and home equally
20	Swati Piramal	Piramal Healthcare	Director	Women have inclusive way of finding solutions	Work should be source of joy
21	Shyamala Gopinath	Reserve Bank of India	Deputy Governor	Encourages young women to emulate you	Make success of life, not career
22	Tanya Dubash	Godrej	ED, President – Marketing	Not important	Happy family life
23	Usha Narayanan	SEBI	Exec. Director	Can make a difference in others' lives	Be at home both with work and life
24	Vedika Bhandarkar	Credit Lyonnaise Suisse, India	Vice Chairman	Can advise clients on what deals to avoid	Be systematic, ask for help when required
25	Vinita Bali	Britannia Industries	MD	Ability to be impactful within and outside business	Enjoy work, not let it be a burden
26	Vinita Gupta	LupinPharma	Group President and CEO	Young women need to believe there are no limits to potential	Prioritize important issues at work and home
27	Vishakha Mulye	ICICI Venture Funds	MD and CEO	Ability to make a difference	Set priorities and maintain discipline
28	Zarina Mehta	UTV Broadcasting	Chief Creative Officer	Do not believe in being powerful	Good family life reduces pressure
29	Zia Mody	AZB and Partners	Managing Partner	Enables you to bring in change in workplace	De-prioritize the unimportant tasks, accept that micro-management of everything not required
30	Zarin Daruwala	ICICI Bank	Group Executive, Wholesale Banking	Sense of responsibility, knowing your decisions can change lives	Prioritize, strategize, trust people, sell ideas to team

Source: *Business Today*, 28 November 2010, 50–104.

Review of Research on Disparity in Gender Diversity

A review of scholarly literature covering women's issues appearing in over 16 journals in the field of career, management and psychology since 1990 was carried out by O'Neil, Hopkins and Billimoria (2008) and threw up interesting results. One pattern that emerged was that women always seek to find the right fit between work issues and relational concerns and the priorities change depending on whether women are in the early, middle or late part of their career. While women struggle to succeed both personally and professionally, organizations demand separation of work from family concerns. Benefits such as parental leave, flexible work hours, less face-to-face work, alternative career paths, job-sharing and telecommuting are just some of the policies adopted by organizations to ensure better work–life balance. However, women are disadvantaged in their career progression when they avail themselves of these benefits.

Research yields that as managerial positions grow in number, more and more women enter the workforce but the lion's share of leadership positions throughout the world still remains a male preserve. In the US, women make up 46.5 per cent of the workforce of which only 8 per centof women are in top management (Beck and Davis, 2005). Despite extensive legislation and the implementation of equal opportunity policies, there is still widespread structural gender inequality and job segregation (Martin and Saunders, 1995) in Britain. A Dataquest–Jobs Ahead study (2003) conducted on 150,000 Indian IT professionals, found that women constituted over 19 per cent of the total workforce at lower levels (up to three years of experience). The number dropped to 6 per cent of the senior workforce, that is, with more than ten years of experience. An interesting trend observed in western countries was instead of being demoralized by discriminating policies and lack of opportunities in the corporate world, many women employees adopted entrepreneurship (Mattis, 2004).

Five theoretical perspectives from gender literature were identified by Basu (2008) while seeking answers to the question of low representation of women in managerial positions the world over: a) the person-or-gender-centered perspective; b) the situation-centered or the organization–structure perspective; c) the gender–organization perspective; d) the gender organization–system perspective; and e) the gender–context perspective. Basu believes that research which probes perceptions, rather than gender differences, would be far more appropriate in explaining why the differences still exist and how such perceptions could be changed. Gupta, Koshal and Koshal (1998) also studied the issue of perception of women managers in India and arrived at the conclusion that negative stereotypes are responsible for women not advancing in the managerial field. Studies on women have been conducted in different professional fields like science, judiciary and finance. Research by Gupta (2007) indicates that though the nature of problems of women in science in India appear to be similar to those faced by the women in science in the west, the specific form of biases varies, and the cultural context influences the nature of discrimination. Contrary to the claims made by the institutions in deciding who gets to do science, gender figures at various levels in shaping the career of a scientist (Subramanian, 2007). A study exploring the representation of women in two Indian accounting professional bodies' websites revealed that the two professional bodies appeared to be visibly masculine. The representation of women in the two websites was either weak or non-existent and the language referred predominately to the masculine (Kyriacou, Pancholi and Bhaskaran, 2010).

The Government has enacted 41 legislations having direct or indirect bearing on women since India gained independence in 1947. Bansal (2003) concluded that the judiciary in India has exhibited a positive attitude towards women-related issues. Women are increasingly becoming aware of their rights and take legal recoursefor redressal of their grievances.

The goals of human development cannot be achieved without the development and empowerment of women. However, the reality that women face is that of disparities in access to and control over resources. The need to include gender sensitive measures of human development was recognized and in 1995, the United Nations Development Programme (UNDP) introduced two new indices: a Gender-related Development Index (GDI) and a Gender Empowerment Measure (GEM). In a workshop on 'Building a Framework for Measuring Gender Equity' organized by Singamma Srinivasan Foundation in Bangalore in 1996, a group of Indian women economists argued that while it was commendable that UNDP had produced a report which was more women centred, the GDI and GEM developed by UNDP needed to be recast to realistically capture the gender gaps in the development and empowerment in the third world. It was argued that these indices had not taken into account the Indian perspective. GDI did not reflect measures that were required in countries with high unemployment and high levels of poverty and inequality. Similarly, for GEM to be useful it must be created out of institutions which empower the poor and look at exclusion and inclusion in those institutions in order to use the right tools for engendering a change in gender relations. Alternate GDI and GEM were developed at the national level and for major states. The results for India were based on a range of different variables and the computed scores differed significantly from those prepared by UNDP.

Women in India: Social Context

The status of women in India is a kind of paradox. While on the one hand she may be at the peak of success, on the other, she may suffer in silence at the hands of her own family members due to traditional social system. Although the Constitution of India guarantees equality to all irrespective of religion, race, caste and sex (Articles 15, 16, 39), women in India have not been able to fully utilize the fundamental rights conferred upon them. Despite well-defined legal codes, women continue to be a victim of covert discrimination at work (Sharma, 1982). In the post-independence period (since 1947), there has been rapid expansion in facilities for women's education. However, when we compare the figures in the context of gender, especially with respect to higher education, there are significant gaps. With regard to nature and also the level of education, women, in the last few decades have come a long way and have achieved a lot particularly in urban areas. The modern Indian women are equipped to face the challenges of career armoured with education and varied talents and have proven themselves in many walks of life. There are a large number of women IT professionals besides doctors, scientists, engineers and professors in India. However, if one probes deeper, it will emerge that their path to the current level of success has been full of challenges and roadblocks and they still have a long way to reach the board level. Covert discrimination, stereotypes, prejudices and ascribed social roles, high power distance and masculine culture are the biggest stumbling blocks for them in India.

The underrepresentation of women in science and engineering, particularly at higher education and research level in India, has become a serious cause of concern for women scientists and science policy planners (Gupta, 2007). Although there is no explicit discrimination against women in enrolment at the college or university level, lack of competitive spirit and professional aspiration, attitudinal social biases work against them. Also, unsupportive institutional structures have, over the years, operated as powerful forces against talented women realizing their full potential in the pursuit of productive and rewarding careers in science, engineering and technology, though they have done well in teaching, nursing and the medical profession. It has been observed that men do not like to work under woman engineers in a manufacturing plant, therefore, despite relevant education and high achievement in their engineering education and related training they prefer to take up a teaching/research job to a job on the shop floor in a plant. Alternatively, they join a MBA programme to make a career move or simply give up their career and settle as housewife and look after home and family as it is extremely difficult to re-enter a professional career after a break. Besides, part-time job opportunities for women professionals are few and far between, though very few organizations have introduced flexi-hours for them. Therefore, a woman's career generally ends with marriage if the partner is posted at a different location or is in a transferrable job or with the birth of a child (which also is due to social pressure as a childless woman is not appreciated in the Indian social system, even though she may be a professional par excellence). As a result, Indian career women either do not marry or opt out of marriage or have a strong family support or a highly supportive husband to pursue the career. Otherwise they settle for low-level jobs and low career aspirations. Also, the institutional support system for rearing children is weak and work–life balance becomes an issue. This further substantiates the prejudice against professional women that they are not serious about their career and promotions are either denied or they are sidelined in favour of male colleagues who are supposed to be more career-centric and enjoy greater credibility than women irrespective of the merit. Under these circumstances, to reach a board-level position remains a dream for most career women.

An International Labour Organization (ILO) report of 1997 stated that the major factors for women being unable to attain the higher-level managerial jobs were social attitudes, cultural biases and male prejudices. The biological and/or socialization pattern of women have apparently prompted them to exhibit traits and behaviours that are not conducive to their becoming successful managers, as per certain gender-centered theorists (Feather, 1985; Schein, 1973). Despite possessing traits considered necessary for managerial success, women managers are often perceived as not possessing the same. Thus in comparison to men, the number of women in the higher echelons of management is low (Commission of the European Communities, 2009).

Over the years, civil society has undergone substantial transformation. The concept of gender equality is today enshrined in the constitution of leading nations with an aim towards women's advancement in different spheres. Various policies, plans and programmes have been framed by government, non-governmental organizations (NGOs) and human rights associations for the development and empowerment of women across the globe. Progressive organizations/industries are also taking steps to encourage diversity among their workforce and to support equal opportunity in employment. With the globe being interconnected through IT, these international gender-inclusive initiatives have impacted the status of women in India to some extent and have helped many women to make it to the senior management level, breaking the glass ceiling. But this has happened where top management has been supportive. Many women have proved their worth in various fields and have carved out a niche for themselves. In recent years, women have adorned high offices in India in the political sphere, from President (Pratibha Devi Singh Patil) and former Prime Minister of India (Indira Gandhi), Chief Ministers of Delhi (Sheila Dixit),Tamil Nadu (JayaLalitha), Uttar Pradesh (Mayawati), West Bengal (Mamata Banerjee) to many members of Parliament and state legislative assemblies. The Indian Parliament also has a woman speaker (Meira Kumar).

Women in Occupations

An interesting description of the empowered Indian woman is given by Shariff (2009). She is literate, employed, contributes to the household income, manages a bank account and owns some property. Over and above she has the freedom of taking decisions about running the household and providing education and medical facilities to her children. She exercises her voting rights and even participates in local government.

Authentic data on female employment are difficult to get; therefore, this chapter relies on sources which may not be up to date. Table 6.4 provides data on employment of women out of total employment in the organized sector covering both public and private sector organizations.

Table 6.4   Employment of women (figures in Lakhs)

Year	Public sector			Private sector			Total women		
	Women	Total	% of women	Women	Total	% of women	Women	Total	% of women
1990	2256			1390				36.46	
1994	2564	19444.9	13.2	1589.3	7929.9	20.0	4153.9	27374.8	15.2
1998	2762.7	19417.8	14.2	2010.9	8747.9	23.0	4773.6	28165.8	17.0
2002	2886.7	18773.4	15.4	248.7	8432.1	24.3	4935.4	27205.5	18.1
2006	51.21						51.21	269.93	19.0

Source: Ministry of Statistics and Programme Implementation, Government of India.

A perusal of the data presented in Table 6.4 reveals that the percentage of employment of women to total employment has steadily increased in the organized sector both in public and private sector firms over the years. However, employment has been higher in the private sector compared to public sector. Women are found in typical stereotyped professions like teaching, nursing, personal service and social work. The percentage of women school teachers is higher than that at higher and professional education levels. Fewer women are found in the higher echelons of science, technology and management. A study of the role of women in technical and technological innovations by Sharma (1984) revealed that the contribution of women in this field was low due to the nature of education pursued by them which included subjects like education, arts, commerce and science. The bulk of women work in those areas which do not require technical skills.

Their percentage was good in medicine but low in engineering (Ministry of Education: University Grants Commission, 1981). Table 6.5 provides figures on the employment of women in various occupations from 2003–2008.

Table 6.5   Data on employment of women in major industries: 2003–2008

Distribution of women's employment by major industries in India (as on 31 March 2003 to 2008)						
Industry	**Women employment (in thousands)**					
	2003	**2004**	**2005**	**2006**	**2007**	**2008**
Agriculture, hunting, forestry and fishing	466.5	458.7	484.1	498.0	490.63	510.25
Mining and quarrying	60.9	73.3	77.4	85.5	83.73	84.13
Manufacturing	1009.8	949.3	939.3	893.0	944.73	1010.41
Electricity, gas and water	47.7	52.1	53.0	53.7	53.29	49.92
Construction	64.1	66.0	67.0	67.4	65.40	64.87
Wholesale and retail trade and restaurants and hotels	44.5	46.0	49.6	48.6	51.60	63.21
Transport, storage and communication	189	189.4	191.6	192.0	194.92	199.72
Financing, insurance, real estate and business services	274.3	287.3	302.2	331.5	412.49	476.68
Community, social and personal services	2811.6	2812.3	2852.1	2950.8	2960.93	2979.74
Total	4968.4	4934.4	5016.2	5120.5	5257.72	5438.91

Source: Ministry of Labor and Employment, Government of India, 12 March 2009.

Table 6.5 yields that employment of women has been highest in community, social and personal services followed by manufacturing, then agriculture, hunting, forestry and fishing. Considering the nature of employment one can see that these are labour intensive and social/personal service jobs. But an interesting observation is that there has been a marginal increase/fluctuations in women taking up jobs in transport, storage and communication, construction, wholesale and retail trade, as these continues to be male-dominated occupations. There has been a significant increase in financing, insurance, real estate and business services. This is an area where the participation of educated women has increased significantly from 2006; however, these are the areas where the glass ceiling is also observed.

Glass Ceiling

The term 'glass ceiling' refers to situations where the advancement of a qualified person within the hierarchy of an organization is stopped at a lower level because of some form of discrimination, most commonly sexism. The causes of the glass ceiling remain more or less the same around the world which include lack of career counselling and development for women, lack of management development opportunities for them, attitudes of male councillors and managers, the expected role of women in society, conflicts between personal and work life, and the organizational culture within which women work (Camilla and Jeff, 1998). A US Federal Glass Ceiling Commission reported in 1995 that a barrier existed at the highest level of business, rarely penetrated by women or persons of colour. In an interesting exploratory study Nath (2000) has used the term 'Glass Moulding' to describe the attitude of Indian women managers who, instead of attempting to emulate their male colleagues, used their differences to add value to the organization in unique ways. Bal (2005) found that women in their late twenties are under family pressure to get married. When they take time off for child care, making a comeback is always a problem as employment rules frequently tend to have upper age limits for positions. Reva Nayyar, of the Indian Administrative Service, took a prolonged break – eight years at a stretch – to look after her children. Inevitably, she paid a price for it by lagging behind her batch mates in the coveted Indian Administrative Service (IAS) every time she was due for promotion, from the rank of joint secretary to that of secretary to Government of India (*The Tribune*, 31 May 2006; *Times News Network*, 31 July 2007).

Traditional Indian women are generally oriented to compliance to authority or conditioned to be accepting in nature. The curbs on freedom are accepted by them as a way of life and for keeping the image of a 'good girl' they comply with many things for the happiness of their family and thereby their own. The fact that women shy away from accepting that they are subjected to discriminatory behaviour is an unconscious process. When questioned they may say that they believe there exists a glass ceiling. However, when asked whether they have faced it themselves, they will answer in the negative (Jain and Mukherji, 2009).

Genesis of Inequality

The position of women in India has always been paradoxical. Ancient literature has references of practices in early *Vedic* era of an egalitarian society (Sharma, 1992). Famous women scholars of the early *Vedic* age like Lopamudra, Gargi, Maitreyi, Ghosha and Apala indicate that women had the freedom of engaging in scholarly pursuits. The concept of *Shakti* or feminine energy was manifested in the worship of female goddesses – *Kali* (destructive energy), *Durga* (protective energy), *Lakshmi* (nourishing energy) and *Saraswati* (creative energy). The custom of '*swayamvara*' whereby a girl had the right to choose her life partner from amongst several eligible bachelors indicates power enjoyed by women in their personal life in ancient days. Women participated in religious rituals equally with men.

Decline in the status of women began around 1000 BC with the invention of the plough and rise of field agriculture (Tharakan and Tharakan, 1975). The man became the owner of the plough and the farm and the woman could share the wealth but not control it. Foreign invasions during the medieval period (1000 AD) further affected the status of women. To protect women from any atrocities by the invaders, free movement of women was curtailed, a veil system (covering the head and face) was introduced and practice of *sati'* (dying in the dead husband's pyre) and *'jauhar'* (group immolation of women) to protect their honour became popular. The girl child began to be viewed as a burden as she needed extra care and security. Child marriages increased resulting in problems of higher birth rate and high mortality rates of women and children. Restrictions were imposed on the girl child's education.

Under the British rule (1600 AD) which lasted for about 200 years in India, the system of education was revolutionized and learning of English became popular. This created a pool of local human resource to smoothly run the administrative machinery at the middle and lower levels. The spread of education gave rise to reformers like Vidyasagar, Rammohan Roy and Ranade who worked relentlessly to improve the status of women. The practice of *sati* was legally abolished and women got the right to inherit property. Women were able to enjoy the fruits of western education with the spread of educational institutions in major cities. However, society remained male dominated and discriminatory towards women at the time of independence in 1947.

SOCIO-ECONOMIC REALITY

Indian women have traditionally been a homemaker and a man a breadwinner. Accordingly a girl has been groomed to be caring, nurturing and supporting towards the family. This developed soft skills in her and prepared her for a social life rather than a professional life. Observing her mother and elder ladies in the family, she prepared herself for the roles performed by them. Another socio-economic reality in India is the patriarchal family where a girl leaves her parental home after marriage and technically is not part of the paternal family as she adopts the surname of her husband's family.

The motivation of parents to raise and nurture children is often a function of future utility (Becker, 1993). Size of family, gender composition and access to food, health care and education is influenced by consideration of future support from the offspring. The mindset of traditional Indian parents is that a son will stay at home and look after them in their old age and carry on the family enterprise while a daughter will leave home and join another family after her marriage. Investment in sons from a parental point of view is more productive (gives higher returns to parents) than investment in daughters (Tisdell and Regmi, 2005). Thus, the girl child faces neglect and is not treated at par with her male siblings in traditional middle class Indian families.

URBAN–RURAL DIFFERENCES

As at the 2001 census, 72.2 per cent of India's population lives in rural areas as compared to 27.8 per cent in cities. Disparities exist in infrastructure, facilities for quality education, development and employment. Table 6.6 indicates that participation of women in the rural labour force is less than half that of males. Ninety per cent of female labour is engaged in the agriculture and allied sectors. Women are overworked, having dual responsibility of household chores and field work. Women often spend hours sourcing potable water and firewood in many under developed rural/hilly areas. Besides working on the farm, often as landless labour, women are involved in basket, broom, rope-making, tassar silk cocoon rearing, lac cultivation, oil extraction, and bamboo work and fishing net-mending.

Table 6.6   Rural population and labour participation

	Male	Female
Rural population	51.9%	48.1%
Labour participation	51.6%	22.7%

Source: Census of India, 2001.

While 22.7 per cent of the female population of a rural area is engaged in labour work, there are women entrepreneurs who have set up village industry units (Table 6.7) under the Government's employment generation programmes.

Table 6.7   Village industry units set up by women entrepreneurs under the Rural Employment Guarantee scheme: 2007–2010

Year	Total units	Units set up by women entrepreneurs	Percentage of women entrepreneurial units
2007–2008	44,285	12,485	28.20
2008–2009	25,507	6410	25.13
2009–2010	39,335	8640	21.97

Source: Lok Sabha Unstarred Question No. 1154, dated 16 November 2010.

These units have been set up in all the states and union territories of India as given in Table 6.13.

DOWRY SYSTEM

Dowry is a social practice prevalent in parts of India wherein the groom's family is given gifts ranging from cash, consumer durables, vehicles and property at the time of the wedding. Giving of jewellery to the girl is also a mandatory custom. In early times women did not have the right to parental property, thus at the time of marriage these gifts were given to ensure she had some share of the ancestral wealth. The jewellery was also a form of insurance in case of any misfortune. The practice had become institutionalized with the grooms' family making demands as a matter of right. If the girl's parents were unable to meet the demands, it often led to harassment of the girl. Therefore, to put an end to this social evil, the Government brought in prohibitory legislation of dowry in 1961. In view of the above, a girl child was often treated as a financial liability and this led to her discriminatory treatment from childhood onwards.

UPBRINGING AND STEREOTYPING OF ROLES

As mentioned earlier, women acquire a great deal of sex role learning early in life which results in a mindset later in their working life. The docile and submissive impression they have been socialized to give sends out a false impression of being incompetent. Women could be wary about an increase in the time and out-of-hours commitments and frequent travel which may be a necessary role requirement at senior level. Many resolve to avoid the 'Superwoman Syndrome' and accept low-level responsibilities Women's lack of self-confidence often stems from having to balance home and work in an unsupportive environment, confronting subtle humiliations in an intimidating macho culture (Mallon and Cassell, 1999).

Stereotyping is a universal phenomena indulged in by people to reduce the information processing demands on themselves (Basu, 2008). Lippmann (1922) introduced the term 'stereotype' to represent the typical picture that comes to mind when thinking about a particular social group. Words usually associated with female managers would be multi-tasking, emotional, empathetic, intuitive, strong, compassionate, relationship building, collaborative, gossipy, consensus building. When describing male managers, words like arrogant, strong, intelligent, ego driven, powerful, dominant, assertive, competitive would come into play. Most male employees view a transactional style of management as masculine. Therefore, when males exhibit transformational traits as stated above, they are highly valued for qualities such as empathy. For women, transformational traits are expected and commented upon only when absent. Female leaders who attempt to adopt the qualities of the transactional leader to be perceived as being more effective, are often criticized for being 'too masculine'. Behaviours such as assertiveness which attract praise in male leaders are reinterpreted in less favourable terms when exhibited by female leaders. Males are 'assertive' while the female exhibiting similar traits is 'domineering'. Self-confidence is seen as a necessary component of leadership in the male, while women may be accused of over-confidence or 'putting on airs' as a result of stereotypes. This uncertainty about what constitutes effective leadership behaviour and how it is perceived can result in uncertainty and a loss of self-confidence for women.

Motherhood remains a critical element in the life of a woman as in spite of the lofty ideals of shared parenting and household management responsibility, the bulk of this work continues to be done by women. Women who become pregnant during their career-building require a reasonable period of maternity leave and even have to take a break in career to spend time with a pre-school child or to complete their families. Societal expectations require that women take time off work when a child is ill; arrive home early enough to spend time with children and that mothers act as chauffeurs, transporting children to sporting events, dance classes or orthodontic appointments (Strategic Direction, 2008). Employers, therefore, view the appointment of women as a loss in productivity due to maternity and family responsibilities.

Parameters of Inequality

GENDER RATIO

India has been ranked 113th out of 134 countries covered in the World Economic Forum's Global Gender Gap Index 2011. The Indian Census 2011 gender ratio figures of 914 females to 1,000 males is a cause for concern. There has been a decline in the figure which stood at 933 females per 1,000 males in the 2001 census. The concern is that the 2001 census figures had an urban ratio of 900 females to 1,000 males, way below the rural figure of 946 females. Every state in the north and east of India has lower female ratios as compared to states in the south and west. One of the prime reasons for this ratio gap is what Nobel laureate Amartya Sen (2001) referred to as 'natality inequality'. The craving of parents for a newborn to be a boy prevents many a girl child from seeing the light of day. Prenatal sex determination, such as amniocentesis and ultrasound technology was introduced in the 1970s as an effort to improve health conditions of mothers and children; along with this abortion laws were liberalized as a comprehensive family planning strategy. Unfortunately, these facilities were misused for sex selection and brought in pre-meditated discrimination preventing the birth of the girl child. Abortion was considered far less physically or psychologically painful than a pregnancy followed by infanticide.

The next survival obstacle for a girl child was high infant mortality. Infanticide was practised as the last resort to get rid of unwanted births in isolated cases. With improvements in health services, nutrition and better protection against epidemics, life expectancy started to increase after 1920. However, women, in the socio-economically weaker sections of the society remained at a disadvantage with regard to medical and nutritional facilities. The notion that a girl child will eventually get married and live with her husband's family influenced all cost considerations in terms of investment in health, education and development. Mortality rates are higher for female children, 49.14 as compared to general infant mortality rate of 47.57 (India Demographics, 2011), a girl child is often discriminated vis-a-vis a male child in low income families.

STATUS OF EDUCATION

Female education has been impacted by cultural, economic, sociological and also anthropological factors (Sharma, 1982). Social attitudes to female education range from welcoming acceptance to absolute indifference. The majority of middle class families residing in urban areas encourage higher education for women and regard it as an accomplishment, not only for them but also for the family. In rural areas, the misconception that education might alienate girls from traditional and social values and lead to maladjustment and conflicts prevents them from pursing education. Even though the Government has made school education absolutely free for girls and recently has made education 'a right for every child', many girls are not able to attend school as they help their mother with household chores or look after siblings when the mother goes to work and so on. Early marriage and a traditional outlook that women are meant to care for family are other barriers. Schools in the rural areas are often situated at distances and commuting is a concern. The schools often lack adequate separate facilities for girls. There is a prevalence of child labour among girls belonging to socially and economically disadvantaged sections and lack of interest, inflexible timings, safety, breaks in studies due to migrating parents (labour class) are some of the bottlenecks for girls pursuing or continuing education. Also, school dropout rates are high for girls as a result of several reasons mentioned above. Among the lower middle class, if the parents have limited resources, the male child gets preference; a large section of people find it difficult to bear the cost of higher education for girls as they like to save money for the girl's dowry (wedding gifts), a symbol of social status and affluence.

Table 6.8   Male–female literacy rates (%) in India: 1901–2011

Year	Male literacy rate	Female literacy rate	Male:Female ratio
1901	9.83	0.60	16.4
1911	10.56	1.05	10.1
1921	12.21	1.81	7.6
1931	15.59	2.93	5.3
1941	24.90	7.30	3.4
1951	24.95	7.93	3.1
1961	34.44	12.95	2.6
1971	39.45	18.69	2.1
1981	56.50	29.85	1.9
1991	64.13	39.29	1.6
2001	75.85	54.16	1.4
2011	82.14	65.46	1.27

Source: Office of Registrar General and Census Commissioner, India; Women in India: A Statistical Profile, 1978, 117. Adapted from Sharma, R.R. (1982). Education of women in India: inequalities and bottlenecks, *The Education Quarterly*, October, 20–27.

A look at the literacy rate of males and females for the past 100 years from 1901–2011 (Table 6.8) reveals a rise in literacy rates for both but the growth rate has been faster for males compared to females, the reasons for which have been explained above. A possible reason for the rapid growth rate could be that after India's independence in 1947, the then Government of India introduced five-year plans which have facilitated the growth of literacy rates for both males and females from 1951 onwards. This appears to have helped participation of women in employment too. However, 65 per cent of the Indian population lives in rural areas which are not as equipped as the urban areas in terms of education infrastructure.

The results of the 2011 census yield that there has been significant growth in literacy figures in India. The literacy rate in the country is 74.04 per cent of which 82.14 per cent is for males and 65.46 per cent for females. Kerala occupies the top spot in the country both in male literacy at 96.02 per cent and female literacy at 91.98 per cent. Arunachal Pradesh has the lowest male literacy rate of 73.69 per cent and Rajasthan has recorded the lowest literacy rates for females at 52.66 per cent.

However, the gap between male and female literacy gets wider at the higher, technical and professional education levels. The *Times of India*, dated 30 December 2005 quoted a chemical engineering student saying, 'Women in the Indian Institutes of Technology (IITs) are an endangered species', in the first-year batch there were 34 women and over 500 men at IIT, Mumbai. An Indian national daily, the *Hindustan Times*, dated 20 May 2011 reports that in 2010 only 12 per cent of the students passing a Joint Entrance Examination (JEE) (a highly competitive national-level examination for admission to IITs) were girls. The Government appointed a panel to look into the matter which has submitted its recommendations to for consideration. Table 6.9 shows the enrolment of women from diploma level to postgraduate education and research during 2002 to 2005.

Table 6.9 Stage-wise enrolment of women in higher education in India: 2002–2005

Stage	2002–2003			2003–2004			2004–2005		
	Total	Total women	%	Total	Total women	%	Total	Total women	%
Graduate	8,224,417	3,285,544	39.93	8,867,378	3,555,664	40.10	9,315,808	3,764,328	40.10
Postgraduate	846,556	355,893	42.04	913,732	385,440	42.18	986,518	398,452	40.39
Research	62,213	23,609	37.95	65,491	25,569	39.04	68,838	27,523	39.98
Diploma/ Certificate	91,647	30,918	33.74	106,905	36,134	33.80	109,878	44,037	40.08
Total	9,227,833	3,695,964	40.05	9,953,506	4,002,807	40.22	10,481,042	4,234,340	40.40

Source: University Grants Commission.

Demand outweighs supply at the higher/professional education level and getting admission into a good university/college on merit is a challenge for girls, though there are a few exclusive women's colleges and women's universities in India but competition is high there too. Professional education is expensive and not easily affordable by all parents, though there are scholarships but these too are based on merit. Parents do not want to pay for the professional education of girls which is not only expensive but also often requires additional expenditure as a result of the university/college being located in another city. Though there is equality of opportunity, inequality in access to higher education presents a challenge towards girls' progress. If the foundation schooling is weak, getting into a professional education programme is a huge challenge; even educational coaching for admission to professional education is very expensive. There is very high competition in professional education (engineering, medical, management) in India and the ratio of women is low in terms of overall enrolment to higher education. Women generally pursue arts, social science, nursing, education and vocational education programmmes which offer them limited opportunities in limited vocations.

Measures to Mitigate Inequality

In view of the genesis and parameters of inequality discussed above, it is evident that significant and diverse measures need to be taken to mitigate gender inequality in social and professional life.

CONSTITUTIONAL PROVISIONS FOR GENDER EQUALITY

The Indian Constitution adopted in 1950 granted equality to women and empowered the state to adopt measures of positive discrimination in favour of women.

Table 6.10 Important provisions under the Constitution of India

Article	Subject
Article 14	Equality before law for women
Article 15(i)	The state not to discriminate against any citizen on grounds only of religion, race, caste, sex, place of birth or any of them.
Article 15(3)	The state to make any special provision in favour of women and children.
Article 16	Equality of opportunity for all citizens in matters relating to employment or appointment to any office under the state
Article 39 (a)	The state to direct its policy towards securing for men and women equally the right to an adequate means of livelihood.
Article 39 (d)	Equal pay for equal work for both men and women.
Article 42	The state to make provision for securing just and humane conditions of work and for maternity relief
Article 46	The state to promote with special care the educational and economic interests of the weaker sections of the people and to protect them from social injustice and all forms of exploitation
Article 51(A) (e)	To promote harmony and the spirit of common brotherhood amongst all the people of India and to renounce practices derogatory to the dignity of women

Article	Subject
Article 243 D(3)	Not less than one-third (including the number of seats reserved for women belonging to the Scheduled Castes and the Scheduled Tribes) of the total number of seats to be filled by direct election in every Panchayat to be reserved for women and such seats to be allotted by rotation to different constituencies in a Panchayat
Article 243 D(3)	Not less than one-third of the total number of offices of chairpersons in the Panchayats at each level to be reserved for women

Article 45 of the Constitution of India which originally stated that 'the state shall endeavour to provide, free and compulsory education for all children until the age of fourteen years' has now been amended. The 86th amendment of the Constitution has made education a fundamental right for children between the ages of 6–14.

In January 1992, the Government setup the National Commission for Women, a statutory body with a specific mandate to study and monitor all matters relating to the constitutional and legal safeguards provided for women, review the existing legislation and suggest amendments wherever necessary. The Ministry of Women and Child Development (MWCD), Government of India, was created in January 2006 with the objective of ensuring overall survival, development, protection and participation of women and children of the country. Various legislations have been enacted and programmes implemented with the support of state governments and NGOs. The battle for gender equality, however, is still far from over; women are still subjected to covert discrimination in the workplace and society at large.

COMBATING GENDER RATIO DISPARITY

The Pre Natal Diagonostic Technique Act (PNDT) was enacted in 1994 prohibiting doctors and clinics from using prenatal diagnostic techniques to determine the sex of a foetus. First offenders faced a penalty of up to three years of imprisonment and a fine of INR 10,000 (US$ 230), and repeat offenders risked a five-year imprisonment and a fine of INR 50,000. Another provision of the law established the presumption that women were compelled to perform sex determination by their husband or another relative, who could in turn couldbe similarly subjected to a three-year imprisonment and a fine of INR 10,000.

Table 6.11 Affirmative schemes for girls

Scheme	Year of introduction	Provision
Dhanalakshmi	2008–2009	Cash transfer to family of a girl child on fulfilling conditions relating to registration of birth, immunization, enrolment and retention in school until class VIII. Insurance coverage if girl remains unmarried till the age of 18.
Ladli	2008	Cash payment of birth and thereafter on reaching educational milestones for two girl children per family.

Nutrition Programme for Adolescent Girls	2009–2010	Undernourished girls (11–19 years) provided 6 kg free food grains per month.
Kishori Shakti Yojana	2009–2010	Address needs of self-development, nutrition, literacy and vocational skills of adolescent girls.

COMBATING EDUCATIONAL DISPARITY

The SarvaShikshaAbhiyan (Literacy for All) scheme, discussed earlier, has been introduced at school level. Various initiatives given in Table 6.11 and others have been taken by the Government, ranging from providing cycles to girl students for commuting to school to waiving tuition fees for girls from Class VI to graduate and postgraduate levels. Scholarships are available to girls for regular undergraduate courses as well as engineering and medical studies. University Grants Commission (UGC) scholarships are available for girls who are first- and second-rank holders at undergraduate level to pursue higher studies.

EMPOWERMENT OF WOMEN

One of the most important steps towards the empowerment of women was taken in 1992 through the 73rd amendment to the Constitution, when 33 per centof the seats in local village councils (*Panchayat*) were reserved for women. The goal was to empower women at the grass root level and give an impetus to the political participation of women. This paved the way for bringing women into the decision-making process for the welfare of the community at the village, block and district levels. The *panchayat* or the village council is an elected body of five persons and is seen as the pillar of rural government in India. As more women are inducted into local government, they, in turn, will help improve the lot of rural women and children in the country by focusing on issues close to their hearts like education and healthcare.

The percentage of women representatives at *gram panchayat* (village council) level in 2010 was 38.40 as compared to 31.37 per cent in 2000. In August 2009 the Government decided to bring a Bill to amend Article 243(D) of the Constitution to enhance reservation for women in *panchayats* at all tiers to at least 50 per cent. In the beginning, several elected women remained at home while their husbands attended the *panchayat* meetings and performed the official duties on their behalf. It has taken time for the situation to change but now the women are coming forward with grit and determination to bring about development resisting vested interests. Volunteer organizations have helped educate these women and made them aware of their responsibilities. The elected women have demonstrated their ability to better utilize the resources available to them and focus on girls' education and improving sanitation in the village. They also work towards reducing alcohol consumption and its after effect – domestic violence. The fact is that even if a *pradhan*or *sarpanch* (head of a village council) is honest, they sometimes have to deal with corrupt officers who refuse to release funds without taking part as commission. Several women *pradhans* have strongly voiced their opposition to this at their open meetings and training programmes. The success of these women had an impact on other women who are now eager to participate more actively in village affairs and contribute to the welfare of the community at large. This is a very positive step in the empowerment of women at the grass root level.

The other important political initiative is the 'Women Reservation Bill' which seeks to reserve for women one-third of the seats in the Indian Parliament and state assemblies on a rotational basis for 15 years. First introduced in 1996, this 108th Constitutional Amendment Bill had been on hold for 14 years. On 9 March 2010 the Bill was finally passed in the Upper house of Parliament. Once it is passed in the Lower House, it will be sent to the President of India for final approval and will then become law. A number of regional political parties have been opposing the Bill as they want further reservations for the minority community and backward castes. The Bill, however, has not been passed in the Lower House as yet.

The Government of India has been undertaking various programmes for political and economic empowerment of women. The schemes range from employment generation, pension schemes, housing for women to role in village and district level councils, and support for setting up village industrial units by female entrepreneurs (Tables 6.12 and 6.13).

Table 6.12   Employment of women under various schemes: 1999–2001

Schemes	2000–2001	1999–2001
Women benefit in SGSY scheme	416,690	58,019
National old age pension programme benefit	1,175,725	1,426,122
National family benefit scheme	29,130	29,541
Houses constructed for women	—	69,170
Employment generated for women (lac/day)	—	14,582.38
Employment assured scheme (EAS)	745.24 (lac days)	1136.09
Women in gram panchayat (village council)	681,258	655,629
Gram panchayat samiti (village-level body)	37,109	37,523
Women in zila parishad (district-level body)	3,153	3,161

Source: Indian Cooperative Movement – A Profile 2002, National Cooperative Union of India.

Units: 1 Lakh (or Lac) = INR 100,000.

Note: The Ministry of Rural Development, Government of India had launched a programme known as 'Swarnjayanti Gram Swarozgar Yojana' (SGSY) on 1 April 1999 by restructuring the then existing schemes; Integrated Rural Development Programme (IRDP), Training of Rural Youth for Self Employment (TRYSEM), Development of Women & Children in Rural Areas (DWCRA), Supply of Improved Toolkits to Rural Artisans (SITRA), Ganga Kalyan Yojana (GKY), and Million Wells Scheme (MWS).

Table 6.13 State-wise village industrial units set up in India by female entrepreneurs under the Rural Employment Generation Programme (REGP) during 2006–2007

State/union territory	Number of units
Chandigarh	19
Delhi	11
Haryana	4,497
Himachal Pradesh	3,975
Jammu and Kashmir	2,103
Punjab	6,237
Rajasthan	9,718
Andaman and Nicobar Islands	62
Bihar	1,155
Jharkhand	131
Orissa	1,992
West Bengal	3,175
Arunachal Pradesh	75
Assam	3,700
Manipur	8
Meghalaya	85
Mizoram	5,129
Nagaland	1,516
Andhra Pradesh	12,493
Karnataka	4,436
Kerala	5,846
Tamil Nadu	4,093
Goa	446
Gujarat	2,232
Maharashtra	777
Chhattisgarh	1,554
Madhya Pradesh	2,582
Uttarakhand	1,390
Uttar Pradesh	5,908
India	**85,345**

Source: Lok Sabha Unstarred Question No. 4481, dated 8 May 2007.

Details of various other programmes adopted by the Government are given in Table 6.14 which range from awareness generation programmes to short stay homes and working women's hostels.

Table 6.14 Funds allocated and released for development of women under various schemes in India (as at 31 December 2008)

Scheme	INR in Lakh (1 lakh = 1,00000)	
	Funds allocated	Funds released (up to 31 December 2008)
STEP	3700.00	1040.59
Swayamsiddha – Phase I	*	*
Swadhar	2000.00	522.95
Working Women Hostel	2000.00	213.59
Ujjawala**	1000.00	280.00
Short Stay Home	1750.00	794.80
Awareness Generation Project	600.00	268.85
Condensed Course of Education	700.00	315.00
Priyadarshini	2300.00	***

Source: LokSabhaUnstarred Question No. 466, dated 20 February, 2009.

Notes:

*   The Scheme ended on 31 March, 2008.

**   The Scheme was approved in December, 2007.

***   The Scheme was approved in November, 2008.

Table 6.15 presents development of cooperatives exclusively for women from 1989–90 and 1999–2000. It can be observed that there has been steady rise in number of societies from 1989–90 to 1997–8 but the membership increase was seen until 1993–4. Thereafter the pattern has been erratic. A similar trend can also be observed for working capital. This erratic phenomenon can be explained that women might be taking a break due to primary responsibilities of home and children and re-joining the cooperatives later. Marriage could be another factor which would take them to another location where her husband and his family reside. Many traditional Indian families do not allow women to work after the marriage.

Table 6.15 Growth of women cooperatives in India (1989–1990 to 1999–2000)

(Membership in thousands, Rs. in millions)				
Year	Turnover	Membership	Working capital	Number of societies
1989–1990	286.9	539.3	596.2	5478.0
1990–1991	326.9	580.3	684.9	5799.0
1991–1992	224.0	586.4	1053.3	5772.0
1992–1993	342.8	685.4	1295.4	6175.0
1993–1994	446.2	715.7	1406.1	6866.0
1994–1995	592.6	591.7	1478.9	7195.0

1995–1996	811.3	692.6	1408.1	8171.0
1997–1998	984.5	897.8	2041.4	8714.0
1998–1999	922.0	828.6	1167.9	8006.0
1999–2000	884.1	842.3	1160.4	8393.0

Source: Indian Cooperative Movement – A Profile 2002, National Cooperative Union of India.

India now has a separate Ministry for Women and Child Development and there are dedicated university departments focusing on women studies in addition to institutions addressing the concerns for female development. As well as these, there are a large number of voluntary organizations (NGOs) engaged in mobilizing self-help groups for women, providing training and helping women become self-employed. The abovementioned measures will go a long way in removing inequality and paving the way for social-economic, educational and professional development of women in India. While significant constitutional, legal, administrative and policy-related decisions have been taken for upliftment of women at large, the need of the houris affirmative action from corporate India to ensure that women are provided adequate opportunities and facilities for development which will enable them to reach the top levels of management. Corporate boards in India will need to have an appropriate ratio of gender diversity for company directors.

Conclusions

The chapter presents a comprehensive account of diversity in India in social, educational and industrial sectors. Tracing the genesis of gender inequality, the chapter highlights that in the ancient *Vedic* era women enjoyed equal status with men in social, religious and educational matters and a woman had the choice to select their life partner from amongst eligible bachelors. However, the decline in status of women began around 1000 BC with the invention of the plough and rise of field agriculture (Tharakan and Tharakan, 1975). The man became the owner of the plough and the farm and the woman could share the wealth but not control it. Foreign invasions during the medieval period (1000 AD) further affected her status. To protect women from any atrocities by the invaders, free movements of women were curtailed; a veil system (covering the head and face) and other social practices were introduced to protect their honour. The foreign rule in the country, the revolutionary change in the education system, changing social roles for women, dowry system, rural–urban differences in infrastructure and socio-economic realities pushed the women behind leading to disparities not only in gender ratio but also in nature and level of education and employment. Stereotypes, prejudices and ascribed social roles, high power distance and masculine culture have been the biggest stumbling blocks for them in India. The Constitutional provisions, legislations and various policies and programmes introduced by the Government of India have been positive developments in improving the status of women. The chapter has suggested measures to mitigate the inequality of women in India so that they are able to optimally utilize their potential and rise to board-level positions.

References

Bal, V. (2005). Women scientists in India: nowhere near the glass ceiling. *Current Science*, 88(6), 872–878.

Banerji, A., Mahtani, S., Sealy, R. andVinnicombe, S. (2010). *Standard Chartered Bank: Women on Corporate Boards in India*. Retrieved 4 April 2011 from http://www.communitybusiness.org.

Bansal, U. (2003). *Women Empowerment in Democratic India: A Myth or Reality?* Proceedings of 1st International Conference Women and Politics in Asia. Halmstad: Sweden.

Basu, S. (2008), *Gender Stereotypes in Corporate India*. New Delhi: Response Books,

Beck, D. and Davis, E. (2005). EEO in senior management: women executives in Westpac. *Asia Pacific Journal of Human Resources*, 43(2), 273–288.

Becker, G. (1993). *Human Capital: A Theoretical and Empirical Analysis, With Special Reference to Education*. University of Chicago Press.

Camilla, V. and Jeff, G. (1998). Smashing into the glass ceiling for women managers. *Journal of Management Development*, 17(1), 17–26.

Commission of the European Communities (2009) *Commission Staff Working Document* – accompanying document to the Report from the Commission to the European Parliament, the Council, the European Economic and Social Committee and the Committee of the Regions – Equality between Women and Men – 2009 {COM(2009) 77 final}. Retrieved on 17 December 2010 from http://eur-lex.europa.eu/LexUriserv/LexUriserv.do?uri=SEC:2009:0165:FIN:EN:DOC.

Feather, N.T. (1985). Attitudes, values, and attributions: explanations of unemployment. *Journal of Personality and Social Psychology*, 48(4), 876–889.

India Demographics (2011). Retrieved on 12 April 2012 from http://www.indexmundi.com/india/demographics_profile.html.

Gupta, N. (2007). Indian women in doctoral education in science and engineering: a study of informal milieu at the reputed Indian Institutes of Technology. *Science, Technology, & Human Values*, 32(5), 507–533.

Gupta, A., Koshal, M. and Koshal, R.K. (1998). Women managers in India: challenges and opportunities. *Equal Opportunities International*, 17(8), 14–26.

Indian Express (2010). *Indian Oil tops Fortune India 500 List*, 9 December 2010. Retrieved 5 February 2011 from http://www.indianexpress.com/news/indian-oil-tops-fortune-india-500-list/722511/.

Jain, N. and Mukherji, S. (2010). The perception of 'glass ceiling' in Indian organizations: an exploratory study. *South Asian Journal of Management*, 17(1), 23–42.

Kyriacou, O., Pancholi, J. and Bbaskaran, A. (2010). Representation of women in Indian accountancy bodies' web sites. *Qualitative Research in Accounting & Management*, 7(3), 329–352.

Lipmann, W. (1922). *Public Opinion*. New York: Macmillan.

Mallon, M. and Cassell, C. (1999). What do women want: the perceived development needs of women managers? *Journal of Management Development*, 18(2), 137–154.

Martin, L. and Saunders, M.N.K. (1995). A decision-making model for analysing how the glass ceiling is maintained: unblocking equal promotion opportunities. *International Journal of Career Management*, 7(2), 21–28.

Mattis, M.C. (2004). Women entrepreneurs: out from under the glass ceiling. *Women in Management Review*, 19(3), 154–163.

Nath, D. (2000). Gently shattering the glass ceiling: experiences of Indian women managers. *Women in Management Review*, 15(1), 44–52.

O'Neil, D.A., Hopkins, M.M. and Bilimoria, D. (2008). Women's careers at the start of the 21st century: patterns and paradoxes. *Journal of Business Ethics*, 80(4), 727–743.

Schein, V.E. (1973). The relationship between sex role stereotypes and requisite management characteristics. *Journal of Applied Psychology*, 57, 95–100.

Sen, A. (2001). Many faces of gender inequality. *Frontline*, 18(22).

Shariff, A. (2009). *Gender Empowerment in India: Concepts and Measurements*. Retrieved on 6 February 2011 from http://salehshariff.blogspot.com/2009/09/gender-empowerment-in-india-concepts.html.

Sharma, L.P. (1992). *History of Ancient India*. New Delhi: Stosius Inc/Advent Books Division.

Sharma, R.R. (1982). Education of women in India: inequalities and bottlenecks, *The Education Quarterly*, October, 20–27.

Sharma, R.R. (1984). *Role of Women in the Assimilation and Spread of Technological Innovations*. Conference Proceedings UNESCO-Sponsored International Workshop, 29 October – 2 November, 157–188.

Strategic Direction (2008). More than ever before, the world needs women leaders. *Strategic Direction*, 24(3), 28.

Subramanian, J. (2007). Perceiving and producing merit: gender and doing science in India. *Indian Journal of Gender Studies*, 14, 259–284.

Subramanian, A. and Sachitanand, R. (2010). The 30 most powerful women, *Business Today*, 28 November, 50–96.

Tisdell, C. and Regmi, (2005) Prejudice against female children: economic and cultural explanations, and Indian evidence, *International Journal of Social Economics*, 32(6), 541–553.

Tharakan, S.M. and Tharakan, M. (1975). Status of women in India: a historical perspective. *Social Scientist*, 4(4/5), 115–123.

The Tribune, 31 May 2006; Retrieved on 6 March 2011.

WILL and KPMG Report (2009). Creating Women Business Leaders: Differentiating Styles of Women Executives: A Case Study of Women in Corporate India. Available from *American Chamber of Commerce in India*. http://www.amchamindia.com/WILL-KPMG%20Survey%20Report.pdf

The Times of India (2006). Next cabinet secy could be a woman. Retrieved on 16 May 2012 from http://articles.timesofindia.indiatimes.com/2006-04-06/india/27796338_1_ias-officer-cabinet-secretary-b-k-chaturvedi

Conceptual Perspectives on Quota Systems

7 *Quotas for Securing Gender Justice*

MARJAN RADJAVI

Introduction

This chapter considers quota policies – policies that make it mandatory for a particular percentage or number of women to be represented in a particular forum – with reference to law, on the one hand, and social practices, on the other. I will examine international laws that have contributed to gender justice movements and state policy-making, thereby impacting quota laws and initiatives. My chapter will address a few conceptual points from the perspective of international law. By using two example countries, namely, Argentina and Pakistan, I will also offer some reflections on the circulating discourses and practices involved in local organizing on gender justice and on the perceived and actual efficacy of quotas. The main question I hope to explore by this cross-case comparison is: 'If states and social movements are subject to the same quota policies and practices determined internationally, why do results vary so much?' In other words, I have selected widely divergent socio-political contexts because if quotas are indeed a beneficial tool in achieving gender equality, as they are deemed to be, then they should withstand the test of different settings.

In this chapter I make three main points. First, I argue that quota laws are the product of a certain time and place, and have not always improved women's conditions. Since the very structure of quota laws does not recognize the importance of context, quotas have fallen short of expectations. Second, I propose that it is not the implementation of law alone that has led to change, but actually the efforts of social activists and advocates and the strength of policies that have served to support quota laws and to help improve conditions for gender justice. Finally, I hope to demonstrate how the foregoing phenomena – the incremental global acceptance of rules and norms through local social practices, the social life of quotas – can best be understood by cross-case comparison, through my analysis of quotas in Argentina and Pakistan.

In some ways, then, this is a chapter about the difference between equality of *opportunities* as provided for in quota law and policies, and equality of *outcomes* that, the international community hopes, occurs when these quotas are applied on the ground. While the explicit intention of quotas is to institute gender equality or a form of gender justice, these outcomes may often remain elusive. I present an explanation of quota successes and failures by accounting for additional factors that play a determinative role.

As a legal anthropologist, I take a somewhat constructivist viewpoint in answering questions about the efficacy of quotas for securing gender justice. I consider quota laws and policies to consist of the sum of their local manifestations; meaning that proposing and operationalizing a quota becomes meaningful only in context. Thus I analyze gender justice and quota discourses and practices as they exist in context. The method is initially archival, making use of background research, and then qualitative, following up with in-depth participant observation, to determine what happens when quotas are applied in the field. This methodology is adopted because, as an anthropologist, I understand change as related to formalized frameworks and institutions, such as international conventions, international and national initiatives, and national quota legislation. However, I also understand change to be influenced by how locals, including local organizations, lobbyists and key individuals, all of whom I call social actors, understand and adopt these frameworks. I take what may be called a 'social movements' approach – one that is ethnographic – and focus on legal and social practices based on laws that are used and reformulated by various locals. How gender justice and equality initiatives are implemented and the processes that result can follow both intentional and direct, but also less predictable but still patterned, trajectories.

In the case of quotas, it is important to highlight the complex and fluid relationships and the intersections between competing discourses and practices that occur in a setting where quotas are applied. The social movements approach I have adopted highlights the various social movements and actors in their constant and often contradictory engagement with quota laws. Quota policies are, as compared to other government policies, highly reliant on locals' engagement and interpretation to bring about the desired outcome and therefore this approach best provides for an assessment of such a policy.

There exists, however, no firm consensus on the success of quotas in improving the situation and status of women. A major hurdle is that gender discrimination is perpetuated even by the very state actors that legislate and implement quotas. Therefore, somewhat paradoxically, implementing a quota asks the state to implement gender justice through its fallible and prejudiced structures; the state then may become the first obstacle. And, in another paradoxical turn, this may contribute to gender justice by providing a centralized focus for the efforts of advocates against state violations. Moreover it might give focus to those otherwise not particularly for or against the state or gender equality, by giving a rallying point to opposition lobbyists, human rights advocates and various women who suddenly have a vested interest. As Sonia Alvarez argues, 'Under different political regimes and at distinct historical conjunctures, the state is potentially a mechanism for either social change or social control in women's lives' (Alvarez, 1990). In this case, the state and its initiatives, such as quotas, may in fact be both restrictive and enabling for women. This dual role of the state is brought forward in the second half of my chapter, by focusing on the case studies.

A Quota is a Product of a Particular Time and Place

Over the last two decades much has been made of the potential for quota laws. In international law, quotas are supported by conventions such as the 1979 Convention on the Elimination of all forms of Discrimination Against Women (hereafter referred to as CEDAW).[1] Quotas have now entered adjacent and intersecting arenas of debate in economic development, political representation and human rights. Up until CEDAW, women's roles and responsibilities discourse had a tendency to focus on motherhood and family rather than on equality, equity or justice; this, although not all women are mothers, and despite the fact that even the mothers amongst them do not want to be defined primarily by their biological role. Women's rights language and feminist theory has to some degree addressed this misrepresentation of women, and the citizenship perspective has also addressed this misrepresentation by envisaging an outcome in which equitable access to justice and the opportunity to participate in democratic decision-making is achieved by all, bringing with it corollary rights and freedoms, including economic rights and also sexual and reproductive rights.

Flowing from the framework provided by international law, true gender equality requires that women enjoy all the fundamental rights on the same basis as men, and that men enjoy the same rights as women. Local and national gender quotas in politics, employment and education act as tools to effectuate this ultimate goal. These instruments recognize women's diverse roles and responsibilities beyond motherhood, and aim to achieve gender equality or some form of gender justice both inside and outside the home. They outline a set of connected and interdependent conditions such as policies, laws, institutional mechanisms and resources for this to occur. However, in their most abstracted form, these instruments cannot account for challenges such as voluntary and subconscious concessions of power and the cultural, religious and economic inclinations of societies that are ever-present and that perpetuate discrimination. Therefore, despite the tremendous political currency of quota talk, as an instrument, a quota is not a panacea.

Affirmative action, of which quotas, as an implementation strategy, are a large part, was introduced in many countries as a way to reform male-led administrative and decision-making bodies. Affirmative action was meant to trickle-down and to increase opportunities for women (and girls). However, there is little agreement on what constitutes success (is it equality, equity or justice?). In other words, the first stage in the social life of a quota is determining if it is meant to effectuate a new version of local gender relations, or women's increased participation, or equality as found in CEDAW and other international instruments such as the Universal Declaration of Human Rights (UDHR). There is also debate on how to measure success in future stages (what proportion of women in institutions is sufficient? Does this constitute true justice for women and men?). Therefore we must elaborate a set of indicators for economic and political bodies, so that we can agree how and when we achieve gender objectives. If quotas are going to work, we must take the time and effort to define what is understood as real sharing and true success in achieving gender goals.

Ideas about justice that concern quotas come with a great deal of baggage. For example, arguing that women and men should be 'equal' regardless of context, can be critiqued from the standpoint that, if we are all expected to be the same, this implies that we all aim for the same goals, and thus our inequalities are masked. Consequently, actual experiences and preferences are ignored. Critics of quotas also point out that they were created by and for men (Hernandez-Truyol, 1996; Cook, 1994; 1995), and that

---

1   Convention on the Elimination of All Forms of Discrimination against Women, G.A. res. 34/180, 34 U.N. GAOR Supp. (No. 46) at 193, U.N. Doc. A/34/46, entered into force 3 September 1981. CEDAW full text available at: http://www.un.org/womenwatch/daw/cedaw/text/econvention.htm, accessed 30 September 2005.

they simply insert a woman into a man's world, and devalue her experiences as a result. According to some detractors, demands for affirmative action are misguided, because achieving true justice is not equivalent to achieving the type of equality that quotas tend to foresee. In this line of argument, the focus on a (male) public sphere devalues care and concern for others, which are core aspects of life, and especially strong aspects of women's socialization. By failing to acknowledge such differences, this abstract voice of justice is male and is falsely represented as neutral. This so-called impartiality then reinforces the status quo where work outside the home is valued more highly than that inside. Quotas, when implemented on their own, perpetuate such devaluing of women's roles and experiences. According to American lawyer Catherine MacKinnon, 'Rights that human beings have by virtue of being human have not been rights to which women have had access, nor have violations of women as such been part of the definition of the violation of the human' (MacKinnon, 2006). Inequalities in power and resources that stem from various local factors and the valuing of public over private (home) spaces, though they may be mentioned in quota policies, are inadequately addressed through a pre-determined vision of equality that is a version that undoubtedly conflates man with human.

Social Advocacy and Policies Help Improve Conditions for Gender Justice

A solution to confronting the above-mentioned challenges is to complement the context-neutral gender quota approach. A combined approach to the social life of quotas offers the possibility to reframe quotas in light of *contextualized* gender justice. In-depth study of socio-political, economic and cultural structures can determine who is considered a full citizen, who is allocated rights traditionally, who controls resources in the public and private realms, and who wields power or manifests opposition. From their efforts combating female illiteracy, to defining what is full citizenship, to reformulating what is considered private or female, social actors on the ground indicate to researchers and advocates how best to establish the measures of success of gender justice. They designate meaning and value to the term 'gender justice' by demonstrating what is to them, the desired outcome of gender relations. Whether gender quotas succeed is influenced by this context.

The study of social movements provides a useful link between the theory and practice of gender quotas. I suggest that this is not only useful for theorists, but also for those interested in gender policy reform on the ground, since it provides a framework to conceptualize the state and social actors and makes explicit the desired outcomes of gender relations in a tangible and site-specific form. In a social movements approach, both the state and social actors are understood as sets of forces competing for control through social conflicts and across cultural orientations (Touraine, 1981, qtd. in Harries-Jones, 1996). What this means is that quotas, and indeed all affirmative action policies, can be understood as part of a set of practices of social formation and reproduction, processes that indicate what are considered proper and just gender relations in a given setting.

A quota can then be understood as a (legal and political) representation of gender relations and relationships, a type of symbol that enters into the field of social organizing to secure women's rights (Messer, 1993). This practical foundation enables us to view quotas as a composite of the desired activities, roles and responsibilities of women and men. In fact, viewed this way, how quotas are adopted, subverted or innovated upon, gives us a very real picture of the relationships between women and men, between women and women, and between men and men in any given society.

This does not mean, however, that we must attend to very idiosyncratic particularities of a situation. To redress gender inequality, there should be some balance between adopting the abstract ideals (of affirmative action and quotas) and the contextual factors that pertain to successful implementation of those ideals. These factors consist of the actual needs voiced by women and men through assessment and consultation, and their patterned and explicable practices. To study and to advocate for quotas requires proponents to strike a fine balance between abstract and concrete and between gendered perspectives.

Quota implementation is attractive to all sorts of institutions because it seems straightforward, and also because this instrument purports to solve the problems of discrimination without considering a host of existing deep-rooted socio-cultural and political inequalities. Abstraction (as in quotas) is traditionally presented as virtuous in that it represents a blindness to difference that is crucial in achieving impartiality and ultimately justice. However, this impartiality tends to endorse the status quo and reinforce existing privileges. Asking for seats to be reserved for women in business and government is a discrete demand; while on the other hand, asking a state to change long-standing patterns of socio-cultural and political engagement and inequality is far more ambitious. This is part of the challenge of making quota implementation more than a simple numerical increase.

To elaborate using CEDAW as an illustration, equality principles from the convention can on occasion be relatively straightforwardly drafted into national legislation. But these principles can only be safeguarded by lobbying for implementation. Lobbying serves to open up the debate and establish a critical mass of informed and qualified proponents of gender equality that contribute to social movements. Such awareness about gender discrimination requires a backdrop of literacy, which also contributes to political literacy and leads to the formulation of ideas about citizenship. Achieving gender equality becomes more likely with the presence of gender advocates in politics, in education, and in economic affairs, all of whom can champion these transformations. Therefore, if quotas are going to work, it is necessary to address these essential contextual factors of gendered illiteracy and attitudinal and institutional discrimination of women in politics and social, economic and cultural decision-making at the same time.

Legal scholar Onora O'Neill proposes a manner of conceiving international gender justice which combines elements of abstraction with particularity (O'Neill, 1990), echoing this social movements/citizenship framework I have outlined to examine the social life of quotas. She suggests that accounting for history, tradition and local context need not tacitly support traditional sexist or nationalist structures. The abstract goal of equality, actual gender conditions and state sovereignty must not be idealized. She recommends that the principles of justice (beliefs, traditions and practices) in particular societies be examined to avoid both impositions from on high in the guise of abstract justice and accommodations from below in the guise of local, culturally-appropriate justice.

In this framework, *justice* is defined as principles practicable for any plurality of interacting individuals. No principles that victimize or undercut the capabilities of others can be adopted. O'Neill puts forward that justice is achieved when a variety of interacting agents with finite capacities determine arrangements through consent. Consent is the key word, and O'Neill makes it clear that consent is often not legitimate. True consent means that an individual has not been coerced and could have effortlessly chosen otherwise. This definition is meaningful only when we analyze actual situations where women select motherhood over employment or public engagement over home-making, depending on the economic, social and cultural factors they face. In this way, achieving justice requires analyzing who is strong, powerful and resource-rich in a given society and what principles underlie consent to that distribution.

In market transactions, the weak are often unable to dissent from arrangements proposed by the economically strong. In family settings, the weak or those lacking in economic entitlements are subject to the authority-bearing family members. If all individuals are to be treated with justice, and if gender justice is to be achieved through the application of quotas, others must not be allowed to impose their will. So before suggesting that equality of opportunities like quotas are a solution, research and preparatory work have to account for the capacities and abilities that both women and men have to actively voice dissent and to transform society.

A Quota is an Abstraction of a Desired Relationship on the Ground

Since gender conditions and expectations in Argentina and Pakistan are different, a cross-case comparison can elucidate the general challenges of applying (abstract) quotas in particular settings. These two nations have variably embraced the principles enshrined in CEDAW, an international convention that promotes equality of genders. CEDAW defines discrimination as both policy that differentiates on the basis of sex without reason, or policy that results in treatment 'impairing or nullifying the recognition, enjoyment, or exercise by women – of human rights and fundamental freedoms in the political, economic, social, cultural, civil or any other field'. Equality is thus measured by access to rights (formalized in law or *de jure*), as well as the real ability to exercise these rights (substantive in fact or de facto). Neither intentional discrimination nor actions that have discriminatory impacts are permitted. Both Pakistan and Argentina are subject to CEDAW since the former acceded in 1996, and the latter became signatory to the convention in 1980 which it ratified in 1985.

Each case is examined not for precise details, but rather to generate factors which support or undermine gender quotas and which ultimately influence how quotas 'succeed' or 'fail' in all countries. This said it is necessary to understand the context of each case. In Pakistan the abstract idea of 'equality' enters a context in which women are considered an economic liability either for their men folk or of the state. Argentina presents a different socio-political and economic setting from Pakistan in that women play a greater public role since their engagement in politics in the 1930s. But this role has also undergone frequent political upheaval and military dictatorship as in Pakistan over the last 30 years. Both countries have introduced the figure of 30 per cent into deliberations of gender and politics recently.

PAKISTAN

Pakistan acceded to CEDAW in 1996 with reservations. The Government and bureaucracy have a unique way of interpreting discrimination against women. The 1973 Pakistani Constitution in Article 25, also called the 'equality clause', articulates the interdiction against discrimination on the basis of 'sex alone' which is sometimes interpreted to mean that discrimination on the basis of sex in conjunction with other factors *is permissible*.[2] This clause is followed by Article 25.3 which states that, 'Nothing in this Article shall prevent the State from making any special provision for the protection of women and children.' This provision suggests that while affirmative action is permitted by the state, it is optional, thereby positioning women and children as beneficiaries at the discretion of state forces and powers. This mimics a culture in which the patriarchal family structure is dominant and according to which women exist as adjuncts to male members of their family (Basu, 2005).

In Pakistan, the Constitution does not describe gender discrimination beyond these provisions. Thus, the application of international standards such as CEDAW, and gender tools such as quotas, can be altered by the country's existing administrative and political bodies. The lack of definition of discrimination against women and the Constitution's frequent references to 'protection' of women, 'morality', and 'public interest' permit strict readings that have conventionally excluded women from political and economic institutions. This counters the very spirit of gender justice as expressed in CEDAW itself.

However, associated with the 1973 Constitution, several measures were designed to increase gender equality, including the introduction of affirmative action and the reservation of ten seats for women in the National Assembly and 10 per cent of seats in the Provincial Assemblies. All Government positions were opened up to women, and women were appointed to several high-ranking posts. The Government created a women's rights committee to recommend measures to improve women's legal, political and economic situation. Nevertheless, the impacts in transforming gender balance and gender relations have been described as minimal (Weiss, 2003). Indeed, with such a low percentage of representation, these measures almost appear to have been face-saving tactics rather than actual political commitments to change. Furthermore, even if they introduced a few women into traditionally male roles and built their capacities, such measures cannot guarantee that women will be empowered and that barriers will be minimized to allow them to *use* their capabilities (UNDP, 1995).

Actual conditions in Pakistan such as lack of public child care and the generally accepted economic inequality of women mean that quotas do not level the playing field between women and men. Even if a certain number of seats are reserved for women in political bodies, existing conditions make it impossible to enjoy this right equally to men, who rarely share in home responsibilities such as child care, cooking and cleaning. Moreover, when women are a new minority of any public decision-making body they will tend to be divided and co-opted by the majority and by the long-established participants whether by party lines or other such institutionalized types of social control.

Anita Weiss remarks, 'While Pakistan does not condone discrimination against women at the constitutional level, agreement on the definition of what constitutes

---

2   Constitution of Islamic Republic of Pakistan, provisions regarding education available at: http://www.right-to-education.org/content/rights_and_remedies/pakistan.html, accessed 23 October 2005.

women's rights seems to end when efforts are made to become more specific and articulate workable, acceptable laws' (Weiss, 2003). Without a set of comprehensive laws and policies geared towards government entities, it is difficult to envisage gender justice in Pakistan. Especially as attitudinal and institutional shift are far from assured.

Further measures were taken to improve the status of women in Pakistan in 2002, when the size of the country's legislative bodies was increased and seats were reserved for women through affirmative action and a provision was made for a 5 per cent quota for women in government in addition to open competition. However, the level of implementation of this quota is not uniform across provinces; two provinces failed to implement entirely, and by 2005, in none of the provinces had the figure of 5 per cent been achieved in the majority of government departments'.[3] Moreover, social practices have repeatedly pigeonholed women as inferiors, have promoted gender stereotypes, and women politicians have been ostracized and labelled as 'abnormal' rather than esteemed as trail-blazers or pioneers in this context.

One relatively recent affirmative action measure was an initiative outside of government. It arose when Pakistan's Supreme Court upheld a decision to reserve a minimum number of seats for women at the medical colleges. Even before they get to college, women's literacy rate is 40 per cent, while men's literacy is 67 per cent (United Nations Statistics Division, 2010).[4] Approximately 30 per cent of boys and 50 per cent of girls never enter school and of those who do, 50 per cent drop out within the first five years (Government of Pakistan and Unicef, 2002; Mukhtar, 1999; Croll, 2001; AEPAM, 1998/1999; Government of Pakistan, 2003). Of those who are 'schooled', the average number of years for girls is lower than that for their companions, brothers and fathers. If quotas are going to work, they will have to address this reality.

How are parliamentary quotas or quotas in boardrooms to work in a context with such low enrolment and low retention rate of girls in schools, where these figures are compounded by poverty, restricted mobility and low educational quality? Moreover, when the honour of male members of the family is thought to be eroded with increasing girls' literacy and worldliness (that is equated with their becoming overly opinionated), how can quotas really enable women to voice their concerns? Economic constraints such as the lack of a state-funded social security system exacerbates male child preference and schooling, because it dictates that family funds are spent preferentially on boys who are considered more likely to financially support elderly parents. In this context where a woman is not considered of comparable capacity and worth to a man in the family and in society she is not accepted as a public persona, quotas carry with them the mindset that the women who benefit from quotas are less capable and less worthy.

Such attitudinal and institutional discriminations are a central focus of the current women's movement which is anchored in the anti-colonial struggles predating the creation of Pakistan in 1947. Early on, the movement demanded the creation of a nation in which women would participate in large numbers, if not around their specific interests as women (Ali, 2000). These demands were made and sustained during an unstable political history marked by several constitutional crises, frequent political upheavals, martial law,

---

3   Consideration of reports submitted by States parties under article 18 of the Convention on the Elimination of All Forms of Discrimination against Women: Combined initial, second and third periodic reports of States parties: Pakistan. 2005. Retrieved on 22 February 2006 from http://daccess-ods.un.org/TMP/1242137.html.

4   Literacy is defined as the ability to read a newspaper, write a simple letter, and perform a simple sum.

thnic and linguistic struggles, provincial autonomy challenges and economic hardships Basu, 2005). In terms of lobbying for equality and justice, educated middle-class urban women formed a number of organizations in the mid-1970s, including the United Front or Women's Rights, the Women's Front, Aurat and Shirkat Gah, which later gave rise to he Women's Action Forum. With the restoration of democracy and elections in 1988, the Women's Action Forum brought out a 'Charter of Demands' presenting a comprehensive women's political programme and circulated it to political parties (Mumtaz and Shaheed, 1987).[5] While privileged women made efforts within governing structures to achieve justice there was no trickle down to the majority of women who were not affiliated with powerful men.

One aspect where political instability has had a particularly wide-reaching impact on women is in their participation in political parties. Parties have been frail and unrepresentative, while military regimes have excluded women from policy-making and have suspended civil bureaucracies where women might have otherwise played an important role. Furthermore, tribal and feudal structures that exclude women have managed to strongly influence Pakistan's central leadership over the years, and fundamentalist movements have curtailed women's participation in the public arena and resulted in reluctance of women to take up even the small percentages reserved for them by quotas.

Today in Pakistan a third of municipal seats are reserved for women, but under such conditions, it is unlikely that women act autonomously to make decisions or to implement justice and equality policies. At the moment, women's major contribution to political (and indeed public including economic) life in Pakistan comes from their vote and from women's movement lobbying. In the movement, many identify state accession to CEDAW as a primary achievement, and see current challenges as comprising fundamentalist political and religious parties, judiciary and state apathy, and the continuing question of whether to engage with corrupt state apparatuses (Shaheed, 2002; Zia and Bara, 1999).[6] Ideologically, they question 'Islam's jurisdictional space in the contemporary political sphere and whether women's rights need necessarily be limited at all by Islamic injunctions' (Weiss, 2003). In practical terms, gender advocates question actual impacts and potential of the revamped state Commission on the Status of Women (2006). They stay committed to increasing women's democratic rights and presence, and know that a shift in values must accompany these changes over the next decades. Otherwise, tools such as quotas which present generic difficulties and abstract away from local conditions, cannot help understand or improve a situation where people will not engage with a corrupt state, or where reservations for women benefit strong families and conservative religious and tribal factions who voice agreements made by and for men.

ARGENTINA

Argentina became a signatory to CEDAW in 1980, which it ratified in 1985, and subsequent administrations have set out policies and initiatives to implement the convention.

5   I would like to thank Khawar Mumtaz, a founding member of Shirkat Gah, who helped me to understand the existing situation.

6   Interviews with Farida Shaheed and Khawar Mumtaz in Lahore, Pakistan conducted between 21 and 28 August 2008.

Moreover, Article 75 of the 1994 Constitution gave human rights treaties such as CEDAW the force of law in Argentina.

Argentina presents a different setting from Pakistan to trace the social life of quotas although some aspects of its recent political and military past are shared. As compared to Pakistan, the illiteracy rate in Argentina is negligible, and there are few gender differences in primary education where enrolment rates and attendance are high. In higher education, the country is 'de-gendering' universities, and also reforming ideas of what are acceptable women's careers and lifestyles (Bonder and Rosenfeld, 2004; Bonder 1999).[7] Over the past two decades, massive transformations have occurred including an influx of women into the marketplace, a further movement towards non-discriminatory access to all levels of education, a slow redistribution of family responsibilities inside the home, and an increase in women's participation in public decision-making. Corollary changes in law, in family structures, and in attendant attitudes and values have meant a rise in economic independence for both men and women.

The women's movement in Argentina played an integral role in critiquing the military dictatorship that lasted until 1989. Although women's groups were factionalized, the focus on democratization unified women in pursuit of a common cause (Guerrero and Guzmán, 1998). The most visible group working against the dictatorship was the Mothers of the Plaza de Mayo, a non-partisan group held together by gender solidarity (Feijoó, 1998). Directly after 1989 and under the first democratic government, the place of non-governmental organizations expanded with encouragement from women in government. This new mass of decision-making women furnished financing for non-governmental meetings and additionally requested participation of gender experts in drafting national reports. This changed the tenor of public institutions in Argentina.

The creation of the 1991 National Program on the Promotion of Equal Opportunity of Women in Education was the first official response by Argentina to the commitments made following the ratification of CEDAW (Stromquist, N.D.).[8] The objective of this programme was to generate an educational renaissance to develop women's capacities and interests and to incorporate women into changing international labour and political institutions on an equal footing with men (Bonder, 1999). Over the following two decades, this programme in education has served in concert with other pro-women initiatives including quotas to instigate measured and deliberate changes to women's access to previously male positions.

Similarly, in 1991, Argentina passed the Quota Law aimed at ensuring equal access of women to elected offices. Argentina became the first country in the world to legislate that women must comprise 30 per cent of all candidates on electoral lists. This quota law was passed as a result of the efforts of key women senators and representatives in Government. In 1989, after the fall of the dictatorship, Senator Margarita Malharro de Torres, and Representatives Norma Allegrone de Fonte and, Florentina Gomez Miranda introduced the quota legislation.[9]

---

7   I would like to thank Gloria Bonder who founded the first Women's Postgraduate Studies Programme at the University of Buenos Aires, and developed a National Program for Women's Equal Opportunities in Education at the Ministry of Culture and Education in Argentina from 1991 to 1995, for her research elucidating these points.

8   Inter-American Commission on Human Rights, see http://www.cidh.org/countryrep/Mujeres98-en/Chapter%203.htm.

9   Law 24.012: Quota Law approved November 6, 1991, article 1.

This is an indication of the validity of the old adage about women and men acting differently in decision-making. In this case, it is possible to argue that women's involvement is indeed a value-added in contributing to a diversity of perspectives and to a different weighting of debates. Ensuring women's representation in government is important because it leads to a higher priority being placed on gender equality and justice issues and eventually influences other spheres of communal life (Jones, 1997). However, just as in the case of Pakistan, without equally educated and confident women, a quota itself will not lead to a higher priority on gender equality and justice.

Unfortunately, at times in Argentina this 30 per cent quota has been interpreted as a ceiling rather than as a minimum due to a lack of political education. Furthermore, when women are designated candidates, as in Pakistan, it frequently stems from their connections to powerful men. This perpetuates hereditary, dynastic power where women are the curious exception rather than a norm. This use of a quota does little for democracy and fair representation which would mandate introducing women based on their independent merits and in the interests of comprehensiveness, and would empower them to participate fully.

In 1992, with the establishment of the National Women's Council attached to the Office of the President, the Government demonstrated its intent to further develop programmes to promote opportunities for women in social, political and economic arenas. One of the biggest changes to electoral lists since the 1991 Quota Law was in the Supreme Court of Justice. New procedures established in 2003 created a participatory mechanism requiring an open comment period for citizens to oppose nominations. In this case, the implementation of the law is coupled with a mechanism for advocacy to ensure positive changes. The push to implement CEDAW instigated this process. The Argentinian women, unified through opposing dictatorship, were able to transfer the participatory method to implement quotas more effectively than in Pakistan where there is only a checkered history of the same.

While the ratification of CEDAW, Government initiatives and citizens' advocacy are prime factors leading to change in favour of women in Argentina, there is more to the story. The country has a strong tradition of women in political parties. The Peronist Party in power from 1946–1955 was actively impacted by the dynamism of First Lady Eva Peron. The party was organized in 'branches': the male branch, the female branch and the trade unions, each with an equal share of representation. These circumstances explain the fact that already in 1954 women held 21.7 per cent of the seats in the House of Representatives and 23.5 per cent in the Senate (Bonder and Marcela, 1995). Furthermore, the powerful style of Eva Peron played a critical role in the legitimization of women's political participation. Peron herself led her husband's campaign for presidency and was popular amongst the underprivileged citizens of Argentina due to her redistribution programmes and her own humble beginnings. This is in sharp contrast to Pakistan where women entering public office are viewed by conservative factions as 'abnormal' although the country was for a time led by a woman prime minister.[10]

In terms of women's movement evolution, early groups were autonomous and met during international meetings where they shared experiences and built a collective feminist identity in the Latin American context (Alvarez et al., 2002). These groups did not aim to impact the central Government or its legislation such as quotas. In the 1990s,

---

10   I.A. Rehman, Director of the Human Rights Commission of Pakistan in interview with the author, August 2008.

however, these meetings were supplanted by advocacy which lent legitimacy to women's rights and citizenship claims, and brought women's experiences closer to attention of state officials and bureaucrats (Alvarez, 2000).

The 2001 economic crisis slowed the advancement of gender equality measures when large numbers of women became beneficiaries of the state. In 2002, in response to Argentina's CEDAW report, the UN Committee noted that the new economy was restricting access, particularly of girls, to public education. Financial strictures were accompanied with efforts to downgrade National Women's Council and to end support to commitments to develop instruments and indicators for women's rights.[11]

At the same time, however, this crisis fueled women's organizing and engagement. Social and economic organizing boosted awareness of rights and of the need to exercise rights. Slowly, the National Women's Council once more began providing training and technical assistance to the provincial and municipal women's offices and to assist organizations in promoting equal rights in relation to paid and unpaid work, to combat violence, to address health concerns and to recognize the value of domestic work (Bonder, Radjavi and Ramirez, 2009). Currently, these efforts bring the administration to account, and the quotas in place have the potential to again improve conditions for gender justice. This demonstrates that even the gains that are made can be eroded by internal and external events, and that advocates only by staying vigilant are able to continue determining what is considered socially and politically acceptable. Indeed, this confirms that social movements are at the very core of ensuring that quotas work, and that quotas should not be employed as one-size-fits-all instruments at the sidelines.

Conclusions

Scholars have pointed out that male participation in politics has itself been possible because of women's labour in the private, domestic sphere. In addition to ideas about women's place, women find it difficult to enter the public arena of politics because their time and energy are taken up by domestic work, and because conventions of male authority limit their autonomy. While in many contexts women have overcome these constraints to enter formal politics and boardrooms, equality in this regard is very rare. In fact, if it is true that men's public sphere positions have been supported by women's private sphere positions, it is logically impossible that quotas for public political and economic institutions solve the problems of inequality and injustice. There would have to be an equal sharing of activities outside, and inside, the home. Maria del Carmen Feijoo, a Latin American feminist, persuasively argues that 'we must make room for a women's agenda that is not a matter of [...] asking for more (more maternity leave, for example) or of helping others, and substitute one that recasts typically feminine tasks so they are no longer only women's responsibilities' (del Carmen Feijoo, 2004).

It is precisely to this task that context-driven social mobilizing around quotas is ideally suited. Social movements driven by citizen's agendas – such as those of discriminated women – produce opportunities to reformulate gender relations and conventions. In this way, each society can find ways for men and women each to take up each other's roles

---

11   NGO Shadow Report of July 2002, to the CEDAW Committee fourth and fifth periodic reports of Argentina (CEDAW/C/ARG/4 and CEDAW/C/ARG/5) at its 584th meeting, on 16 August 2002.

nd responsibilities and share arrangements consensually. This means that the many actors that have been proven to complement and enhance quotas on the ground must lso be part of the equation.

We are headed in the right direction in our examination of the social life of quotas if ve couple quotas with a consideration of two key elements. These elements are power of lecision and action, and resources including education and political education. The first s an essential condition for autonomous, informed decisions and the second is necessary o exercise decisions in a safe, effective and consensual manner (Corrêa and Petchesky, 1994). Quotas are only one part of the equation for achieving non-discrimination, and an work in isolation only as a short-term strategy. In brief, this means that institutions leed not abandon the language of quotas and affirmative action, but should couple it with an understanding of citizen's rights and the role of social movements in advocating for gendered interests. And social theorists would do well to delve into legal theory and anthropology to highlight the unequal semantics and socio-economic, political and cultural structures that have allowed discriminations to occur.

I hope that an open discussion of quotas such as this has the ability to expand the space for public awareness about sharing, because that is what quotas are for. It is through a discussion that addresses both what quotas are meant to achieve and how they can be measured, that quotas can be more effective in securing gender justice. We must move away from quotas as a quick fix to deeply embedded and complex social hierarchies. We need to emphasize the need for thoughtful examination and implementation of quotas in order to avoid misunderstanding, or that unintentional harm be caused to those who are intended to benefit.

References

Academy of Education Planning and Management (AEPAM) (1998/1999). Pakistan School Education Statistics, Retrieved 18 September 2006 from: http://www.aepam.edu.pk/Index.asp?PageId=18#.

Ali, S.S. (2000). 'The women's movement in Pakistan', in S. Rai (ed.), *International Perspective on Gender and Democratisation*. Basingstoke: Palgrave.

Alvarez, S.E. (1990). *Engendering Democracy in Brazil: Women's Movements in Transition Politics*. Princeton, NJ: Princeton University Press.

Alvarez, S.E. (2000). Translating the global: effects of transnational organizing on local feminist discourses and practices in Latin America, *Meridians: Feminism, Race, Transnationalism*, 1(1), 29–67.

Alvarez, S.E., Friedman, E.J., Beckman, E., Blackwell, M., Stoltz, N., Chinchilla, N., Lebon, N.M. and Ríos Tobar, M. (2002). Encountering Latin American and Caribbean feminism, *Signs: Journal of Women in Culture and Society*, 28(2), 537–579.

Basu, A. (2005). *Women, Political Parties and Social Movements in South Asia*, Occasional Paper, 5 July. Geneva, Switzerland: United Nations Research Institute For Social Development.

Bonder, G. (1993). As found in G.C. Riquelme, *Women and Education in Argentina (Mujer y Education en Argentina)*, personal collection of the author.

Bonder, G. (1999). *Gender Equity in Education Policy: Lessons from Experience (La Equidad de Genero en las Políticas Educativas: Lecciones de la Experiencia)*. Buenos Aires, Argentina : Centro de Estudios de la Mujer.

Bonder, G. and Nari, M. (1995). 'The 30 percent quota law: a turning point for women's political participation in Argentina' in A. Brill (ed.), *A Rising Public Voice: Women in Politics Worldwide*, New York: The Feminist Press at City University of New York Press, pp. 183–193.

Bonder, G., Radjavi, M. and Ramirez, C. (2009). Advancing women's sexual health and reproductive rights in Argentina: challenges to implementing international law, *Canadian Women's Studies Journal*, 27(1).

Bonder, G. and Rosenfeld. M. (2004). *Equidad de Genero en Argentina* (*Equity and Gender in Argentina*) Buenos Aires, Argentina: FLACSO Argentina and the United Nations Programme.

Cook, R.J. (1994). Women's international human rights law: the way forward, *Human Rights Quarterly*, 15, 230–261.

Cook, R.C. (1995). Enforcing women's rights through law, *Gender and Development*, 3(2), 8–15.

Corrêa, S. and Petchesky, R. (1994) 'Reproductive and sexual rights: a feminist perspective' in G. Sen, A. Germain and L.C. Chen (eds), *Population Policies Reconsidered*. Cambridge, MA: Harvard University Press, pp. 107–123.

Croll E. (2001). *The Girl Child Project Pakistan; Assessment Report 2001*, UNICEF, Pakistan Office, Islamabad, Retrieved on 20 September 2006 from: http://www.unicef.org/evaldatabase/index_14201.html.

Feijoo, M.C. (1994). 'From family ties to political action: women's experiences in Argentina', in B.J. Nelson and N. Chowdhury (eds), *Women and Politics Worldwide*. New Haven: Yale University Press, pp. 60–72.

Feijoó, M.C. (1998). 'Democratic participation and women in Argentina', in J. Jaquette and S. Wolchik (eds), *Women and Democracy: Latin America and Central Eastern Europe*. Baltimore and London: The Johns Hopkins University Press.

Jeffery, P and Basu, J.P. eds. (1998). *Appropriating Gender: Women's Activism and Politicized Religion in South Asia*. New York/London: Routledge.

Government of Pakistan (2003). *National Plan of Action on Education for All (2000–2015)*. Pakistan, Ministry of Education, GoP, Islamabad, 14 August 2001.

Government of Pakistan and UNICEF (2002). *Facts and Figures Pakistan 2002*. Ministry of Education, EFA Wing, Islamabad, Retrieved on 25 September 2006 from http://www.moe.gov.pk/factsnfigures.htm.

Guerrero, E. and Guzmán, V. (1998). 'El caso de Chile y del Cono Sur' in *Caminos a Beijing: IV Conferencia Mundial de la Mujer en América Latina y el Caribe*. V. Vargas Valente (ed.), Lima: Unicef, Flora Tristan Editions, Unifem, pp. 173–205

Harries-Jones, P. (1996). 'Affirmative theory: voice and counter-voice at the Oxford Decennial', in H.L. Moore (ed.), *The Future of Anthropological Knowledge*. London: Routledge, pp. 156–172.

Hernandez-Truyol, B.E. (1996). Women's rights as human rights – rules, realities and the role of culture: a formula for reform, *Brooklyn Journal of International Law*, 21, 605–677.

Jones, M.P. (1997). Legislator gender and legislator policy priorities in the Argentine Chamber of Deputies and the United States House of Representatives, *Policy Studies Journal*, 25(4), 613–629.

MacKinnon, C.A. (1994). Rape, genocide, and women's human rights, *Harvard Women's Law Journal*, 17, 5–16.

MacKinnon, C.A. (2006). *Are Women Human?: and Other International Dialogues*. Cambridge, MA: Harvard University Press.

Messer, E. (1993). Anthropology and human rights, *Annual Review of Anthropology*, 22, 221–249.

Mukhtar, E.M. (1999). *Basic Education in Pakistan*, UNESCO, September, 1999, Retrieved on 25 September 2006 from http://unesdoc.unesco.org/Ulis/cgi-bin/ulis.pl?database=&lin=1&ll=1&gp=1&look=default&sc1=1&sc2=1&nl=1&req=2&au=Mujahid-Mukhtar,%20Eshya.

Mumtaz, K. and Shaheed, F. (1987). *Women of Pakistan: Two Steps Forward, One Step Back?* Lahore, Pakistan: Vanguard.

O'Neill, O. (1990). Justice, gender and international boundaries, *British Journal of Political Science*, 20(4), 439–459.

Shaheed, F. (2002). *Imagined Citizenship: Women, State and Politics in Pakistan*. Lahore, Pakistan: Shirkat Gah, Women's' Resource Centre.

Stromquist, N.P. (N.D.). *Gender, Equity and Emancipatory Education in Latin America*. Inter-American Council for Integral Development. Retrieved om 10 October 2005 from http://www.cidi.oas.org/InteramerStromNel.htm.

United Nations Development Programme (1995). *Human Development Report*. New York and Oxford: Oxford University Press.

United Nations Statistics Division (2010). *Social Indicators*. Retrieved on 20 February 2010 from http://unstats.un.org/unsd/demographic/products/socind/default.htm.

Weiss, A. (2003). Interpreting Islam and women's rights, *International Sociology*, 18(3), 581–600.

Zia, S. and Bari, F. 1999. *Baseline Report on Women's Participation in Political and Public Life in Pakistan*. Islamabad, Pakistan: Aurat Publications and Information Service Foundation, a Project of International Women's Rights Action Watch.

8 Gender Diversity on UK Boards: Exploring Resistance to Quotas

ELENA DOLDOR

Introduction

Gender diversity on UK boards has been intensively scrutinized and researched, yet a retrospective look at the country's demographic trends reveals low numbers of women on boards and a slow pace of change for over a decade. Several corporate governance reforms have attempted to address these disparities, yet prospects for change are grim if numbers continue to increase at this pace. In an international context where there is increasing pressure and legal action for more gender-balanced boards, more forceful legislation and particularly quotas have been recently considered in the UK as a possible solution for change.

However, as everywhere, in the UK quotas are fraught with controversy. This chapter examines some of the discursive controversies surrounding the principle and the implementation of board quotas, drawing on a range of psychological theories to unpack the causes of resistance to quotas and to provide suggestions for a more persuasive positioning of quotas. The chapter focuses on two major categories of obstacles creating resistance to quotas: tendency to deny or minimize inequality and fear of backlash effects. Denial of inequality is fostered by individuals' in-group bias, as well as their belief in a just world and their system justification propensity. Anticipated backlash effects are related to a fear of negative perceptions if one expresses frustration with ongoing gender inequalities, and concerns about tokenism and negative perceptions of women's competence once quotas are implemented.

Further on, introducing the distinction between distributive and procedural justice, the chapter exposes the shortcomings of how quotas are positioned as a policy mechanism, arguing that by focusing on gender inequality as an outcome, quotas leave unexamined the social and organizational processes that actually generate this inequality. An increased focus on procedural justice has the potential to appeal more strongly to individuals' sense of fairness and to convey more accurately the actual problems quotas are aiming to address, namely the factors obstructing women's access to boards.

Women on UK Corporate Boards: State of Play and Prospects for Change

Lack of diversity on boards remains persistently documented across the world (Vinnicombe et al., 2008). In recent years, scholarly attention has particularly focused on gender diversity in the context of boards. Within Europe, gender representation on corporate boards ranges from 0.8 per cent in Portugal to 40.2 per cent in Norway (European Professional Women's Network, 2008). In the US and Canada, women's directorships represent only 14.6 per cent and 15.1 per cent respectively of all board seats (Joy, 2008; Burke and Leblanc, 2008). In the UK, women currently occupy 12.5 per cent of directorships on FTSE 100 boards (Vinnicombe et al., 2011). This translates into 117 female non-executive directorships out of a total of 750 FTSE non-executive directorships and only 18 female executive directorships out of 327 FTSE executive directorships overall. Despite widespread belief that women stand a better chance of holding directorships in smaller companies, figures only become worse as one looks lower in the rankings of smaller companies: only 7.8 per cent of FTSE 250 board directorships are occupied by women.

Clearly, women's presence in the corporate elite remains peripheral across western countries overall. Despite incremental progress, many feel that change is excessively slow and becomes more difficult the higher one tries to penetrate the corporate hierarchy (Daily, Certo and Dalton, 1999). In effect, women's access into the top corporate and public power ranks has not followed a linearly ascending trend historically, and backslide effects are to be expected if change is not proactively encouraged (Eagly and Carli, 2007). Although general awareness of persistent gender inequalities is increasing worldwide, corrective action in many countries is slowed down by an ongoing belief that gender disparities will be eradicated by the mere passing of time. This assumption is likely to paralyze social change. Idly waiting for change to occur at its current pace would mean postponing the prospect of gender equality unduly for several decades. Cranfield's International Centre for Women Leaders has been monitoring the percentage of women on the boards of FTSE-listed companies since 1999. From 7 per cent in 1999, women's representation on boards has risen to only 12.5 per cent in 2011. This change of only 5.5 per cent in 12 years suggests that at the current rate of change, it will take more than 80 years to achieve gender-balanced boards of directors on UK's FTSE 100 companies. The change is modest at best. In effect, a retrospective look at the number of women on boards suggests that in the last few years, progress seems to have stalled in the UK (see Figure 8.1).

Slow progress on UK's FTSE boards is confirmed not only by the number of women sitting on boards, but also by the turnover rate for board directorships. In 2010, only 13.3 per cent of new board appointments went to female candidates. A retrospective look at the rate of women in new FTSE 100 board appointments points to a plateau at this level as well. Figures for female appointments range from 17 per cent in 2004 to 13 per cent in 2010, with an all time high of 20 per cent new directorships going to women in 2007 (see Figure 8.2). This suggests that despite increased scrutiny into the issue of gender diversity on boards, the appointment process – a key vehicle for change – is failing to become more inclusive and to open up to female candidates.

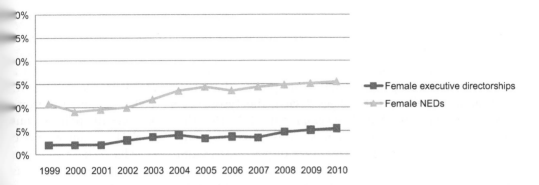

Figure 8.1   Women on FTSE 100 boards – plateaued progress
Source: Cranfield Female FTSE Report 2010 (Vinnicombe et al., 2010).

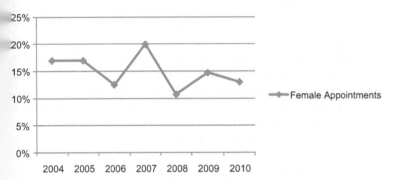

Figure 8.2   Rate of female appointments on FTSE 100 boards
Source: Cranfield Female FTSE Reports 2004–2010.

Corrective Measures: From a Consensual Approach to the Threat of Quotas

These trends conveying a lethargic pace of change on UK's boards are quite surprising, given that for more than a decade there has been constant monitoring and research, governmental support, business initiatives and media attention dedicated to the issue of women on boards. Cranfield's Female FTSE Report in the UK, along with Catalyst in the US, pioneered gender monitoring on boards. After a decade of monitoring and public scrutiny, the numbers of women on boards seem to have stalled in both countries, disputing the managerial motto 'What gets measured gets done'.

In addition to monitoring, in the UK efforts have been made to tackle the issue of gender diversity on boards, in the context of corporate governance reforms. A round of corporate failure and governance scandals in the 1990s generated a wave of mistrust in corporations and their boards, and gave rise to the recommendations of the Higgs Review and the Tyson Report in the UK, which paralleled the Sarbanes-Oxley Report in the US. The Higgs Review (2003) into the role and effectiveness of Non-Executive Directors (NEDs) adopted a relatively non-prescriptive stance by embracing the principle of 'comply or explain'. Calling for higher proportions of NEDs compared to Executive Directors (EDs) the review found that current practices in the selection of board directors overlooked qualified candidates. The report laid out more stringent criteria for the selection and evaluation of independent directors. Derek Higgs particularly insisted on the need for a more open and transparent appointment process that draws on a broader pool of talent.

Commissioned after the Higgs Review, the Tyson Report (2003) examined in more depth the recruitment and development of NEDs. The report clearly pointed out that 'diversity in the backgrounds, skills, and experiences of NEDs enhances board effectiveness by bringing a wider range of perspectives and knowledge to bear on issues of company performance, strategy and risk'. Furthermore, it suggested that more rigorous and transparent selection processes could foster diversity to a greater extent, pointing towards the key role of executive search firms in identifying more diverse candidates.

More recently, the new UK Corporate Governance Code required companies to 'pay due regard for the benefits of diversity on the board, including gender' when selecting NEDs (Financial Reporting Council, 2010). Many argued that the recommendation was timid and ineffectual, particularly when viewed in an international context where several countries such as Norway, Spain and France are adopting increasingly forceful legal measures to tackle women's underrepresentation on boards. Criticism from media and public opinion was echoed by a qualitative inquiry into the views of 14 Chairmen of 17 major FTSE corporations concerning the recent gender diversity principle. The study, published in the most recent Female FTSE Report (Vinnicombe et al., 2010), indicates that these chairmen perceived the clause as insufficient to foster any significant change. Some of them saw it, at best, as a useful acknowledgement for companies where there good practice exists ('I'm rather of the view that boards who do pay consideration are happy to see it in writing') or a reminder for companies who lag behind on the issue of board diversity ('It will underscore it for those who are not at the forefront'). Labelled as a 'wishy-washy' approach by one chairman, the clause was anticipated to 'make a difference in a modest way'. One chairman commented on the principle: 'It's a signal that this is the good direction to go in if you want to, no more than that. The Code is still "comply or explain". I would say it's a weak acknowledgement of an issue.'

With the recent change of government in the UK, a new inquiry into the lack of women on boards was led by Lord Davies. Perhaps not surprisingly, with an increasingly heated public debate on the topic and rising pressure to improve women's representation on boards, Lord Davies seriously considered quotas as a possible corrective measure:

> What we need is a fundamental change in the attitude of chairmen in terms of board representations. There is a range of options. One of them is to bring in a direct quota or a timeline that leads to a quota. My view is that to say 20 per cent of people on a board should be women is not enough. It has to be 30 per cent or 40 per cent to make a real change.

The Davies Report, released in February 2011, refrained from recommending quotas as a way forward, placing the onus once again on companies (particularly on chairmen and CEOs) to increase gender diversity on their boards. Its key recommendations require companies to set aspirational targets for women on boards and to have an explicit policy for boardroom diversity; chairmen and search consultants must also report on their efforts to increase diversity through the appointment process. The steering board led by Lord Davies is to convene every six months to monitor the UK's trends on board diversity, with a view to report annually on the progress – or lack thereof – businesses have made. The Davies report states however that:

> ... *government must reserve the right to introduce more prescriptive alternatives if the recommended business-led approach does not achieve significant change.*

It thus appears that for the first time in the UK, the prospect of board quotas becomes a plausible one. While outlining guidelines for best practice on boards in 2003, the Higgs Review expressed scepticism towards more mandatory legal action, commenting that 'the brittleness and rigidity of legislation cannot dictate the behaviour, or foster the trust' necessary for the good functioning of boards. In contrast, stated the report, a philosophy of 'comply or explain' offers 'flexibility and intelligent discretion' in boardroom practice. Eight years later, in light of little improvement in the figures of women on boards, one thing is clear: the UK's corporate governance rules have not lacked flexibility and discretion, yet the business-driven approach has so far failed to deliver. In a country that has always favoured a consensual approach and strived to include all stakeholders in changing the landscape of male-dominated boards, quotas are emerging as a last, and fairly imminent, resort for change.

Perceptions of Quotas as Vehicle for Change

The UK's attempt to increase gender diversity on boards is by no means unique. In recent years, several countries have grappled with the issue, tackling it with legislation ranging from mandatory to advisory. Among the advisory approaches, in 2010 Australia and Iceland have asked companies to legally operate under a 'comply or explain' or 'if not, why not' disclosure requirement. After women's presence on Fortune 500 boards remained entrenched at about 15 per cent during the last few years, the US has passed a law asking public companies and mutual funds to explain if and how diversity is being considered when new board directors are being selected. At the opposite extreme, mandatory approaches have been pioneered by Norway with its 2003 compulsory quota law requiring a minimum 40 per cent of board members to be of either sex. The trend seems to be spreading. In January 2011, the French Parliament gave final approval to legislation imposing 40 per cent women on the boards of CAC 40 companies within six years. Other countries currently considering quota legislation are Belgium, Canada, Italy, Netherlands and Sweden. At EU level, the Fundamental Rights Commissioner Viviane Reding has threatened to pass legislation mandating at least 20 per cent women on boards, unless numbers improve (Catalyst, 2010).

Despite widespread awareness of gender disparities on boards in most western countries, corrective mandatory legislation is often met with resistance, even in very egalitarian countries such as Norway (Hoel, 2008). Business retains a general hostility to state-driven regulation, particularly in free-market economies. In the UK, Cranfield's study into the views of FTSE chairmen indicated that most chairmen interviewed were opposed to quotas. One of them commented: 'I'm sure it was right not to go the prescriptive Scandinavian route for instance with 40 per cent requirement.' In addition, media coverage is infused with rampant criticism of quotas measures, perceived to be repudiating the principle of meritocracy. Whether the UK will end up adopting board quotas or not, exploring the discursive controversies surrounding the principle and the implementation of quotas is essential to understanding reactions to quotas, as well as the broader consequences of such legal measures. While a plethora of research has documented the business case for board diversity (Bilimoria, 2000; Nielsen and Huse, 2010; Singh and Vinnicombe, 2004; Terjesen, Sealy, and Singh, 2009), given the relative novelty of legal measures to address this issue, it is perhaps not surprising that little research has so far explored the causes of general resistance to quotas. Nevertheless, several theories and concepts from the field of social psychology can provide useful insights into what causes attitudinal resistance to quotas, as well as pointers for a more persuasive positioning of quotas. Drawing on these theories, subsequent sections of this chapter discuss two categories of obstacles creating resistance to quotas: tendency to deny or minimize inequality and fear of backlash effects. While the points are illustrated with examples pertaining to UK corporate boards, the psychological mechanisms discussed transcend national or business contexts.

DENIAL OF INEQUALITY AND RESISTANCE TO QUOTAS

Awareness of inequality is a precondition for addressing it. In most developed countries, public awareness about women's scarcity in business leadership in general and on boards in particular is raised via monitoring and research conducted by media, academics, non-governmental organizations (NGOs) or governmental bodies. Whilst social and legal norms convey an increasing intransigence in the face of persisting inequalities in the workplace, a range of psychological mechanisms that impede individuals to fully acknowledge and address inequality have remained largely unexplored in the context of boards. Particularly relevant to understanding perceptions of gender inequality as related to boards is individuals' inherent tendency to deny or minimize inequality due to a) in-group bias; and b) the belief in a just world and the propensity to perceive the status quo as legitimate, even when it is to their disadvantage.

Social identity theory (Tajfel, 1982) and group justification theories (Jost and Banaji, 1994) posit that individuals are motivated to maintain a positive image of themselves and their respective in-groups. Based on the assumption that in-group favouritism is an endemic tendency, these theories suggest that in order to preserve group status and identity, the socially advantaged are motivated to ignore inequality and to minimize their responsibility for it (Deutsch, 2006). Confirming this differential sensitivity to gender inequality triggered by in-group bias, a study into the careers of US and Canadian top executive women found that women identified as most significant barriers stereotyping, exclusion from male networks and unwelcoming organizational cultures, whilst their male CEOs considered that women do not advance because they lack the adequate skills and experience and because of not having been in the pipeline long enough (Catalyst, 1996). This perspective explains why women's scarcity on boards might not be seen as problematic by key stakeholders of the male-dominated corporate elite (top leaders, board directors, chairmen, CEOs) and why corrective measures such as quotas are perceived by these elite as unnecessary or threatening. Given the criticality of the appointment process in fostering change, it is particularly important that the gatekeepers of this process – chairmen and nomination committees – become aware of gender inequalities on boards and committed to addressing them. However, over the last 12 years, women constituted only 1.1 per cent of the UK's FTSE 100 chairmen. Such exceptionally skewed demographics are certainly not likely to counterbalance in-group tendencies. Illustrating this effect, a Heidrick and Struggles report (2008) found that larger and more diverse nomination committees tend to tap into a more diverse pool of candidates when selecting NEDs. In addition, insensitivity to gender inequality created by in-group biases can be compounded by organizational-level factors. Taking a five-year retrospective view on companies who have performed well and not so well in terms of board diversity, the most recent Female FTSE Report has exposed 11 companies that have had at least 20 per cent women on their boards on average and eight companies that have consistently failed to include women on their boards during this period (Vinnicombe et al., 2010). Interestingly, companies with diverse boards had relatively diverse executive committees, and the 'zeros' had very low female representation at this level as well. This trend points towards an institutionalized indifference to gender inequality, whereby in-group bias created by male-dominated leadership structures is exacerbated by organizational inertia.

In addition to in-group bias, perceptions of inequality can also be shaped by individuals' overarching need to believe in a just world. Lerner (1980) proposed that in order to preserve their own motivation and efforts in pursuing various goals in life, individuals need to believe in a just world where people fundamentally get what they deserve. This need triggers biased interpretations of evidence threatening the concept of a just world, such as ongoing social inequalities. This theoretical lens provides insight into why social inequalities tend to be 'explained away' by both the advantaged and the disadvantaged. In particular, the notion of a just world transpires in the way women's scarcity on boards is often 'explained away' by resorting to concepts such as 'merit' or 'choice'. These explanations are particularly appealing in more individualistic countries such as the US, where individual effort and merit is touted as the unique cause of success. An excessive focus on the individual conceals structural and organizational processes behind women's disadvantage and allows the 'blame' for women's absence to be put upon the women themselves (Lewis and Simpson, 2010), for the sake of preserving a sense of justice and deservingness about the process of getting on boards. A recent study into perceptions of meritocracy among senior women in banking found that adherence to the notion of meritocracy decreased and shifted with time and experience, as merit became increasingly defined not only by human capital factors (skill, experience), but also by social capital factors (social and political skills) (Sealy, 2010).

Reinforcing and refining the just world hypothesis, system justification theory postulates that individuals are ideologically motivated to endorse and justify the status quo, even when existing social arrangements are at the expense of personal and group interest (Jost, Banaji and Nosek, 2004). A review of psychological research in this area has highlighted a range of system-justification beliefs and mechanisms: rationalization of the status quo, out-group favouritism, and depressed entitlement amongst the disadvantaged (Jost, Banaji and Nosek, 2004). In the context of boards, this explains why women sitting on boards or aspiring to board directorships could be motivated to deny inequality and reject interventionist measures reinforcing the idea that inequality exists.

Findings suggesting that the status quo exerts a powerful influence on individuals, whether it benefits them or not, shed light on why the notion of a meritocratic system is an impediment to more diverse boards. Both men and women have criticized quotas for allegedly parachuting women into board directorships on grounds other than merit. What remains unspoken and unchallenged in this frequent criticism of quotas is the assumption that the current system *is* a fair one, one in which those who get on boards –

mostly men – achieve this solely based on merit, and those who fail to get on boards – mostly women – simply lack merit. The pipeline argument, which proposes that women's absence on boards is due to a shortage of qualified female candidates, relies on the same underpinning assumption. Debunking this hypothesis in the UK, the Female FTSE Report has consistently revealed a significant pipeline of women directors, just below the board level (Sealy, Vinnicombe and Doldor, 2009; Vinnicombe et al., 2010).

Based on Sealy's study previously quoted, one might speculate that women are more likely to question the status quo as their perceptions of meritocracy change and their experiences expose them to the gendered realities of the corporate world. Further research is necessary to ascertain if and how women's perceptions concerning the legitimacy and fairness of board processes evolve. This would perhaps indicate how tendencies to endorse and justify the status quo of corporate governance can be counteracted. Paradoxically, the scepticism towards old ways of doing business created by the current economic downturn can be seen as an opportunity to encourage questioning of the status quo of corporate boards and eventually, to push for corrective action.

FEAR OF BACKLASH AND RESISTANCE TO QUOTAS

While a number of business women in the UK have spoken against quotas, one cannot presume that this resistance is exclusively due to system justification tendencies. Certainly, many seasoned business women are acutely aware of the gender obstacles to be faced on the way to boards. One of Cranfield's Female FTSE Reports found that female directors had fairly pessimistic views about the future of women on boards (Sealy, Vinnicombe and Singh, 2008). One female director commented

> They (my chairman/CEO) keep talking about getting a female non-exec but they haven't so far. I've got my views ... they recruit very much in their existing mould of years of older white men.

While many of these women declared themselves against quotas, some did feel that more voluntary action was needed:

> I'm not a big fan of quotas ... I do believe in a meritocracy ... Insofar as we've had many years of equal opportunities and we're still having these conversations maybe that means we do have to do something more directive.

One female director singled out quotas as the last resort to change:

> Emotionally I think it should be non-interventionist ... but I know from the work I've done that unless you have targets/quotas it doesn't change.

If (at least some) business women are aware of inequalities in the context of boards and of the need to address them, why are quotas not endorsed to a greater extent? Three possible reasons are proposed below. A first possible apprehension could be that women avoid being too vocal in their criticism of the status quo due to social perception concerns. Anecdotal evidence suggests that women fear to be perceived as 'victims' or 'agitators' when flagging out gender disparities and supporting forceful legal measures to redress them. Reporting resentment about social injustice is often seen as socially undesirable

Olson and Hafer, 2001) and critics of the status quo are often given less credibility than endorsers of the status quo (Robinson and Kray, 2001). Given the challenges women face in establishing credibility, particularly at senior levels in business, raising gender equality concerns could certainly have more negative individual consequences than benefits.

In addition, both men and women have raised some pertinent concerns about the backlash effects quotas might have once implemented. Therefore, a second apprehension concerns fear of tokenism. With less than 15 per cent women on boards, female directors risk being perceived as representative of their social group and are more likely to be judged in light of gender stereotypes (Kanter, 1977). In line with these findings, some have recommended that a critical mass of at least three women on boards is needed so that boards can truly embrace diversity (Erkut, Kramer and Konrad, 2008). Exposure to rare exemplars of women directors is unlikely to eradicate gender stereotypes and to change the male-dominated cultures that characterize boards. In effect, a Catalyst study (2005) found that people who reported to senior female managers actually held stronger gender stereotypes than people who didn't report to female bosses; female bosses were also judged more harshly in male-typed sectors, suggesting that women are more exposed to stereotyping when they are underrepresented. This indicates that numbers alone are not the whole story. In the aftermath of getting the numbers right with quotas, more subtle yet pervasive challenges (sex stereotypes, gendered cultures) are likely to persist and will need to be tackled.

A last apprehended backlash effect of quotas concerns perceptions of competence for women getting board directorships in the context of such legal action. This concern is substantiated by evidence from social psychology. Laboratory studies examining perceptions of females hired under affirmative action provision in the US indicated that women tend to be perceived as less competent when their hiring was associated with affirmative action, particularly by the dominant group or by non-beneficiaries of these policies, usually men (Heilman, Block and Stathatos, 1997; Heilman, McCullough and Gilbert, 1996). Maio, Bell and Esses (1996) found that stigmatizing effects can extend to the group level as well. Extrapolating these findings, it appears that the risk of stigma due to mandated quotas concerns not only individual female directors, but also the group of female directors as a whole. Overlooking this threat when advocating gender quotas can place women in precarious positions. This risk can be mitigated by ensuring that their competency is made explicit.

This array of evidence emerging from psychological research provides powerful insights into how people are likely to make sense of the lack of gender diversity on boards and how they react to corrective measures such as quotas. A first category of psychological motives, ranging from in-group bias to the need to justify the status quo of the current corporate system, leads individuals to deny or minimize the existence of gender inequalities on boards. In this case, corrective legal measures such as quotas are inevitably seen as unwarranted. Even when gender inequality concerns are acknowledged, a second category of psychological motives prevents individuals from embracing quotas as corrective intervention. This is mainly due to three categories of anticipated backlash effects: negative social perceptions when expressing discontent with gender inequalities, risk of tokenism and diminished perceptions of competence of newly appointed female directors. The public and academic debate on quotas only partially alludes to some of these psychological barriers, particularly with its focus on the issue of merit. The next section of this chapter proposes that some of these obstacles can be addressed by reframing the debate on quotas.

REFOCUSING THE QUOTA DEBATE ON PROCEDURAL JUSTICE

The attitudinal resistance discussed above might be exacerbated by the nature and positioning of quotas in particular, as a legal strategy to enhance gender diversity. Constant monitoring of gender demographics on boards exposes an indisputable inequality of representation. However, while sheer numbers convey an inequality of outcome, they say nothing about the factors and processes generating inequitable outcomes across genders. Research on board diversity has often been criticized for being atheoretical and insufficiently mature in its attempt to go 'beyond numbers' and explain why so few women make it onto boards (Doldor, Vinnicombe, and Sealy, 2010). Whilst many countries currently concur that a more proactive approach is needed to increase diversity on boards, action needs to be underpinned by a clear understanding of what exactly causes the lack of diversity. Shortcomings in focusing scholarly and public attention on what goes on beyond gender disparity in numbers have direct implications into how quotas are researched and implemented, given that the problems quotas are attempting to address remain poorly defined.

A useful conceptual tool in framing gender issues occurring beyond numbers is the distinction between procedural and distributive justice. Whilst distributive justice refers to the fairness of outcomes individuals receive, procedural justice is concerned with the perceived fairness of rules and processes generating these outcomes. Research into the psychology of justice indicates that, perhaps counter-intuitively, individuals are far more concerned with fairness in how decisions are made, rather than fairness in the results of these decisions (Tyler, 1987; Barett-Howard and Tyler, 1986). Applied to quotas, this suggests that individuals are likely to be more attuned to issues of fairness related to the rules and processes restricting women's access on boards, rather than to the mere fact that there are fewer women on boards. However, due to the controversy triggered by their mandatory nature, quotas run the risk of deflecting attention from the actual impediments to board diversity, or in other words the problems they are trying to address. By focusing attention on distributive justice rather than procedural justice, quota measures actually fail to leverage on people's sensitivities in terms of justice. This also leads to quotas being easily misconstrued as preferential treatment instead of being seen as a remedy to an exclusionary system.

For example, a plethora of research suggests that one of the major factors perpetuating the status quo of gender inequality on boards is the appointment process of NEDs. This process was often criticized for its exclusionary practices (lack of transparency in advertising openings and short-listing candidates, unclear selection criteria), susceptible to ruling out qualified female candidates (Terjesen, Sealy and Singh, 2009). In a study of Fortune 500 companies, Westphal and Zajac (1995) found that newly appointed directors tend to be demographically similar to CEOs and to incumbent board members. In the UK, the Higgs Review criticized the excessive reliance on informal network when selecting NEDs. In addition, Dulewicz and Herbert (2008) found that during the appointment process, very few nomination committees of FTSE 350 companies actually predefined high performance criteria for the role. As a reaction to these biased and exclusionary practices, numerous researchers have called for an objectification of the appointment process of corporate directors, by making skills and qualifications more explicit (Burgess and Tharenou, 2002; Ragins and Sundstrom, 1989).

When discussing quotas as corrective action, increased scrutiny into these matters would bring issues of procedural justice to the forefront of debate and action concerning board diversity, leading perhaps to a greater acceptance of quotas and a better understanding of the actual problems they aim to address. In effect, focusing on procedural justice arguments can counteract to some degree resistance to quotas by the psychological obstacles discussed above. The first category of obstacles relate to the inherent tendency of individuals to legitimize and endorse the status quo by minimizing the seriousness of gender inequalities. More than a decade of gender monitoring on UK boards has brought to the forefront gender inequalities by highlighting the outcome (disparities in numbers), yet this seems insufficient to catalyze significant change. Increased public attention to the issue of board diversity and the current threat of quotas provide an opportunity to frame gender equality challenges in more procedural terms, by exposing structural bias that puts women at a disadvantage, in board-related processes. This could lead to a greater questioning of the status quo.

The second category of obstacles is concerned with anticipated backlash if quotas are defended and implemented. Of particular importance are the risks women face of being perceived as 'agitators' when defending quotas and being perceived as less competent when they take on directorships under quota provisions. Again, linking quotas to the need to optimize board processes would help counteract these psychological barriers by shifting attention from women as the cause and the beneficiaries of the quota system, to the broader system of corporate governance and its exclusionary practices.

Conclusion

The need to diversify corporate boards is obvious in the UK, and worldwide. In the last few years, many countries have implemented or at least considered more forceful legal action to improve the gender balance of boards. While the current 'quota fever' is in many ways an encouraging sign of an increased appetite for change, quotas as legal measures are generally fraught with controversy. Understanding what shapes attitudes toward quotas is essential for the acceptance and the successful implementation of quota legislation. This chapter analyzed a range of psychological mechanisms creating entrenched resistance to quotas, suggesting that quotas are likely to be met with resistance due to a deep-seated psychological need to deny or minimize inequality, as well as a result of the anticipated backlash effects quotas might have. In addition, examining quotas through the lens of justice arguments, the chapter proposed that introducing the notion of distributive justice in the debate and positioning of quotas would be beneficial not only for the acceptance of quotas, but also for making sure that the underlying obstacles women face on their way to boards are gradually shattered.

References

Barett-Howard, E. and Tyler, T. (1986). Procedural justice as a criterion in allocating decisions, *Journal of Personality and Social Psychology*, 50(2), 296–304.

Bilimoria, D. (2000). 'Building the business case for women corporate directors', in R.J. Burke and M. Mattis (eds), *Women on Corporate Boards of Directors: International Challenges and Opportunities* Dordrecht: Kluwer, pp. 25–40.

Burgess, Z. and Tharenou, P. (2002). Women board directors: characteristics of the few, *Journal of Business Ethics*, 37(1), 39.

Burke, R.J. and Leblanc, R. (2008). 'Women on corporate boards of directors: the Canadian perspective', in S. Vinnicombe, V. Singh, R.J. Burke, D. Bilimoria and M. Huse (eds), *Women on Corporate Boards of Directors. International Research and Practice*. Cheltenham: Edward Elgar Publishing, pp. 24–37.

Catalyst (1996). *Women in Corporate Leadership: Progress and Prospects*. New York: Catalyst.

Catalyst (2005). *Women 'Take Care', Men 'Take Charge'. Stereotyping of US Business Leaders Exposed.* New York: Catalyst.

Catalyst (2010). *Women on Boards*, New York: Catalyst.

Daily, C.M., Certo, S.T., and Dalton, D.R. (1999). A decade of corporate women: Some progress in the boardroom, none in the executive suite. *Strategic Management Journal*, 20(1), 93–99.

Deutsch, M. (2006). A framework for thinking about oppression and its change, *Social Justice Research*, 19(1), 7–41.

Doldor, E., Sealy, R., and Vinnicombe, S. (2010). Increasing gender diversity on public and private boards: Obstacles and Initiatives, *Academy of Management Conference*, Montreal, Canada.

Dulewicz, V. and Herbert, P. (2008).Current practice of FTSE 350 Boards concerning the appointment, evaluation and development of directors, boards and committees post the Combined Code, *International Journal of Business Governance and Ethics*, 4(1), 9.

Eagly, A.H and Carli, L.L. (2007) 'Women and the Labyrinth of Leadership', *Harvard Business Review*, 85(9), 63–71.

Erkut, S., Kramer, V.W. and Konrad, A.M. (2008). 'Critical mass: does the number of women on a corporate board make a difference?', in S. Vinnicombe, V. Singh, R.J. Burke, D. Bilimoria and M. Huse (eds), *Women on Corporate Boards of Directors. International Research and Practice*, Northampton, MA: Edward Elgar Publishing, pp. 222–233.

European Professional Women's Network (2008). *Third Bi-annual European PWN Board Monitor*, Egon Zehnder International.

Financial Reporting Council (2010). *The UK Corporate Governance Code*. London: FRC.

Fondas, N. and Sassalos, S. (2000). A different voice in the boardroom: how the presence of women directors affects board influence over management, *Global Focus*, 12, 13–22.

Heilman, M.E., Block, C.J. and Stathatos, P. (1997). The Affirmative Action Stigma of Incompetence: Effects of Performance Information Ambiguity, *Academy of Management Journal*, 40(3), 603–625.

Heidrick & Struggles (2008). *Route to the Top: What Does it Take for Women to Get on to FTSE100 Boards?* London: Heidrick & Struggles.

Heilman, M., McCullough, W. and Gilbert, D. (1996). The other side of affirmative action: reactions of non-beneficiaries to sex-based preferential selection, *Journal of Applied Psychology*, 81(4), 346–357.

Higgs, D. (2003). *Review of The Role and Effectiveness of Nonexecutive Directors*. London: Department of Trade & Industry.

Hoel, M. (2008). 'The quota story: five years of change in Norway', in S. Vinnicombe, V. Singh, R.J. Burke, D. Bilimoria and M. Huse (eds), *Women on Corporate Boards of Directors. International Research and Practice*, Cheltenham: Edward Elgar Publishing, pp. 79–88.

Joy, L. (2008). 'Women board directors in the United States: an eleven year retrospective', in S. Vinnicombe, V. Singh, R.J. Burke, D. Bilimoria and M. Huse (eds), *Women on Corporate Boards of Directors: International Research and Practice*, Cheltenham: Edward Elgar, pp. 15–23.

ost, J.T. and Banaji, M.R. (1994). The role of stereotyping in system-justification and the production of false consciousness, *British Journal of Social Psychology*, 33(1), 1–27.

ost, J.T., Banaji, M.R., and Nosek, B.A. (2004). A decade of system-justification theory: accumulated evidence of conscious and unconscious bolstering of the status quo, *Political Psychology*, 25(6), 881–919.

Kanter, R.M. (1977). *Men and Women of the Corporation*. New York: Basic Books.

Lerner, M.J. (1980). *The Belief in a Just World: A Fundamental Delusion*. New York: Plenum Press.

Lewis, P. and Simpson, R. (2010). 'Introduction: theoretical insights into practices of revealing and concealing gender within organizations', in *Revealing and Concealing Gender: Issues of Visibility in Organizations*, Basingstoke: Palgrave Macmillan, pp. 1–22.

Maio, G., Bell, D. and Esses, V. (1996). Ambivalence and persuasion: the processing of messages about immigrant groups, *Journal of Experimental Social Psychology*, 32(6), 513–536.

Nielsen, S. and Huse, M. (2010). The contributions of women directors on boards: going beyond the surface, *Corporate Governance: An International Review*, 18(2), 136–148.

Olson, J. M., and Hafer, C. L. (2001). 'Tolerance of personal deprivation'. In J.T. Jost and B. Major (eds), *The Psychology of Legitimacy: Emerging Perspectives on Ideology, Justice, and Intergroup Relations*. Cambridge, UK: Cambridge University Press, pp. 157–175.

Ragins, B.R. and Sundstrom, E. (1989). Gender and power in organizations: a longitudinal perspective', *Psychological Bulletin*, 105(1), 51–88.

Robinson, R. and Kray, L. (2001). 'Status versus quo: naive realism and the search for social change and perceived legitimacy', in J. Jost and B. Major (eds), *The Psychology of Legitimacy*, Cambridge, UK: Cambridge University Press, pp. 135–157.

Sealy, R. (2010). Changing perceptions of meritocracy in senior women's careers, *Gender in Management: An International Journal*, 25(3), 184–197.

Sealy, R., Singh, V. and Vinnicombe, S. (2007). *The Female FTSE Report 2007: A Year of Encouraging Progress*, Cranfield: Cranfield School of Management.

Singh, V. and Vinnicombe, S. (2004). Why so few women directors in top UK boardrooms? Evidence and Theoretical Explanations, *Corporate Governance: An International Review*, 12(4), 479–488.

Sealy, R., Vinnicombe, S. and Doldor, E. (2009). *The Female FTSE Board Report 2009: Norway and Spain Join our Census to Benchmark Corporate Boards*, Cranfield: Cranfield School of Management.

Sealy, R., Vinnicombe, S. and Singh, V. (2008). *The Female FTSE Report 2008: A Decade of Delay*, Cranfield: Cranfield School of Management.

Tajfel, H. (1982). Social psychology of intergroup relations, *Annual Review of Psychology*, 33, 1–39.

Terjesen, S.A., Sealy, R. and Singh, V. (2009). Women directors on corporate boards: a review and research agenda, *Corporate Governance: An International Review*, 17(3), 320–337.

Tyler, T. (1987). Procedural justice research, *Social Justice Research*, 1(1), 41–65.

Vinnicombe, S., Sealy, R., Graham, J. and Doldor, E. (2010). *The Female FTSE Report 2010: Opening Up The Appointment Process*. Cranfield: Cranfield School of Management.

Tyson, L. (2003). *The Tyson Report on the Recruitment and Development of Non-Executive Directors*. London: London Business School.

Vinnicombe, S., Singh, V., Burke, R., Bilimoria, D. and Huse, M. (eds) (2008). *Women on Corporate Boards of Directors: International Research and Practice*. Cheltenham: Edward Elgar.

Westphal, J.D. and Zajac, E.J. (1995). Who shall govern? CEO/board power, demographic similarity, and new director selection, *Administrative Science Quarterly*, 40(1), 60.

9 The Construction of Workplace Identities for Women: Some Reflections on the Impact of Female Quotas and Role Models

JUNKO TAKAGI AND SHORA MOTEABBED

Introduction

Gender quotas are being introduced in countries across Europe as a means to combat underrepresentation of women in upper-level management and also to introduce more ethical concerns to corporate decision-making processes. In this chapter, we discuss some of the implications of this trend on the development of professional identities of women aspiring to leadership positions in firms. We summarize recent literature on women and leadership and on role models, and introduce another avenue of research concerning women on corporate boards, which has so far tended to focus on corporate strategies for meeting quota guidelines and the impact of quotas on firm performance. We propose that setting female quotas will increase the likelihood of more viable role models for women aspiring to leadership positions. At the same time, we nuance this positive trend by differentiating between executive and non-executive board members and the consequences of this differentiation on role models for women.

Women and Leadership

Both the academic and practitioner literature on women and leadership in management continue to find that women are scarce in the upper tiers of management (Colaco, Myers and Nitkin, 2011; McKinsey Report, 2007; 2008). The former investigates the causes of this underrepresentation (for example, Terjesen, Sealy and Singh , 2009) and has identified factors such as differences in self- and other-expectations (Eagly and Johnson, 1990; Ridgeway and Smith-Lovin, 1999) and managerial and leadership expectations in particular (Bosak and Sczesny, 2011; Taylor and Hood, 2010), differences in leadership styles between men and women (Madero, 2011; Vanderbroeck, 2010; Vinkenberg et al., 2011), and systemic factors including causes such as the glass-ceiling effect (Morrison and Von Glinow, 1990) that compound the difficulties for women to access leadership position (Lyness and Thompson, 2000). The latter tends to highlight the business case for greater gender diversity in upper-level management and focuses on strategies for attaining increased equality (Catalyst, 2000; 2003; McKinsey Report, 2007; 2008).

In relation to perceptions around leadership, studies have found that there are indeed discrepancies between womens' self-expectations of leadership qualities and others' expectations, indicating that stereotypical beliefs persist regarding women and leadership. For example, perceivers report higher incongruencies for women than for men in their beliefs regarding gender roles and leadership (Bosak and Sczesny, 2011). A study by Taylor and Hood (2011) on leaders' emotional and social competencies also reports that while male and female managers predict their own leadership competencies similarly, others' perceptions of the same competencies differ for men and women. This has potential consequences for women, who have more difficulty predicting others' ratings of their leadership competencies, in terms of developing a coherent and legitimate professional identity. Davies, Spencer and Steele (2005) studied the impact of gender stereotypes on women's leadership aspirations and found that women who are primed on gender stereotypical images undermine their own aspirations on a leadership task. They also reported that when women are in an identity safe environment, the impact of stereotypical images on leadership aspirations is diminished. At the same time, studies also indicate a recent trend of women participating more in governance activities in firms with increasing aspirations for a more expanded role (Colaco, Myers and Nitkin, 2011), and diminishing gender differences in management practices between male and female managers (Madero, 2011). The literature suggests that while more women have leadership aspirations than in the past, they are still caught between not only differences between self and other-expectations of leadership possibilities which have been found to impact gatekeepers in their selection of executives (Oakley, 2000), but also between gender stereotypes that they have internalized and their individual aspirations.

These perceptions of gender differences have also generated a literature on differences in leadership styles between men and women. The second McKinsey Report which focuses on leadership issues identifies women as having leadership behaviours that encourage people development through a participative style and that build respect by emphasizing the ethical consequences of their decisions (Eagly and Johnson, 1990; McKinsey Report, 2008). Similarly, some studies emphasize the emotional, social and ethical contributions of women to the process of management (Barsh, Cranston and Craske, 2008; Binns, 2008). When considering leadership styles, the literature thus identifies different skill-sets for women and men. However, other studies suggest that a common pitfall for women leaders is that they and others expect them to have the same leadership skill-sets as men (Cames, Vinnicombe and Singh, 2001) and are consequently comparatively penalized (Vanderbroeck, 2010). Female leadership styles are less recognized and legitimate in the eyes of both men and women, As Eagly (Eagly and Carli, 2003; Eagly, 2005) points out, although women may have some advantages in certain leadership styles, it is important to take into account followers' perceptions of the legitimacy of the occupant in the leader position where prejudicial evaluation of women's competencies as leaders persist.

Establishing a clear relationship between women and leadership continues to be problematic due to perceptual issues and the question of legitimacy. Studies continue to find that incongruencies exist within and between self- and other-expectations which lead to perceptual biases, and the underrecognition of women in a leadership role and/ or their skill-sets. We argue that these elements complicate the process of establishing a coherent workplace identity for women in upper-level management.

Role Models

Role models are considered to be essential for task or career transitions in several studies (Ibarra, 1999; Gibson, 2003). A role model represents possible selves that individuals may wish to become and goals that they would like to attain in their professional life (Gibson, 2003; Ibarra, 1999). Through illustrating possible future goals and how to attain them, role models help individuals to develop their identity at work by showing what is possible (Gibson, 2003; Ibarra, 1999; Sealy and Singh, 2006; 2010). In this section we will review the literature on role models and their impact in shaping work identities specifically for women in the organizations.

The importance of having female role models in upper-level management in order for women to develop a clear and coherent professional identity to progress in their careers, and the difficulty as a result of the lack of adequate role models are expressed in several studies (for example, Eagly, 2005, Ibarra, 1999, Singh, Vinnicombe and James, 2006; Sealy and Singh, 2010). As a result of the dearth of senior women generally, women aspiring to be leaders require more effort than their male counterparts to cognitively process role models from fragmented sources to create upward professional images (Sealy and Singh, 2006). Men on the other hand are able to choose from attributes already legitimated by the organization and to add them to their personal repertoires. The resulting images for women are less likely to be fully acknowledged by others although, as a result of the increased cognitive effort, they tend to be more 'true-to-self' (Ibarra, 1999).

In her study of professional identity in the finance and consulting industries, Ibarra (1999) observed that scarce representation of women in senior positions constrained female managers' abilities to find feasible or attractive identity matches in their observations. Singh, Vinnicombe and James (2006) conducted a qualitative study to investigate role models of young female managers in an organization that had a predominantly male senior management. They discovered that these young women managers were not successful in finding adequate female role models and found it difficult to identify with senior male managers. The study reports frustration on the part of women seeking to learn from the personal characteristics and styles of role models in order to identify with and develop a feminine management style and characteristics (Singh, Vinnicombe and James, 2006). These studies demonstrate the importance of perceived availability, that is 'the degree to which individuals think they are sufficiently similar to others in their environment that they can observe and perhaps emulate', as a basis for role modelling (Gibson, 2003).

Gibson (2003) gives a taxonomy of role models based on qualitative data collected through interviews with employees in their early, middle and late career stages. He claims that individuals mainly interpret role models along four dimensions. Two cognitive dimensions identified by Gibson are positive/negative and global/specific role model construction. Two structural dimensions include close/distant, and up/across/down (Gibson, 2003; 2004). The positive dimension is compatible with what we typically have in mind when we think of role models: observation of behaviours and following someone in what you want to become. Negative role model construction refers to how not to be in general or how not to behave in a particular situation. Global role model constructions relate to overall attributes in a role model to be emulated, while specific constructions refer to drawing on a specific attribute in a role model in a specific context (Sealy and Singh, 2010). Defining the structural dimensions of the role model, Gibson (2003) explains that close role models refer to someone well known to the individual, whereas distant role models lie outside of normal interactions.

Gibson (2003; 2004) suggests that at each career stage, individuals have different expectations from the identification process with the role model. In the early career stage, individuals seek to acquire a viable professional identity through global emulation of close role models. In the mid-career stage, they seek to refine their existing professional identity by selecting specific attributes of roles models, and in the late career stage, individuals seek to affirm and enhance their professional identity by acquiring specific skills attached to specific objectives (Gibson, 2003; 2004). Gibson (2003) suggests that individuals are more likely to identify with positive as opposed to negative role models, although in the mid and late career stages, individuals may also use negative role models to enhance their sense of uniqueness. At the same time interviewees in their middle and late career stages in Gibson's study (2003; 2004) emphasized that one important reason that they do not identify with positive role models is a result of a lack of perceived availability of such role models.

Although Gibson (2003; 2004) does not address gender issues, he suggests that since women typically have fewer available same-sex role models, we may want to take into consideration gender differences. According to Ibarra (1999) and Gibson (2003; 2004) women moving into upper-level management positions have difficulty finding an appropriate general role model and are more likely to develop specific modelling strategies rather than global ones. As a result of a general lack of appropriate role models, women engage in translating male role model behaviour into behaviour that works for them. The pool of role model material available for women is restricted, leaving them with lower-quality information than that available to men (Sealy and Singh, 2010).

Ibarra (1999) notes that while men tend to develop a general strategy of role modelling based on a few integral role models, women are more likely to combine characteristics from multiple role models and to craft a more 'true-to-self' persona.

Men, on the other hand, are more able to activate global role modelling strategies due in part to the abundance of male role models (Gibson, 2003; 2004; Sealy and Singh, 2010).

Sealy and Singh (2010) note that the demographic scarcity of women in senior management leads to the increased likelihood of negative role models. Studies investigating the underrepresentation of women in top management consistently report the negative impact of senior women on other women's perceptions (Gibson and Cordova, 1999; Liff and Ward, 2001). In these studies, senior women were perceived by other women in the firm as 'not very nice' or 'unnatural', and also as having 'lost their femininity'. Takagi (2010) came across instances of negative female role models whose impact on other women was not so much to affirm their uniqueness or to identify attributes they did not want to emulate, but to push them towards or to confirm professional choices that were more traditional. Female middle managers reported that they 'did not want to be like' the female senior managers who were perceived as 'unattractive', 'tough' and 'not having the important portfolios'. As Sealy and Singh (2006) suggest, what makes it difficult for women to find role models is a 'lack of women perceived to be similar to the women seeking role models, or a lack of role models to whom they would desire to be similar'.

In accordance with our discussion on women and leadership, the literature on women and role models also indicates that the paucity of women leaders creates a fragile environment for women to find appropriate role models who are able to create upward possibilities, and whom they can emulate either globally or specifically in order to create stable and legitimate professional identities. In the next section we will argue about the impact of gender quotas in general and on corporate boards and how they can impact the process of role modelling and shaping women's work identity.

Gender Quotas

There is a growing literature on women on corporate boards (Branson, 2007; Burke and Mattis, 2000; Huse, 2007; Thomson and Graham, 2005; Vinnicombe et al., 2008) which has been triggered in part by the implementation of gender quotas in certain European countries. They highlight the overall slow progress of women to senior management levels, including the slow increase of women on corporate boards, the persistence of gender-biases and 'old-boys' networks' which still dominate board elections, and call for the improvement of the quality of board deliberations and overall corporate governance by increasing board diversity. A gender quota was initially introduced in Norway in 2003, and Norwegian firms have already met the 40 percent guideline proposed by the law. Gender quotas have since been introduced in Spain and France, and are under consideration in other countries such as Germany and Holland.

Studies on boards' gender composition have focused on measuring the impact of boards' gender diversity on the financial performance of firms (for example Campbell and Minguez-Vera, 2008; Carter, Simkins and Simpson, 2003). What remains under-examined is the impact of the number of women on a corporate board on other women working in the same company. One way that senior women including women on corporate boards can assist other women at work is through acting as a role model (Ely, 1995; Ibarra, 1999). Sealy and Singh (2010) argue that increasing the number of visible women in authority positions may be associated with women's aspirations and change in gender-based expectations.

In our previous discussion, we identified the need for more senior women role models in order to establish stable and legitimate professional identities for other women. In addition to inconsistencies in self- and other-expectations and lack of legitimacy, women aspiring to senior positions continue to struggle to build professional self-concepts from fragmented role model attributes. In this section, we discuss the potential impact of gender quotas on the construction of professional identity for women aspiring to leadership positions.

Kanter (1977) demonstrated that when women are situated in a numerical minority of less than 15 percent, they are entirely marginalized by the dominant male group and become what she called 'the token women'. Ragins and Sundstorm (1989) along with Kanter (1977) suggest that the exceptional situation of these women lead to exaggerated publicity of their individual activities such that they become 'one of the boys' leading to a more favourable evaluation of masculine as opposed to feminine attributes. They project an unfavourable evaluation to their in-group, and the identification between women in the firm may decrease. Particularly in the case of success, these token women may desire to remain visible and hinder other women from replicating their success and are reluctant to serve as mentors or close role model for other women.

The scarcity of women in top management may also impact their leadership style and thus how they are perceived as potential role models. In a meta-analysis of studies on leadership style and gender, Eagly and Johnson (1990) deduced that women had a general tendency to pursue feminine styles of leadership. This is characterized by concern for the morale and welfare of people in the workplace and consideration of others' viewpoints when making decisions. Women tend to have more of a participative leadership style, with high interpersonal concerns and caring compared to men. However, when they were a clear minority in leadership roles and hence had the status of token in organizations or groups, women were found to abandon stereotypically feminine styles. One possible reason suggests that women may tend to lose authority if they adopt distinctively feminine styles of leadership in extremely male-dominated roles. As a result women who survive in such roles need to adopt the styles typical of male role occupants, whereas in a gender-balanced setting they are more at liberty to take on their own leadership style. The problem is that other women do not find such role models appropriate but they find them non-feminine and aggressive, and have a hard time identifying with them as a role model (Gibson and Cordova, 1999; Liff and Ward, 2001; Singh et al., 2006).

Ely (1994; 1995) specifically examined the effect of women's proportional representation in the upper echelons of organizations on the relationships between these women and their social constructions of gender differences and gender identity at work. She discovered that women in male-dominated firms accept more masculine stereotypes, have weaker relationship with other women and have a worse idea of their own competencies than women in more gender-equal firms. Focusing on the relationships between professional women, she found that individuals in firms with few senior women were less likely to perceive senior women as role models with legitimate authority, more likely to perceive competition in relationships with women peers, and less likely to find support in within-gender relationships compared to women in firms with a more gender-equal distribution of senior women (Ely, 1994). She also discovered that, in firms with more balanced gender representation at the top, the opposite was true conclusively.

This would indicate that increasing the number of women at the top should lead to more balanced perceptions of other women and their competencies. However, the mere presence of women in top management is not enough. It is also important to consider the gender ratio, or more specifically the number of women on a board. Studies have examined the direct impact of board gender diversity on firm financial performance and found that companies with at least three women board directors performed significantly better than average in terms of return on equity, return on sales and return on invested capital (Joy et al., 2007). This result was not supported in companies with fewer women on the corporate board. Konrad, Kramer and Erkut (2008) studied groups with one, two or three women and found that a critical mass of three is necessary for women to feel supported by the group and freer to raise issues and be active. Erkut et al. (2008) consider that women are invisible when there is only one woman in a group, and they are perceived to conspire when there are two. Only when there are three is their presence considered to be normal by the group, and women are empowered by the group to make effective contributions. These findings may be extended to the role of women on corporate boards as potential role models for other women in the firm. Discarding the token status may not only lead to better performance due to the normalization of gender and the possibility for women board members to 'be themselves', but also to their being perceived as attractive role models for women aspiring to authority positions.

Conclusion

The literature on gender diversity in groups and gender quotas leads us to the conclusion that we need to take into consideration the notion of critical mass regarding female representation. Gender quotas that ensure at least three women in groups and corporate boards enable these women to contribute in an effective and 'true-to-self' manner, independent of gender stereotypes and counter-stereotypes. This critical mass 'normalizes' gender as a characteristic of the group, and encourages women to be empowered by the group. Such a supportive work environment enhances centrality as identified by Barsh, Cranston and Craske (2008) as a key element for women leaders to thrive. The critical mass may also lead to the legitimation of female leaders and their skill-sets so that they gain what Eagly (2005) terms authenticity. The increased presence of female leaders who are able to bring alternative characteristics to top management positions through gender quotas will have a significant impact in terms of filling gaps in role models available to women aspiring to leadership.

We also need to take into account the type of positions on the board that are available to women. There are two groups of board members: executive and non-executive (Burgess and Tharenou, 2002). Executive Directors (EDs) are senior managers who gain a place on the board because of their position within the company. Non-Executive Directors (NEDs) are members who primarily work somewhere else and hold a position on the board based on their specialist expertise, industry contacts or prior experience (Burgess and Tharenou, 2002). Based on Gibson's role model framework, EDs can act as close (as opposed to distant) role models, since they are also integral members of the firm and interact more often with their subordinates. Non-executive members are more distant, since they interact very little or not at all with other non-board members of the firm.

Referring to Gibson's model, role models could be both close or distant and global or specific. In the early stages of a career, employees normally observe close and global role models (Gibson, 2003). We can predict that at this stage women usually choose their direct bosses as direct role models and normally there are enough female role models for them in the lower ranks of organizations (Gibson, 2003). In middle and late career stages thus the role of females on the board becomes critical in shaping women's identity. Singh and Vinnicombe (2003) found that since women could not find enough similar and same sex role models inside their workplace and department, they were obliged to use a selection of role models from other domains, many of them from outside the workplace, to help them build appropriate identities. Studies also show that individuals in their middle/late stages of career facing the uncertainty in the workplace look for more specific attributes of role models performing in certain tasks and situations. This increases the need for closer interactions with the available role models.

Building on this argument, non-executive board members may be less useful as role models for women in their middle/late career stages since they are more likely to be distant and also global models. They have worked in different companies and have different backgrounds thus lacking in perceived similarity for women inside of the company. Also they are likely to have limited opportunities of interactions with non-board members of the firm. We can conclude that in this regard executive members of the boards could serve better as role models for women inside of the organizations.

Experience from countries that have met their gender quotas for corporate boards indicate that non-executive female board members play a key role (see Chapter 1 in this book), There are not enough women executives to fill the corporate board seats that have become available to them. Thus, while we can celebrate the success of quota laws in some countries in increasing female participation on board decisions, from the perspective of role models and the development of leadership identities for women, there is still much room for development. We would argue that the next step for those countries where the gender quota has been met is to work on the number of female executive members. For countries working on meeting the gender quota, it is important to take into consideration the role of female executive board members on developing the pipeline for the next generation of board members.

References

Barsh, J., Cranston, S. and Craske, R. (2008). Centered leadership: how talented women thrive. *McKinsey Quarterly*, 4, 35–36.

Binns, J. (2008). The ethics of relational leading: gender matters. *Gender, Work and Organisation*, 15(6), 600–620.

Bosak, J. and Sczesny, S. (2011). Exploring the dynamics of incongruent beliefs about women and leaders. *British Journal of Management*, 22(2), 254–269.

Branson, D. (2007) *No Seat at the Table: How Corporate Governance and Law Keep Women out of the Boardroom*, New York : New York University Press.

Burgess, Z. and Tharenou, P. (2002), Women board directors: characteristics of the few, *Journal of Business Ethics*, 37(1), 39–49.

Burke, R.J. and Mattis, M. (2000), 'Women on corporate boards of directors: Where do we go from here?', *Women on corporate boards: International challenges and opportunities*, Kluwer, Dordrecht, 3–10.

Cames, I., Vinnicombe, S., Singh, V. (2001), "Profiles of 'successful managers' held by male and female banking managers across Europe", *Women in Management Review*, 16(3), 108–17.

Campbell, J.L. and Minguez-Vera, A. (2008). Gender diversity in the board room and firm financial performance, *Journal of Business Ethics*, 83(3), 435–451.

Carter, D.A., Simkins, B.J. and Simpson, W.G. (2003). Corporate governance, board diversity, and firm value, *Financial Review*, 38(1), 33–53.

Catalyst and Opportunity Now (2000). *Breaking the Barriers: Women in Senior Management in the UK*. London: Business in the Community.

Catalyst/Conference Board (2003). *Women in Leadership: Comparing European and US Women Executives*. New York: Catalyst/Conference Board.

Colaco, H.M.J., Myers, P. and Nitkin, M.R. (2011). Pathways to leadership: board independence, diversity and the emerging pipeline in the United States for women directors. *International Journal of Disclosure and Governance*, 8(2), 122–147.

Davies, P. G., Spencer, S. J., & Steele, C. M. (2005). Clearing the air: Identity safety moderates the effects of stereotype threat on women's leadership aspirations. *Journal of Personality and Social Psychology*, 88, 276–287.

Eagly, A.H. (2005). Achieving relational authenticity in leadership: does gender matter? *Leadership Quarterly*, 16(3), 459–474.

Eagly, A.H. and Carli, L.L. (2003). The female leadership advantage: an evaluation of the evidence. *Leadership Quarterly*, 14(6), 807–835.

Eagly, A.H. and Johnson, B.T. (1990). Gender and leadership style: a meta-analysis, *Psychological Bulletin*, 108(2), 233–256.

Ely, R.J. (1994). The effects of organizational demographics and social identity on relationships among professional women. *Administrative Science Quarterly*, 39(2), 203–238.

Ely, R.J. (1995). The power in demography: women's social constructions of gender identity at work. *The Academy of Management Journal*, 38(3), 589–634.

Erkut, S., V. Kramer , W. and Konrad, A. M. (2008), 'Critical Mass: Does the Number of Women on a Corporate Board Make a Difference?', in S. Vinnicombe, V. Singh, R. Burke, D. Bilimoria and M. Huse (eds), *Women on Corporate Boards of Directors: International Research and Practice*. London, UK: Edward Elgar, 222–232.

Gibson, D.E. (2003). Developing the professional self-concept: role model construals in early, middle, and late career stages, *Organization Science*, 14(5), 591–610.

Gibson, D.E. (2004). Role models in career development: new directions for theory and research. *Journal of Vocational Behavior*, 65(1), 134–156.

Gibson, D.E. and Cordova, D. (1999). 'Women's and men's role models: the importance of exemplars.' in A.J. Murrel, F.J Crosby and R.J. Ely (eds), *Mentoring Dilemmas: Developmental Relationships within Multicultural Organizations*, Mahwah, NJ: Erlbaum, 121–142.

Huse, M. (2007). *Boards, Governance and Value Creation: The Human Side of Corporate Governance*. Cambridge, UK: Cambridge University Press.

Ibarra, H. (1999). Provisional selves: experimenting with image and identity in professional adaptation. *Administrative Science Quarterly*, 44(4), 764.

Joy, L., Carter, N.M., Wagner, H.M. and Narayanan, S. (2007). *The Bottom Line: Corporate Performance and Women's Representation on Boards*. New York: Catalyst Inc.

Kanter, R.M. (1977). *Men and Women of the Corporation*. New York: Basic Books.

Kelman, H.C. (1961). Processes of opinion change, *Public Opinion Quarterly*, 25(1), 57–78.

Konrad, A. M., Kramer, V. and Erkut, S. (2008) Critical mass: The impact of three or more women on corporate boards, *Organizational Dynamics*, 37(2), 145–64.

Liff, S. and Ward K. (2001). Distorted views through the glass ceiling: the construction of women's understandings of promotion and senior management positions, *Gender, Work and Organization*, 8(1), 19–36.

Lyness, K.S. and Thompson, D.E. (2000). Climbing the corporate ladder: do female and male executives follow the same route? *Journal of Applied Psychology*, 85(1), 86–101.

Madero, E. (2011). Are workplaces with many women in management run differently? *Journal of Business Research*, 64(4), 385–393.

McKinsey Report (2007). Women Matter 1.

McKinsey Report (2008). Women Matter 2.

Morrison, A.M. and Von Glinow, M.A. (1990). Women and minorities in management, *American Psychologist*, 45(2), 200–208.

Oakley, J. (2000). Gender-based barriers to senior management positions: understanding the scarcity of female CEOs. *Journal of Business Ethics*, 27(4), 321–334.

Ragins, B.R. and Sundstrom, E. (1989). Gender and power in organizations: a longitudinal perspective, *Psychological Bulletin*, 105(1), 51–88.

Ridgeway, C. and Smith-Lovin, L. (1999). The gender system and interaction, *Annual Review of Sociology*, 25(1), 191–217.

Sealy, R. and Singh, V. (2006). *Role Models, Work Identity and Senior Women's Career Progression – Why are Role Models Important?* Best Paper Proceedings of the Academy of Management Annual Meeting, Atlanta, GA.

Sealy, R. and Singh, V. (2010). The importance of role models and demographic context for senior women's work identity development, *International Journal of Management Reviews*, 12(3), 284–300

Singh, V. and Vinnicombe, S. (2003) The 2002 Female FTSE Index and woman directors, *Women in Management Review*, 18(7), 349–58.

Singh, V., Vinnicombe, S. and James, K. (2006), Constructing a professional identity: how young female managers use role models. *Women In Management Review*, 21(1), 67–81.

Takagi, J. (2010). Aachen paper.

Taylor, S.N. and Hood, J. (2010). It may not be what you think: gender differences in predicting emotional and social competence. *Human Relations*, 64(5), 627–652.

Terjesen, S., Sealy, R. Singh, V. (2009). Women Directors on Corporate Boards: A Review and Research Agenda, *Corporate Governance: An International Review* 17(3), 320–337.

Thomson, P., Graham, J. (2005). *A Woman's Place is in the Boardroom.* New York: Palgrave Macmillan.

Vanderbroeck, P. (2010). The trap that keeps women from reaching the top and how to avoid them. *Journal of Management Development*, 29(9), 764–770.

Vinkenberg, C.J., van Engen, M.L., Eagly, A.H. and Johannesen-Schmidt, M.C. (2011). An exploration of stereotypical beliefs about leadership styles: is transformational leadership a route to women's promotion? *Leadership Quarterly*, 22(1), 10–21.

Vinnicombe, S., Singh, V. Burke, R. Bilimoria, D. and Huse, M. (2008), *Women on corporate boards of directors: International research and practice.* Cheltenham: Edward Elgar.

10 Down for the Count: How Meritocratic Ideology Stigmatizes Quotas in the United States and Some Alternative Paths to Equity

MAUREEN A. SCULLY

Introduction

All remedies to inequality must be grounded in the argument that the inequality is illegitimate and unfairly produced. In the United States, the dominant ideology of meritocracy provides a competing explanation that inequality is the result of a fair contest. Against this backdrop, it is difficult for advocates for change to legitimate proposed remedies to inequality. This chapter proceeds in two main parts. In the first part, I set the stage by introducing the idea of meritocracy and the history of quotas. Specifically, I explain the main tenets of meritocracy and the particular romance with this idea in the US. I then briefly summarize how gender and race discrimination remain serious departures from meritocratic promises in organizations, to establish that remedies to inequality remain relevant. I introduce when and how quotas have been invoked as a remedy, and where they have been distorted and polemicized to provoke objections to affirmative action. I close this first part by noting studies that show how quota systems can stigmatize women and people of colour who advance in organizations, both to themselves and to others. Faith in meritocracy obscures the root problems of gender and racial inequality, leaving quotas to look like unfair departures from meritocracy rather than remedies intended to restore meritocracy.

In the second part, I consider two trends and a promising new direction in the US, which have arisen to address gender and race inequality in organizations and society. The two trends are situated by the shift in organizations from using the language of quotas and affirmative action to using the language of 'diversity' and 'inclusion' (Kelly and Dobbin, 2001). 'Quotas' and 'diversity' are two distinct streams of discourse and practice in the

United States now. The same advocates for gender and race inequity may invoke both of them, but strategically in different moments and different settings. The overarching term of this book 'Diversity Quotas' is not one that is heard in the US. Rather, it is not unusual for an organization now to have a Diversity Office that operates separately from the Affirmative Action Office.

As the language and logic of diversity displaced the language and logic of affirmative action, activists in organizations found new ways to address inequality. Two resulting trends that I consider – deep cultural analyses and employee network groups – have the advantage that they dig into the root causes of gender and race inequality, often proving the differential impacts of facially neutral but subtly gendered and raced policies. But these trends run the risk that, in leaving behind the logic of quotas, they are not attentive to concrete numerical gains for women and people of colour in organizations. The promising new direction that I consider places attention squarely on the material facts of inequality. It involves linking root problems of inequality across domains, such as schooling, housing and employment, to create deeper structural solutions. By introducing this approach here, in a series of papers focused mainly on the workplace, I pull some insights from the domain of social policy analysis into the domain of organization studies. I assess these three approaches (deep cultural analyses, employee network groups and linked domains of inequality) with respect to the initial goals of quota systems and affirmative action programmes: reducing inequality that unfairly limits the well-being and life chances of women, people of colour and their families.

Meritocracy, Quotas and Where they Meet

THE MAIN TENETS OF MERITOCRACY

Meritocracy refers to achievement and governance by the most qualified (Scully, 1997). It is an ideal invoked specifically in contrast to aristocracy, where standing is inherited, not earned. The particular history of the US, including the lack of a feudal heritage (Hartz, 1955) and immigrant aspirations to pursue the American Dream and become a 'self-made man' have made meritocracy a deep cultural logic. This cultural logic infuses popular media, politics, schools and the workplace.

Philosophers have distilled three main principles of meritocracy as a distributive system (Daniels, 1978). First, there are meaningful and definable measures of merit. Second, everyone has an equal opportunity to develop and display their merits and to advance on the basis of merit. Third, there are valued rewards (such as income or high-status occupations) attached to positions that are vertically stratified by merit. Discrimination on the basis of gender, race or other factors means that a system is not a meritocracy. Passage of affirmative action legislation, while always highly politically contested, may have initially succeeded in the US because of the abiding aspiration to be a meritocracy. Debate rages over the extent of the departures from meritocracy, but not over the value of meritocracy.

DEPARTURES FROM MERITOCRACY THAT WARRANT REMEDIES

Discrimination can arise regarding any of the three main principles of meritocracy. First, standards of 'merit' may arise that do not actually relate to the education or job that an applicant is seeking, and moreover, that favour one group over another. For example, the LSAT test is a timed, standardized test taken for admission to law school. Minority students have historically performed lower on the LSAT exam, and debates have raged over whether minority applicants should be admitted with lower LSAT scores, to ensure educational opportunity and enhance diversity in the classroom. A new angle on this debate asks whether LSAT scores are a relevant merit for performance in law school in the first place (Henderson, 2004). Findings show that LSAT scores are good predictors of what they test: How students will do in law school on timed, in-class tests. They are not good predictors, for white or minority students, of performance on take-home exams, essay exams, papers, classroom preparedness and comments, nor later performance in a law career. Thus, the debates over special admission criteria for minority students, which served to diminish the merits and compromise the confidence of minority students, prove to be misplaced, because the metric of merit was not robust.

Second, opportunities to develop and display merit, and be advanced on the basis of merit, are another site of discrimination or differential impact (for example, Cox and Nkomo, 1986). For example, women professors in the sciences at Massachusetts Institute of Technology (MIT) in the 1990s began to see that their opportunities to succeed were unfairly limited. They literally measured the size of the laboratory spaces assigned to women scientists and found them to be smaller than those assigned to men scientists. Unlike office size in corporations, which can be a mere display of status, laboratory size bears a direct impact on research productivity. With larger laboratories, a scientist can conduct more experiments concurrently, employ more graduate students and postdoctoral fellows, produce more articles and win more grants, which in turn fuel further status and productivity. The lab size constraint proved to be the tip of the iceberg in investigations of measurable and not so easily measurable impediments to women faculty, as they worked to develop and display merit, and be promoted on the basis of merit, at MIT. The women scientists were initially staunch believers that sheer merit would propel their careers in an objective field like science. They began to see systemic patterns, beyond what individual hard work and determination alone could surmount, and documented how the 'accumulation of slight disadvantages' (Bailyn, 1999) impeded them relative to male scientists.

Third, differential rewards may be assigned to the same position in a system that is supposed to be stratified by merit. In the 1970s, the focus was on 'equal pay for equal work', with women lobbying to get paid the same when they attained the same position. Such evident cases of inequality are rarer today, but differential rewards persist in subtle forms. For example, where variable pay, such as stock options, is part of the pay package, women are likely to receive lower rewards, because subjective managerial assessment carries favouritism towards men (Elvira and Graham, 2002). As another example, idiosyncratic job titles, where only one person holds a special title, are more likely to be held by men and to be more highly rewarded than titles in the same organization in which comparably skilled men and women are paid the same (Baron and Bielby, 1986 Miner, 1987). That is, while male and female software engineers may be paid the same, a man with similar credentials but holding the title 'special software analyst' might be paid more, without evidently violating the 'equal pay for equal work' principle.

Specifying these types of departures from meritocracy is a useful first step in thinking about quotas. Objections to quotas often arise from a taken-for-granted assumption that meritocracy already prevails, so any interventions compromise assessment and advancement on the basis of merit. Over time, it has been the persistence of discrimination, documented in stories and studies like the above, that has kept alive the quest for legislative and organizational remedies. When meritocracy is shown to be compromised, that nags at broad American sensibilities about what is fair, and wedges open the door for change efforts.

QUOTAS: REPAIRING OR IMPEDING MERITOCRACY?

After passage of the Civil Rights Act of 1964 in the US, many employment systems were scrutinized, including those of the federal government, unions and large corporations. Counting the numbers of employees from different racial groups was a natural first step to assess how far a workforce deviated from the racial composition of the available population of workers. This difference indicated the extent of discrimination in hiring. Quotas represent numerical targets for what a system would look like were equity to be achieved. They were meant to be informative and aspirational, but have come to be seen as prescriptive, rigid and limiting. In the US, quotas were mainly applied to the pursuit of racial equity. Prohibiting discrimination on the basis of sex was added to the Civil Rights Act by politicians trying to subvert its passage. Immediately after its passage, greater attention was paid to racial discrimination, but the door was opened for later attention to sex discrimination, which often took the gross form of occupational segregation by sex (Reskin, 1993).

Quotas per se cannot survive legal challenges and are not favoured in principle in the US (Twomey, 2009), specifically where quotas are thought to require hiring someone mainly or solely on the basis of their race or sex. Disincentives to using quotas come from the logic of disparate impact itself, from cases in employment law and from organizational efforts to legitimate their broader approach to affirmative action (Stryker, 2001). The spirit behind quotas remains pertinent, that numerical evidence can reveal where discrimination is operating, in impact if not demonstrably in intent. The logic of quotas was one of accountability. The unspoken assumption behind quotas is that all racial groups have merit, so that if any group is disproportionately underrepresented in hiring and promotions, there must be a departure from meritocracy. Thus, the idea was not to hire people on the basis of their race or sex, thereby ignoring their merits, but quite the opposite: to make sure that race or sex did not obscure the merits of members of a group.

Ironically, however, meritocracy is more often invoked as an objection to quotas, rather than as an aspiration that quotas might help to realize. In practice, quotas became embroiled in sharp distributive contests. Limited places in the reward structure – whether winning a government contract, a spot in a union apprentice programme, an entry-level job or a seat in university – become contested terrain. Consider an example of the type typically raised when quotas are hotly debated. There may be 20 open slots in a system, and the aim may be that two slots be awarded to racial minorities, in a region where 10 per cent of the population are of that racial group. Among white applicants, 18 may be selected with scores on some test of merit that range from 85 to 95, out of 100. A likely but ignored backdrop to this story might be that a person from a racial minority with a potential score of 97 was discouraged from even taking the test, and another person from that racial group took the test without benefit of the preparation programme that typically adds ten points to one's score and nonetheless managed to score 80. But these types of factors, which reveal the root discrimination in the first instance, are ignored. Instead, the focus of popular discourse falls on the person from the group historically discriminated against who gains a slot with a score of 83. The nineteenth best white applicant, who scored 84, is denied a slot, and this result becomes the flash point of anger and contention. The effort at redistribution of opportunities, which may be applauded in broad terms at a macro level, is bitterly fought over local, individualistic results. Particular 'winners' and particular 'losers' in the contests for particular slots draw attention away from the broader goals of quotas.

Because applying the logic of quotas at a broad, systemic level to address patterns of discrimination was subverted by local battles such as these, quotas were replaced with the concepts of 'goals' and 'timetables'. These were to be affirmatively, or proactively, pursued to remedy inequality. Organizations were pressed to present plans as much as outcomes. The idea was for organizations to have locally sensible mechanisms for checking their composition against the pipeline of people available for hiring or promotion. The move away from a strict logic of quotas was intended to increase the legitimacy of efforts to change the composition of organizations.

This temperate approach nonetheless continues to stir strong feelings. Researchers have probed why many Americans continue to struggle with affirmative action. White Americans and black Americans alike express ambivalence, though from different standpoints. These debates tend to rage more intensely in the US around issues of race, but they can arise in discussions of gender as well. Assessing white American's distrust of affirmative action or belief that it is not warranted, one view is that they are prejudiced or underestimate the extent of discrimination (Crosby, 2004). Another view is that these factors are in play, but more nuanced factors, such as unconscious bias, may explain why people who claim not be prejudiced might behave in discriminatory ways (Greenwald and Banaji, 1995). Still another approach documents how common folks, white and black, are able to talk together about the complex distributive dilemmas that are involved, as affirmative action aims to reset a broad system while limiting unintended penalties to qualified individuals, white and black, along the way (Gamson, 1992). This last perspective was born in response to the tendency to blame the working class for prejudice and for failures of affirmative action, because many contests erupt where the few working class jobs with decent pay and conditions have many claimants, such as in police and fire departments. Many people are capable of appreciating these dilemmas and reasoning beyond their own group's self-interest, but policy-making nonetheless remains challenging.

At the same time, the rejoinder that affirmative action is 'reverse discrimination' (replacing favouritism towards whites with favouritism towards blacks) is readily invoked by many white Americans. Lessons about affirmative action in the business school classroom are often made impossible when vocal students are misinformed but insistent about reverse discrimination (Rodin, 2009) and lack the rigorous empirical grounding to understand the presenting problem of discrimination (Reskin, 1998). The tenacity of the belief that hard work and ability govern success in the US (Kluegel and Smith, 1998) make it hard to see both discrimination and forms of white privilege and easier to believe in reverse discrimination. Indeed, the worry that hiring women might look like reverse discrimination creates a 'paradox of meritocracy' whereby managers who are reminded of an organization's meritocratic promises become less likely to select a woman for a position (Castilla and Benard, 2010).

Black ambivalence about affirmative action stems from this simmering debate over whether affirmative action restores or departs from meritocracy (for example, Carter, 1992). Many black professionals describe needing to be 'twice as good to get half as far', only to detect the suspicion from colleagues that they got their latest promotion only because of their race. They experience organizations entirely differently than their white counterparts, at once celebrating and masking what their racial identity could contribute to learning from diversity at work (for example, Bell and Nkomo, 2001). Having affirmative action policies on the books in organizations creates a backdrop against which many black employees feel they cannot escape from this subtle, and sometimes not-so-subtle, judgment and cannot be appreciated for their merits. Investigations of this experience have led to research on stigmatization from myths about quotas, which I situate in the context of meritocratic ideology.

MERITOCRATIC IDEOLOGY AND STIGMATIZATION FROM MYTHS ABOUT QUOTAS

Meritocracy is more than a descriptor of a type of distributive and governance system. It is an ideology that is invoked politically in arguments about whether redistribution is or is not warranted. As an ideology, it functions like a logical syllogism (Huber and Form, 1973). That is, there is a starting premise that there is a meritocracy in place, correctly sorting people on the basis of merit. From there, an inference can be drawn that anyone in a lower position must not be meritorious. The dominant view in economics argues that systems reset themselves to a meritocratic equilibrium, because organizations that select for merit will out-compete those where biases divert jobs to the less meritorious. From this standpoint, which might be called a dominant ideology, meritocracy prevails and systems do not need fixing. Those who have fared poorly are in lower positions by dint of lower merit.

This line of reasoning, treating meritocracy like a logical syllogism, was invoked famously by former Harvard University president Larry Summers. In seeking to explain the scarcity of women in maths and science, he referred to the lower frequency of high mathematical talent among women as a possible indicator of women's lower innate merit. Advocates for women quickly retorted that systemic obstacles for women were a stronger explanation. It has been difficult to remedy gender discrimination, in academia and elsewhere, because of this sticky belief that low numbers simply reflect lower merit. Even when new organizational policies aim to address underlying systemic problems that stall women, they generate a widespread perception that women's numbers are increasing because of unearned preferential treatment for women, not because women's merits are finally being recognized (Zernike, 2011).

Knowing that this attribution is readily available, many women and racial minorities come to dislike affirmative action programmes. The existence of such programmes – in a context where meritocracy is treated like a logical syllogism – raises doubts about their qualifications, even where they are evidently qualified, or even overqualified, for a position and receive no special consideration. They feel more highly scrutinized, s if colleagues are sceptically checking for evidence of merit. Moreover, they feel their performance has to represent the deservingness of their entire group. These pressures add up to 'stereotype threat' (Spencer, Steele and Quinn, 1999), which causes women and racial minorities to perform worse on tests (and conversely, to perform better when cues for stereotype threat are removed). Thus, cross-group performance differences can be seen as endogenous to the system of discrimination, not as an external difference in merit for which adjustments and exceptions are needed.

In broad strokes, 90 per cent of the top positions in the Fortune 500 companies in the US are held by white men, who represent 40 per cent of the US population. To conclude that affirmative action or other remedies are not needed is essentially to conclude that this broad statistic means that women and people of colour are just not sufficiently motivated or meritorious for these positions (Bell, 2006). Such a conclusion might be jarring to even the staunchest advocate that the US has realized its meritocratic promise.

Alternative Paths to Equity

Alternative paths to equity have become relevant in the face of limited efficacy of legislative and judicial approaches to eliminating discrimination. Evidence of disparate impact of hiring and promotion practices might have led the way to a search for root causes and appropriate fixes. Instead, affirmative action became more superficial and compliance oriented. The standard of proof subtly shifted so that employers could inoculate themselves by showing no intent of disparate treatment. With the American faith in meritocracy infusing employment law and workplace culture, remedies to discrimination were increasingly viewed as disruptions of meritocracy. The Civil Rights Act of 1991 was meant to codify disparate impact doctrine, but left the door open for challenges that weakened it (DeSario, 2003). Thus, it may not be surprising that, at around this time in the mid-1990s, alternative approaches to addressing discrimination emerged.

ANALYSIS OF DEEPLY EMBEDDED CULTURAL PRACTICES

Through the courts, many cases of overt discrimination were addressed in large companies in the 1970s. Remaining patterns of discrimination were more subtle. Handling 'second generation employment discrimination' required naming nuanced problems and finding locally appropriate solutions inside the workplace, while creating structures to retain the accountability and oversight that external regulation had provided (Sturm, 2001). Studying these more nuanced sources of discrimination required researchers and concerned organizational activists to work together. New methods such as 'collaborative interactive action research' (Rapoport et al., 2002) involved joint sense-making with organizational members to see how everyday workplace practices hampered gender equity. The focus shifted from looking mainly at employment benefits that might support women, such as maternity leaves or on-site child care, to looking at employment practices themselves as carriers of gender inequity.

An example shows what can be uncovered through this approach (Scully, 2004). Executives at a high technology company wondered why there were few women in the Senior Software Architect position. Numerical counts revealed the problem, but simply enforcing promotion quotas was not the solution. A research team interviewed women about their experiences at this company, eliciting details about how they did their work (Scully and Segal, 2002). They found that the way to be promoted to senior software architect seemed to be to cultivate a reputation for problem-solving, which took the specific form of dramatic fixes to software bugs at the eleventh hour before a product or upgrade was to launch. These 'cowboy' stories were told often by employees, and always told about men, often to explain a man's rise in the programmer hierarchy.

The women took a different approach to their work, which had three distinct features. First, they were conscious that there were few women programmers in this predominantly male occupation, so they coded very carefully in order to minimize the chances of any bugs later, always remembering to 'comment their code' in order to reduce bugs that might arise as colleagues used or linked to it. In doing so, ironically, they closed the door to later heroic fixes of bugs. Second, they worked at a steady pace, because a series of all-nighters before launch would be difficult for their work and family balancing. They could not manage the midnight rescue efforts, so paced themselves in order to avoid them, again ironically writing themselves out of a part in the 'cowboy' stories. Third, they befriended the women in the mostly female quality testing and assurance department, learning from their experiences about some best practices that would prevent bugs. They respectfully engaged with this group in a way not done by most male programmers. The men saw that department as second class, which is common where occupational sex segregation persists. Altogether, these practices engaged in by the women – which appear gendered at first look – were actually best practices for workplace productivity for everyone. Indeed, these three ways of working might be considered indicators of merit for programmers – minimizing errors, pacing the work and consulting over quality control.

Upon presentation of these findings, executives realized that all the madcap fixes were problematic to corporate strategies for announcing and delivering new products on time. They saw that it would be misguided to 'mentor' the women programmers to make them more like the men programmers and thereby more promotable. A quota system (though not practised by this company) would have elevated women without an accompanying story about the merits of their work practices, thereby delegitimating their achievement. The outcome instead was to diffuse the women's ways of working as new standard operating practices.

This approach to using a gender analysis to uncover areas for improvement more broadly has been called the 'dual agenda' for advancing gender equity *and* work effectiveness (Bailyn and Fletcher, 2003; Kolb and Merrill-Sands, 1999). Problems in an organizational system are often initially detected and felt by historically underrepresented groups, and their remedy ultimately benefits the entire system – the 'canary in the coal mine' effect (Guinier and Torres, 2002).

EMPLOYEE CAUCUS GROUPS

The above approach is often triggered by an external evaluation team working collaboratively with insiders. Another approach to change comes from the grassroots of organizations. Employee caucus groups organize along social identity lines, initially race and gender and now often sexual orientation, age, disability or religion. They may also be called employee network groups or employee affinity groups. They come together to voice shared concerns about barriers to opportunity in the workplace, an approach pioneered by the Black Caucus Group at Xerox Corporation in 1972 (Friedman and

)einard, 1991). Caucus groups form when members of a social identity group realize they ave shared concerns. They may meet during company time or after hours. Their tenor as shifted from grassroots to more formally corporate in recent times. They increasingly write mission statements that link their goals of creating opportunities for members of their group to the corporate business case for diversity. They aim to uncover issues that initially are pertinent to their group but whose resolution may benefit all employees and the company. For example, the Black Caucus Group members noticed that internal jobs were often filled by a favoured candidate before they even knew there was a job opening for which to apply. The resulting job posting system was more transparent, which was appreciated by employees of all races who were seeking promotions, as well as by hiring managers seeking talent.

One of the most significant accomplishments of employee caucus groups is helping members shift their attributions for blocked opportunities from individualistic to more systemic ones. Employees who feel they have not advanced as high as their merits warrant, or as high as an equally or less qualified referent group, try to make sense of this experience. Employee caucus group members often report being surprised that others faced the same barriers, ones they thought they needed to overcome through personal determination alone (Scully and Segal, 2002). Meritocratic ideology encourages individualistic attributions. Employee caucus groups allow a shift to a more collective stance, which is significant in the individualistic culture shaped by meritocratic beliefs. Employees share their stories and discover common patterns. In working together, they can more confidently approach managers with proposed solutions. For example, in one organization in the Northeast of the US, recruiters often said they would hire more black employees if only they could find them. Black employees were discouraged that the company spent money sending recruiters to Europe to find talent but would not pay for recruiters to go to Atlanta and tap the strong black middle class and graduates of historically black colleges and universities. Several individual black employees kept this concern to themselves, but when they finally learned that others shared this concern, they were able to go together to management and craft a summer internship that drew talented black college students and recent graduates to the company.

Employee caucus groups have benefits and limitations. The benefits include having a group of insiders who are sophisticated about the nuances of the problems and the levers for change. They hold managers accountable and seize appropriate moments to advance changes. The limitations are that they can become part of a very superficial effort to make workplaces feel more inclusive. Such efforts lose track of numerical counts that indicate whether the opportunity structure is changing to include greater diversity. One recent study found that diversity training per se did not enhance gender and racial diversity in organizations; only creating metrics that made managerial efforts to increase diversity a part of the performance evaluation system had an impact (Kalev, Dobbin and Kelly, 2006).

RELINKING INEQUALITIES ACROSS SOCIETAL DOMAINS

Thus far, this chapter has talked about employment discrimination and the workplace domain. I now consider a promising new direction: relinking remedies to discrimination across the domains of schooling, housing, education, health care, transportation and employment. Clearly, these factors are related, but they are typically not jointly considered in discussions of workplace discrimination. In the US, which does not have a strong social safety net, the quest for equal employment opportunity may be hampered by broader societal inequities. 'Several previous [studies] have marked the United States as an outlier [among developed nations]: high poverty rates; low public social spending but high private social expenditures; a rather strong belief that people are poor because of laziness or lack of will' (Martin and Koen, 2011:1). Thus, racial discrimination in housing persists in the US, with predominantly black neighbourhoods often having lower performing schools and less access to public transportation. These are root causes that, in turn, limit employment opportunities.

Activists tend to work in one domain or maybe two to alleviate inequality (for example alleviating health care disparities or reducing the impacts of homelessness on children's schooling stability). Researchers also tend to specialize, with studies of the workplace anchored in organizational theory, rarely looking outside work to see the impacts from other domains.

Relinking these domains holds three promises. First, studies of internal workplace conditions and promotion systems need to take external context into account, beyond external labour markets. Employers often believe that corporations simply inherit these external conditions. But they also participate in creating them. Low-wage jobs limit housing options for employees, creating long commutes that might make it difficult to be on time for work and thereby to keep a job. Jobs with little flexibility make it difficult for working parents to attend meetings with teachers at their children's schools. Thus, employers do not just inherit employees who are the products of schooling; they play a role in shaping how effective schooling can be in the first place. Differential opportunities in the workplace shape differential life chances, which in turn shape differential opportunities in the next generation, reproducing inequality.

Second, many approaches to diversity focus on advancement to the highest positions in organizations by relatively more privileged employees. Considering multiple domains returns the focus to the material conditions of inequality across positions. Quota systems are applicable where numbers are larger, typically at the bottom of pyramidal organizations where there are enough positions for statistical looks at the composition to make sense. As attention moves away from quotas, it moves away from these lower positions, with diversity and inclusion efforts aimed at higher-level jobs. One line of reasoning for the focus on advancement of women and racial minorities into the highest positions in organizations is that they will become voices at the top, representing their social identity groups more broadly, perhaps even encouraging corporate community involvement that spans domains. But there is limited evidence of this advocacy, perhaps even less among those who have faced conformity pressures during advancement. Thus, restoring attention directly to the situation of those in the lowest positions, rather than waiting for that to happen through the voices of the few who reach the top, is vital.

Third, where quota systems have been implemented internationally, it is in representational positions, such as legislative bodies or boards of directors. The idea is that, if representatives look more like the population they represent, they will better carry their interests. There is some evidence that, when there are more women on boards of directors, they are less tokenized, more emboldened to bring up community issues to which women might be more closely connected, and more able to turn boardroom conversations towards sustained consideration of multiple stakeholders, beyond shareholders (Kramer et al., 2007). The test of whether women in these representational positions is effective might be, not simply whether there are greater returns to the corporation, but whether there are benefits more broadly across societal domains.

Conclusion

Relinking the multiple domains pivots attention to the broader opportunity structure, where inequality arises and is reproduced. Approaches such as deep cultural analysis and programmes such as employee caucus groups can be considered with respect to the original spirit and aim of quotas. Note that the stories of the women programmers and women scientists did not end with indications of whether the numbers of women went up in either sphere. Deep cultural analyses can uncover the conditions for increasing women's numbers, while stopping short of creating needed mechanisms for sustaining and measuring results (Sturm, 2001) and actually increasing numbers. Both trends considered in this chapter have the capacity to shake assumptions and provoke significant changes in organizations, but both are vulnerable to becoming symbolic exercises in inclusion that cost companies nothing, instead of tools for redistribution whose costs signify serious change.

Quota systems have a distinct aim, which can be summarized as: Increase the numbers of underrepresented groups in the valued jobs and positions in a society. Those increased numbers mean increased access to the 'goods' of society, from income to housing to health care to higher education. This improved access spreads societal benefits more broadly and fairly. The 'American Dream' of equal opportunity is a mere myth without continuous and active monitoring to protect equality of opportunity. Remedying inequality requires redistribution, which invariably provokes political tension (Scully, 2002). The political tensions surrounding quotas and affirmative action have spurred not just backlash but new approaches, but these new approaches must continually be assessed through the original aims of quotas: increasing numbers, access, opportunity and quality of life.

References

Bailyn, L. (1999). *Momentum of Report [of the Committees on Women Faculty in the School of Science] Needs to be Extended to the Entire Institute*. Faculty News Letter. http://web.mit.edu/fnl/women/bailyn.html.

Bailyn, L. and Fletcher, J.K. (2003). The equity imperative: reaching effectiveness through the dual agenda, *CGO Insights*, 18(July), 1–4.

Baron, J.N. and Bielby, W.T. (1986). The proliferation of job titles in organizations. *Administrative Science Quarterly*, 31(4), 561–586.

Bell, E.L.J. and Nkomo, S.M. (2001). *Our Separate Ways: Black and White Women and the Struggle for Professional Identity*. Boston: Harvard Business School Press.

Bell, M. (2006). *Diversity in Organizations*. Cincinnati, OH: Cengage.

Carter, S.L. (1992). *Reflections of an Affirmative Action Baby*. New York: Basic Books.

Castilla, E.J. and Benard, S. (2010). The paradox of meritocracy in organizations, *Administrative Science Quarterly*, 55(4), 543–576.

Cox, T. and Nkomo, S.M. (1986). Differential performance appraisal criteria: a field study of black and white managers, *Group and Organization Management*, 11(1–2), 101–119.

Crosby, F.J. (2004). *Affirmative Action is Dead; Long Live Affirmative Action*. New Haven, CT: Yale University Press.

Daniels, N. (1978). Merit and meritocracy, *Philosophy and Public Affairs*, 7(3), 206–223.

DeSario, N.J. (2003). Reconceptualizing meritocracy: the decline of disparate impact discrimination law, *Harvard Civil Rights – Civil Liberties Law Review*, 38(2), 479–510.

Elvira, M.M. and Graham, M.E. (2002). Not just a formality: pay system formalization and sex-related earnings effects, *Organization Science*, 13(6), 601–617.

Friedman, R.A. and Deinard, C. (1991). *Black Caucus Groups at Xerox Corporation*, (A) and (B). Cases no. 491-047 and 491-048. Boston, MA: Harvard Business School Publishing.

Gamson, W.A. (1992). *Talking Politics*. Cambridge: Cambridge University Press.

Greenwald, A.G. and Banaji, M.R. (1995). Implicit social cognition: attitudes, self-esteem, and stereotypes. *Psychological review*, 102(1), 4–27.

Guinier, L. and Torres, G. (2002). *The Miner's Canary: Enlisting Race, Resisting Power, Transforming Democracy*. Cambridge, MA: Harvard University Press.

Hartz, L. (1955). *The Liberal Tradition in America: An Interpretation of American Political Thought since the Revolution*. New York: Harcourt Brace.

Henderson, W.D. (2004). The LSAT, law school exams and meritocracy: the surprising and undertheorized role of test-taking speed, *Texas Law Review*, 82(4) IU Law-Bloomington Research Paper (20), 975–1052.

Huber, W. and Form, J. (1973). *Income and Ideology: An Analysis of the American Political Formula*. New York: Free Press.

Kalev, A., Dobbin, F. and Kelly, E. (2006). Best practices or best guesses? Diversity management and the remediation of inequality, *American Sociological Review*, 71(4), 589–617.

Kelly, R. and Dobbin, F. (2001). 'How affirmative action became diversity management', in J.D. Skrentny (ed.), *Color Lines: Affirmative Action, Immigration and Civil Rights Options for America*, Chicago, IL: University of Chicago Press, 87–117.

Kluegel, J. and Smith, E. (1986). *Beliefs about Inequality: Americans' View of What is and What Ought to Be*. New York: Aldine de Guyter.

Kolb, D.M. and Merrill-Sands, D. (1999). Waiting for outcomes: anchoring a dual agenda for change to cultural assumptions, *Women in Management Review*, 14(5), 194–203.

Kramer, V.W., Konrad, A.M., Erkut, S. and Hooper, M.J. (2007). Critical mass on corporate boards: why three or more women enhance governance, *Directors Monthly*, February, 19–22.

Martin, M.C. and Koen, C. (2011). Welfare reform in the US: a policy overview analysis, *Poverty and Public Policy*, 3(1). http://www.psocommons.org/ppp/vol3/iss1/art8.

Miner, A.S. (1987). Idiosyncratic jobs in formalized organizations. *Administrative Science Quarterly*, 32(3), 327–351.

Rapoport, R., Bailyn, L., Fletcher, J.K. and Pruitt, B.H. (2002). *Beyond Work-Family Balance: Advancing Gender Equity and Workplace Performance*. San Francisco, CA: Jossey-Bass.

Reskin, B.F. (1993). Sex segregation in the workplace, *Annual Review of Sociology*, 19(August), 241–269.

Reskin, B.F. (1998). *The Realities of Affirmative Action in Employment*. Washington D.C.: American Sociological Association.

Rodin, J. (2009). 'Teaching the truth about affirmative action', in R.A. Oglesby and M.G. Adams (eds), *Business Research Yearbook: Global Business Perspectives*, Vol. 16. Beltsville: International Academy of Business Disciplines, pp. 497–502.

Scully, M.A. (1997). 'Meritocracy', in R.E. Freeman and P.H. Werhane (eds), *The Blackwell Encyclopedia of Management: Business Ethics, Vol. 11*, London: Blackwell, pp. 413–414.

Scully, M.A. (2002). Confronting errors in the meritocracy, *Organization*, 9(3), 396–401.

Scully, M.A. (2004). Rethinking management: what's gender got to do with it? *CGO Commentaries*, 1(March), 1–9.

Scully, M. and Segal, A. (2002). 'Passion with an umbrella: grassroots activists in the workplace', in M. Lounsbury and M.J. Ventresca (eds), *Research in the Sociology of Organizations*, Oxford: JAI Press, Vol.19, 127–170.

Spencer, S.J., Steele, C.M. and Quinn, D.M. (1999). Stereotype threat and women's math performance, *Journal of Experimental Social Psychology*, 35(1), 4–28.

Stryker, R. (2001). Disparate impact and the quota debates: law, labor market sociology, and equal employment policies. *Sociological Quarterly*, 42(1), 13–46.

Sturm, S. (2001). Second generation employment discrimination: a structural approach, *Columbia Law Review*, 101(3), 458–568.

Twomey, D.P. (2009). *Labor and Employment Law: Text and Cases*, 14th edition. Cincinnati, OH: Cengage.

Zernike, K. (2011). Gains, and drawbacks, for female professors, 21 March, *New York Times*.

11 *The Gender Issue: Identity and Differences Revisited*

LAURENT BIBARD

Introduction

The predominantly social-political literature on 'gender' has opened up the question of the subtle relations between sexualities and their cultural variations, reflecting the deeply embedded humanistic assumptions of sexuality which is now never considered entirely 'natural', and may even be thought not at all 'natural'. This literature's approach to addressing sexualities is, moreover, one that is usually constructed explicitly against the very idea of 'nature', which is one of the highly ideologically-charged ideas and concepts in civilizations where segregation was a fact of life (cf. Kojève, 1969; Aristotle, 1995. In this context, it is vital that the literature on gender originating from North America should penetrate the old continent of Europe and its biases. This is currently occurring, with the benefit of bringing about greater equality (although still too slowly) in the social, economic and political conditions of existence for women and men in the workplace and elsewhere.

Yet it would be just as unilaterally problematic for a reflection of sexualities and the required dynamic balance between them if the literature on gender and its premises failed to incorporate the possibility of a fundamental questioning of sexualities in the sense of native philosophy. This chapter outlines the possibility of such an interaction between, on the one hand the presuppositions of the literature on gender, and on the other, those of the 'traditional' European philosophical literature on what, for the latter, is the relatively new theme of sexualities. To do so, I shall discuss the following in turn, with reference to my essay *Sexualité et Mondialisation:*[1]

- the concept of 'globalization';
- a few points on method concerning the approach to the theme of sexualities in the sphere of political philosophy;
- some difficulties concerning sexualities generated by the humanist intent for control over nature;
- a fundamental hypothesis given the hidden issues of the contemporary structural dynamic of sexualities;

---

1   L'Harmattan, Paris, 2010. The book is currently being translated into English. The title will probably be *Sexuality and Globalization.*

- highlighting the cross-dynamics of sexualities;
- and lastly, a juxtaposition between the understanding of sexualities as briefly presented here and certain elements of the Taoist approach to the same theme.

Globalization

The purpose of this work is to present and explain the way sexualities and globalization are linked. There can be no doubt that the most important aspect of globalization is *uncertainty*. A characteristic feature of globalization is the increasing confrontation between nations on economic and geopolitical fronts. This confrontation generates the unexpected and is based on unexpected events – either human or 'natural' – that are increasing in number and with expanding dynamics and consequences: financial and political crises reflect the growing complexity and unpredictability of the course of things, as do natural events such as the tsunami of 2004. We could go so far as to say that man's globalized environment is in chaotic evolution. This chaos can be described as an equivalence of possibilities: anything can take place without any possibility of determining an order in which events will occur, and very small events or decisions may have major consequences on a scale that at first sight is incommensurable with those events or decisions. So globalization leads to growing uncertainty, and a declining possibility of control or command by human beings over their immediate or distant environment.

Methods

The approach to the question of sexualities and globalization is facilitated by three basic premises and elements of method:

- First premise: One of the decisive aspects of globalization is that it is the setting for achieving equality for women and men in recognition of their human dignity and work.
- Second premise: Political life begins by sexual life.
- Methodological premise: In some circumstances, the smallest and greatest elements on a political level are in direct, even commensurable interaction.

FIRST PREMISE

One of the decisive aspects of globalization is that it is the setting for achieving equality for women and men in recognition of their human dignity and work.

This requires little exemplification or argument to be accepted with little risk of error. Although globalization is characterized by the intensification of economic, social and geopolitical tensions at an international level, it is just as importantly the arena for a fundamental dynamic, not to say battle, for equal recognition for women and men in their human dignity and at work.

SECOND PREMISE

Political life begins by sexual life.
This second premise is more questionable. In the context of this chapter, it takes us back to the Aristotelian assertion that political life begins by conjugal life:

> *The first form of association naturally instituted for the satisfaction of daily recurrent needs is thus the family, and the members of the family are accordingly termed by Charondas 'associates of the breadchest', as they are also termed by Epimenides the Cretan 'associates of the manger'.*
> (Aristotle, 1995: 1252b15; 1252a24 to 1262b17)

> *One of the factors underlying this 'classic' assertion of western and non-western political philosophy is that for a long time, in order for human communities to live, that is, defend themselves and produce the goods needed to survive, it was necessary to 'produce' citizens, and therefore to make love. In other words, a duly regulated and ordered heterosexual life lies at the basis of human communities that have no weapons or science and techniques enabling them to defend themselves and produce regardless of their numbers.[2]*

The Aristotelian assertion referred to is undermined not only by the contemporary proliferation of weapons of mass destruction and sciences and techniques in general, but also by the foundations of modern political science. The bases of modern political science, which can be traced back to the English philosopher Thomas Hobbes, are established in direct opposition to the Aristotelian bases of classical political thought. They assert that political life begins with the establishment of a 'social contract' between individuals who are free, equal among themselves and rational, independently of any consideration of sex, ethnic origin, age and so on.

Notwithstanding these limitations, we start from the premise that political life begins with sexual life, even if we are now concerned with 'gendered' life rather than directly sexual life. In other words, what is decisive in sexual life for understanding political life is no longer the possibility of reproducing the human, but its internal differentiation. Consequently, from the standpoint adopted here, homosexuality, and also impotence or celibacy, do not form an obstacle to political life as such.

---

2   Understanding clearly the Aristotelian statement on conjugal life can be favoured paying special attention to the very beginning of his *Politics* (1252a1), in the horizon of 1253a2 : 'From these considerations it is evident that the city belongs to the class of things that exist by nature, and that man is by nature a political animal', and 1253a25. Such an understanding demands that the real Aristotelian understanding of slavery and of gender issues be grasped as well. This may be facilitated by a specific consideration to 1254b27, in the light of 1253b14, 1254a13, 1255b1 and sq. concerning slavery. See 1259a37 and sq. concerning genders, in the specific light of the discussion of the difference between the statesman and a king restated 1259b32. See the last – but not least – statement 1260b8 on the relation between these issues and political regimes: 'We must therefore consider the constitution before we proceed to deal with the training of children and women – at any rate if we hold that the goodness of children and women makes any difference to the goodness of the city. And it must make a difference. Women are a half of the free population: children grow up to be partners of the constitution.' It appears evident that Aristotle aims at being seemingly compliant with taken for granted opinions on genders and slavery of his time. However, a close examination of his wording highlights that in fact, he takes some significant distance with these opinions (on a similar form of writing, see Strauss L., *Persecution and the Art of Writing*, Chapter 2).

METHODOLOGICAL PREMISE

In some circumstances, the smallest and greatest elements on a political level are in direct, even commensurable interaction.

Just as the previous premise had serious limitations, this one is sociologically false: the smallest and greatest on a political level are inherently incommensurable, to the extent that the dynamics of life for a couple and the world, for example, have nothing in common in everyday life. Yet it may happen, in certain highly unusual circumstances, that the smallest and the greatest not only echo each other, but are directly correlated. At least, this is what Plato has Socrates suppose in his *Republic* when the intention of examining the concept of justice is explained (Plato, 2009). The argument is as 'simple' as this: since justice is easier to consider at the level of the city, that is what will be examined, rather than man or the individual, in order to identify what human justice is :

> 'It looks to me as though the investigation we are undertaking is no ordinary thing, but one for a man who sees sharply. Since we're not clever men,' I said, 'in my opinion we should make this kind of investigation of it: if someone had, for example, ordered men who don't see very sharply to read little letters from afar and then someone had the thought that the same letters are somewhere else also, but bigger and in a bigger place, I suppose it would look like a godsend to be able to consider the littler ones after having read these first, if, of course, they do happen to be the same.'
>
> 'Most certainly,' said Adeimantus, 'but, Socrates, what do you notice in the investigation of the just that is like this?'
>
> 'I'll tell you,' I said. 'there is, we say, justice of one man; and there is, surely, justice of a whole city too?'
>
> 'Certainly,' he said
>
> 'Is a city bigger than one man?'
>
> 'Yes, it is bigger;' he said.
>
> 'So then, perhaps – there would be more justice in the bigger and it would be easier to observe closely. If you want, first we will investigate what justice is like in the cities. Then, we will also go on to consider it in individuals, considering the likeness of the bigger in the idea of the smaller?'
>
> 'What you say seems fine to me,' he said.
>
> 'If we should watch a city coming into being in speech,' I said, 'would we also see its justice coming into being, and its injustice?'
>
> 'Probably,' he said.
>
> 'When this has been done, can we hope to see what we're looking for more easily?'
>
> 'Far more easily.'
>
> 'Is it resolved that we must try to carry this out? I suppose it is no small task, so consider it.'
>
> 'It has been considered,' said Adeimantus. 'don't do anything else.'
>
> (Plato, 2009: 368b–369b)

I shall adopt a similar point of view to the opinion Plato gives the characters in his dialogue on a just republic, but taking the opposite starting point. Since examination of the political is easier at the quasi-individual level of a couple or gendered life, I examine globalization from the starting point of human sexuality.

These, then, are the three fundamental methodological premises of this presentation on sexualities.

Past Difficulties

Beginning by discussing sexualities is more difficult in our times, as the accessibility of the concept is affected by universalization of the humanist intent for control over nature that can be traced back to the Renaissance.

Of course, European humanism's intent cannot be summed up as the intent for control over nature, but control of nature is indeed part of it. 'Humanism' consists in the claim, expressed in many different ways and through a large number of arts, that humanity has its rightful place 'here below', and is at home on earth. One of the implications of being at home is, among other things, deposing the theological and political power of the Christian Church which reigned at the time, and 'controlling and possessing' nature as Descartes put it in his *Discours de la Méthode* (Descartes, 1956).

That such 'control and possession' will eventually arise and replace 'God', or to put it another way, that humanists will eventually become atheists either in reality or potentially, and that the humanist dream will consciously or unconsciously take on Faustian airs even at its inception, is more than likely. That it will guide the future towards control over nature, considered hostile because it foments suffering, pain and death as much as enjoyment, happiness and life, is even more likely. Finally, that the intent for control over nature through its 'control and possession' should be expressed as a *universal masculinization* of humans towards nature is decisive for sexualities and the recognition of their relative differences.

We can observe such signs of the universalization of human beings' new masculinity in the approach to nature in the title of Francis Bacon's *The Masculine Birth of Time* (Bacon, 1603), or when Machiavelli foreshadows the Cartesian concepts of control and possession in his comparison at the end of Chapter XXV of *The Prince* between 'fortune' and 'feminine', which both need to be 'beaten and ill-used' to be held in submission (Machiavelli, 1981). However, it is no longer the masculine virility used in *combat* that will control and possess nature in a virile way, or beat and ill-use fortune. It is instead masculinity understood as the *voluntarism of humans wishing to control nature* – human and non-human – through new sciences and techniques, in other words through work. But in contrast to what is suggested by Machiavelli's approach to the question at the end of the chapter of *The Prince* referred to earlier, this masculinity, related to work rather than fighting, concerns women just as much as men, and is particularly symbolized by the triumph of mankind over the female reproductive cycle. That contraception was perfected almost at the same time point in history as man – in this case, males, but representing all of humanity – was finally setting foot on the moon is symbolic of the effects of a decision made a few centuries earlier.

The difficulty now is that the universal masculinization of humanity, understood as an active intent to control and possess nature that is both the driver and the consequence of certain nodal aspects of globalization, progressively obstructs and stifles access to what masculine and feminine sexualities are, 'beyond' that contemporary universal masculinization.

Before proceeding further, two points should be emphasized in relation to what has just been said.

- First of all, the reason masculinization of men and women is becoming globalized or universalized so easily is because the need for control over his environment by the animal that represents the *homo sapiens* species is anthropologically 'hard-wired' into his memory. At this level, the modern rationalism that derives from European humanism meets and converges unexpectedly with the most fundamental animal emotions, including *fear*.
- Next, 'globalization' must in this context be interpreted not as a unilateral universalization of the intent to control nature, but as the tension between the intent for control and the assertion that nature is 'uncontrollable' – just as much as 'god' or gods are uncontrollable. In other words, 'globalization' is a tension, between the 'west' or a control-focused attitude, and the 'non-west' understood as an assertion of the ultimately not (entirely) controllable nature of human and non-human things.

Sexuality and Globalization: A Fundamental, Founding Hypothesis

My modest but exacting preamble here on the question of sexualities is fundamental in theme, and a founding factor of the movement it seeks to set in motion.

There is nothing more inevitable than that sexuality as a theme for examination should be deemed fundamental, if it is accepted that until a new biotechnological order arises life comes to the human rather than the contrary, at least insofar as its coming is unconscious, involuntary and therefore received. The past participle used to describe being 'born' expresses this receptive dynamic. What is received in this way is life itself, through a dynamic that pervades and mobilizes sexuality. What humans call 'self-awareness', free will, rationality, in no way diminishes the natural 'remainder' we can discuss in the footsteps of Leo Strauss for example (1952), which concerns the way humans reproduce.

Here, I expand upon attributes given to sexualities. The 'hypothesis' of my work is that *it is through sexualities that freedom, language, time and human reason are possible.*

To bring out the space of understanding from the fact that feminine and masculine sexualities are, by their dynamics and interrelatedness, at the root of man's humanity itself, we must break free of any presupposed confinement to the 'scientific' categories and pre-existing philosophical and ideological frameworks. If we were to seek a resemblance between this intent and a recognizable philosophical intent, the least illegitimate suggestion would be to compare it with that of Heidegger's second period. But for that comparison to be meaningful, we must completely ignore the specific limitations of the Heideggerian view on sexualities.[3]

In any case, I do not seek to propose some sort of 'description' of sexualities in the light of the question of globalization in general; instead I propose an exercise to make space, time and freedom to question the very origins of humanity and the meaning of its future and what it is to become. *For this exercise, the question under examination must be 'inhabited'. The examiner must be willing to be inhabited, so he or she can inhabit the question.*

The aim is to make the hypothesis possible and active.

---

3   Heidegger's opinion on sexualities is presented between the lines in his utmost important work *Being and Time*.

Sexualities

It is time to sketch out the dynamic of sexualities under this approach, in an attempt to address the hypothesis touched on earlier.

Detection of sexualities as differentiated ways of existing in the world has two counterpoints, one of which is the humanist intent as such, as expressed by Machiavelli, the other the Freudian interpretation of female sexuality.

- When Machiavelli's *The Prince* (1981) compares fortune to the feminine, despite its apparent unimportance and coarseness towards women, this is more than a superficial remark: he has in mind the feminine as a capacity for gestation. If fortune must be 'beaten and ill-used' to be kept in submission, 'because it is a woman and as a woman prefers adventurous young men to coldly prudent older men', then steps must be taken to control the very coming into existence of a human life, symbolized by the event of any pregnancy. 'Beating and ill-using' fortune, which will gradually extend to all spheres of human life, comes down to the principle of controlling births from their very origin, that is, conception, and their coming, which involves gestation. I approach the notion of sexualities by taking into consideration the simple event of birth, which presupposes previous human gestation.[4]
- The ultimate understanding of female sexuality, the 'dark continent' of psychoanalysis in the words of Freud himself, is an understanding *via* the negative: little girls are supposed to all feel their 'lack of a penis' sooner or later, and ultimately see their sexuality constructed on the basis of that lack. I see this as the expression of a deep, modern (potentially over-modern) blindness to the event of gestation, and of any birth. And just as Heidegger talks of the 'morning' event of thought without going so far as to speak of its birth, Freud talks of sexuality in a way that fundamentally abandons half of the human race to the structures and dynamics of the other half.[5]

Gestation can be taken as the basis of construction of sexualities through difference. Gestation, and the fact that until a new biotechnological order arises, it is strictly a woman's act or at any rate a formation of female origin, brings out the following obvious observation. While any little girl eventually knows consciously or unconsciously that she can repeat what her mother did for her, bearing a child, a little boy is similarly eventually inhabited by the opposite certainty. In other words, a woman's sexuality is ultimately conditioned in its origin, dynamic, desires and questions by the certainty of being able to do what her mother did, like any other woman. If this is well-founded, it is certain for the little girl that she advances in *continuity*, through a kind of identification with her mother, which comes down to the fundamental, founding possibility of carrying and giving life.

Matters are quite different for the little boy, who ultimately feels with varying degrees of consciousness that he is *not* from the same world as his mother although she is the world he comes from. He feels therefore that he is 'pushed out' or that he is outside the feminine or life; that he is in a world with no certainty other than the certainty of *not* being immediately 'somewhere' that makes sense. That he is thus in a place of difference,

---

4   This 'humanity' depends on the *duration* of gestation for Taoists.

5   On these last considerations, see the importance Heidegger gives to death as a means for humans to reach humanity.

doubt and questioning, not completely correlated with life as such, life in this sense as the origin and renewal of the self. The little boy will need the mediation of a non-intense relationship with his father or men in general to trigger the process of rest, developing identity, recognition and foundation at a different level from that of his vital origins. Reciprocally, it is through her relationship or relationships with the masculine in general that a little girl will develop her sense of otherness, openness, risk-talking and moving beyond the inherent identity of which she is the primordial setting.

More generally, it can be said that as sexuality is the place of all desire, including sexual desire naturally but, if psychoanalysis is right at all on this point, as the framework or root of all other desires, in sexuality lies desire itself in the form of a 'lack'. We only desire what we lack, in quality, quantity or relationships. Each of the sexualities, which is desire above all, is therefore the desire for what it is not. Difference for the feminine, which is experienced first as identicalness, and identicalness for the masculine which is initially received as a difference.

If this too is true, then it appears that the feminine wants difference, and finds it in the masculine, while the masculine wants identicalness and finds it in the feminine. In doing so, each of the sexualities seeks in the other what the other seeks to abandon of himself or herself. The dynamics of the feminine lead her to seek herself in difference, while the dynamics of the masculine lead him to seek identicalness. In all, each of the sexualities ideally – that is, for itself – wishes to find in the other what the other wishes to separate from (identicalness for the feminine) or abandon (difference for the masculine). In short, if each sexuality succeeded in 'keeping' the other sexuality in what it wants from it, it would lock the other into the infancy of its desire, generating the most serious frustrations with potentially deadly consequences.

To put it differently again, the total solipsistic expression of each of the sexualities, in relation to and in view of the other, potentially causes its alienation, slavery or death. The balance of the sexualities in their inherent dynamic is quite simply crucial for each one.

This is nothing less than fundamental for mankind's very humanity, and clearly at least for its very existence. I shall end by commenting on this last point through consideration of the question of sexualities as a counterpoint to certain Taoist teachings on the question.

Yin and Yang, or how Globalization has come full circle

The two following common-sense assertions are found sooner or later in traditional Chinese medicine:

- Every individual is always both masculine (seat of the Yang energy) and feminine (seat of the Yin energy), or feminine and masculine, because he or she is the result of a 'heterogendered' encounter – whether truly heterosexual in its fullest sense, or simply involving the two sexes. Like certain points examined earlier, until a new biotechnological order arises, this point remains true today: an encounter between male and female gametes is necessary to start the process that will result in a small man or woman.
- More radically yet than the previous observation, life itself, in its health, corresponds to a harmonious dynamic balance between masculine and feminine, or feminine

and masculine. In other words, if an imbalance arises health may deteriorate or be fundamentally compromised.

How does the above enhance our previous assertion that it is at the level of sexualities that the human begins and is forged?

Just as History was for a while interpreted as the history of a slavery from which mankind freed itself, it can also be interpreted as a dynamic by which mankind frees itself of nature – in other words of sexualities as inherently spontaneous and spontaneously dual expressions of what is Human. If the history of the liberation of Slaves can be understood to have an End, even if it is potentially 'comic' (Kojève, 1969), the history of the liberation of Humanity from its spontaneity, *and thus its dual sexuation*, suffers the same fate but leads to a 'tragic' End, in the sense that in such a case human lives would be absurd. To put it another way: the Silence of Mankind resulting from the End of History, understood as an End to Slavery, would apparently still be filled with meaning (Kojève, 1969). The Silence of Mankind resulting from the End of its History, understood as the setting for the combined dynamic action of its 'gendered' duality, would certainly be a totally absurd silence. Totally absurd, for it would then be filled with no memory and driven by no desire as such – not even the desire for Living which underpins mankind's Humanity. Paradoxically, it is because humans' 'gendered' desire springs up from the animal in mankind that it creates the fundamental possibility of indefinite emergence of meaning for that same animal. And in contrast, it is because it is based on a non-animal desire, that the desire for recognition that lies at the root of slavery conditions the dynamics of a History than can be ended without threatening the humanity of human life at its roots.[6]

In other words, the fundamental founding Misunderstanding through which the two sexuations of mankind dynamise each other is the genesis of the possibility of all surprise, doubt, all explicit, conscious, deliberate questioning, all dialogue, all discussion and all meaning. To express it in the Greek way following Socrates, we cannot know what Meaning (or Justice) is without knowing what at least the possibility of Non-Meaning (or injustice) is. To say this from the perspective of a theological eschatology that is implicit in the west, there is no Meaning without awareness of the remarkable possibility of Non-Meaning, *nor Understandings without a Misunderstanding*, fundamental and founding. History is thus a domestic row that is constantly repeated, and this is how it oscillates between Non-Meaning and Meaning. For this to be true, in other words for Meaning to remain possible, Non-Meaning must remain just as possible. As going beyond the possibility of Non-Meaning would correspond to total control and possession over nature by mankind, the post-humanist universalization of masculinity discussed earlier, which comes about through original development of modern sciences and techniques, is the representation par excellence of such a possibility. And it is because it works to bring out dynamically, through the very event of reading it, the space and time of an immediate examination of Meaning through the fundamental and founding possibility of Non-Meaning, that *Sexualité et Mondialisation* expresses a major hypothesis on the future of mankind.

---

6   This can be considered as the full commentary on the *two* notes Alexandre Kojève devotes to the End of History and its meaning or lack of meaning, in his *Introduction to the Reading of Hegel* (Kojève, 1969, pp. 433–437).

Contrary to the aims of Machiavelli and his fellows, it is desirable that at least on a symbolic level, total transparency of nature to Man, the cognitive correlation of his control by action, should never actually happen. Since the question of whether it is possible remains as yet unanswered, it is relevant to meditate on the meaning of the Heraclitean assertion that 'nature loves to hide', a meaning it is doubtless relevant to hear in the Taoist horizon of the following Taoist proposal by which we open the future of our questioning:

In the darkness, make the darkness even deeper.

Conclusion

Through the difficulties it engenders for contemporary life, 'globalization' is a time and place of exceptionally fertile circumstances for humanity to take itself in hand and understand itself. Not that this has never taken 'place' before, at another given moment in time and elsewhere. The fact remains that the contemporary conditions of general chaos foster:

- Tension between the greater and the smaller, such that individuals' everyday life can be legitimately considered epistemologically as an opportunity for truth in the strongest sense for mankind; when the greatest and the smallest echo each other on anthropological, political and psychological levels, the most complete and the most fragmentary resonate also on the cognitive level, and the most understanding and the most enigmatic on the level of meaning.
- A *mise en abîme* of the human as a dynamic of control over nature taking into consideration the availability to what arises when anticipation is neither possible nor desired.
- Cross-fertilization of worlds which successively break up and regress to their initial expressions, causing cultural interdependencies commensurate with cultural clashes that foster a grasp of the most archaic facets of humanity. In the perspective of this fundamental possibility, we can understand the encounter with the 'west' – in the sense not only of a possibility of control over nature, but also as a world that is 'European' in origin.

These circumstances are those of a possible meeting between the west as a paradoxical forgetting of sexualities, and the east as a source of fertilisation of such questioning.

A meeting that should be the starting point for a dialectical and certainly permanent move beyond the concept of the 'End of History'. But that is another story, resulting from rediscovery of sexualities as the place par excellence of Mankind understood as Word.

References

Aristotle (1995). *Politics*. Oxford: Oxford University Press.

Bacon F. (1603). *The Masculine Birth of Time*. (Unfinished), Chicago: University of Chicago Press, 1964.

Bibard L. (2010). *Sexualité et Mondialisation (Sexuality and Globalization)*. Paris: L'Harmattan.

Descartes, R. (1956). *Discourse on Method*. New Jersey: Prentice Hall.

Heidegger, M. (1962), *Time and Being*. New York: Harper & Row.

Machiavelli, N. (1981). *The Prince*. New York: Penguin Books.

Plato (2009). *The Republic*, Allan Bloom translation. New York: Basic Books.

Kojève A. (1969). *Introduction to the Reading of Hegel*. New York: Basic Books. Original French publication 1947, *Introduction à la Lecture de Hegel*. Paris: Gallimard.

Strauss, L. (1952). *Persecution and the Art of Writing*. Illinois: The Free Press.

Index